ISTANBUL BOY

Part III

Modern Middle East

Literature in Translation

Series

ISTANBUL BOY

The Autobiography of Aziz Nesin, Part III

Yokuşun Başi (The Climb)

Translated from Turkish
by Joseph S. Jacobson

Center for Middle Eastern Studies
The University of Texas at Austin

Library of Congress Catalogue Card Number 77-75949

ISBN 0-292-738-64-1

Printed in the United States of America.

Cover drawing: Susana Jacobson

Cover design: Diane Watts

Editor: Annes McCann-Baker

Distributed by arrangement
with University of Texas Press/Box 7819
Austin, Texas 78713

My Father

My father was the world's best father.
Our minds were antagonists,
Our hands were friends.
The only hand in the world I kissed
Was my father's.
"You're past forty and not a man," he said;
I listened with bowed head.
I bowed my head only to my father.
He recited the Koran all night
For my mother's soul,
Believing he would join her.
He called me an unbeliever,
Without rancor.
In the world only I forgave him,
Only he forgave me.
When I got into trouble he looked after my children.
"I really can't die because of you," he said,
"Your children would be left destitute."
He couldn't die for anxiety over me;
He was forced to live on my account.
The fire in his eyes died in his glance;
"May whatever you touch turn to gold," he said.
Only he understood my children.
My father was the world's best father.

My father, Abdulaziz Efendi, died on a Sunday, 11 Feb. 1962, at the age of eighty-four. This poem was written ten years ago, after my father's death.

Aziz Nesin

Acknowledgments

The Center for Middle Eastern Studies at the University of Texas is very proud to bring out Part III of Turkish author Aziz Nesin's autobiography, *Istanbul Boy.* Assistance in the publication of this edition was provided through a gift in memory of Dorothy Beverly, who cared for small lovely things. We are grateful to translator Joseph S. Jacobson, Professor Emeritus at the University of Utah, for being patient with the Center in its search for funds to continue publishing *Istanbul Boy* in its entirety. Thanks should go also to Professor Jacobson's daughter, Susana V. Jacobson, Associate Professor of Painting at Yale University, for her third charming cover sketch of "Nusret." And most of all we are grateful to Aziz Nesin himself.

Annes McCann-Baker
Editor

Foreword

At the end of the first volume of his autobiography, published by the University of Texas at Austin as *Istanbul Boy* Parts I and II, Aziz Nesin says: "My dear readers! You have learned, with almost all the details, my life up to the age of twelve. While relating my memoirs (other than what I have forgotten), I've hidden from you none of my shortcomings, my mistakes, my faults or my disgraces. And if I am able to write subsequent sections of my memoirs, I will continue in the same manner. You have learned from my experiences that my childhood was lived under the oppression of many feelings of inferiority. Not only my childhood, but my youth was like that. Let me repeat a universal truth: the feeling of inferiority either destroys a person or, paradoxically, is a force which pushes him ahead and takes him on to productive efforts. There are years that I believe I put myself to the test with this feeling of inferiority. And I could be wrong in this opinion, but, after all, I do believe it. . . Had it not been so, I couldn't have written my memoirs in all their nakedness, hiding nothing."

In Part III Nesin continues his biographical anecdotes, which concern relatives, friends, acquaintances and life around him during early youth. His mother's grave, falsehoods, army tales, Ataturk, dervishes, truancy, Turkish minorities, raising turkeys, fire prayers, epilepsy, sex education, cock fights, and war with the Greeks are just a few of the wide spectrum of subjects he treats. The reader should be warned that, like an actor who abandons his role on the stage and speaks "asides" to the audience, Nesin sometimes leaves his biography to confide current problems or opinions, a custom in Turkish "theater in the round" for centuries. While Nesin's literary style continues to feature anecdotes as basic building blocks, forming a narrative structure typically Turkish, and the content reflects his life as a public middle-school pupil—and truant, it is rich in socio-historical observations of a keen, eyewitness observer and master reporter-commentator.

The cataclysmic political earthquake that finally destroyed that oriental superpower of the Middle Ages, the Ottoman Empire, and Turkey's desperate attempt to leap into the Twentieth Century and become a modern European nation, has been well covered by historians. However, the human aspects and effects on Turkish society of this revolutionary transformation were scarcely probed until Nesin's memoirs described many of these as they occurred during these radical changes, such as the new alphabet, secular schools, banning of the fez, adoption of hats and European clothes. Nesin doesn't hesitate to leave his life story to reflect on such subjects and repeat the political views of his father, Uncle Galip, and others.

Aziz Nesin autographed the delayed second volume of his autobiography: "My dear friend Joseph S. Jacobson, ten years later, I was able to publish the second volume of *Böyle Gelmiş Böyle Gitmez*. In friendship, 15 September 1976." It has also taken us ten years to get around to the publication of *Istanbul Boy* III. While the hero in the book remained twelve, Nesin and I passed our middle seventies as my daughter Susana, the artist for the cover, moved on from being a graduate student at Stanford to associate professor at Yale University's School of Art. Also, Author Emeritus Nesin has published over twenty more books, completed major buildings at the Nesin Foundation, and now struggles desperately to feed, clothe, shelter, and educate over twenty orphan children from preschool to college age. Your translator, now august Professor Emeritus, continues translating and publishing works of Turkish literature.

Nesin asked me, "Why on earth would a reader be interested in the memoirs of a writer whose works they've never read?" My reply included many of the things I've mentioned in this foreword. Now, after more than ten years, Nesin's works should be a little better known as more than twenty of my translations of Nesin stories have appeared in print and reached thousands of readers, particularly through the bimonthly periodical, *Short Story International*. Other Nesin publishers include: *Contemporary Literature In Translation*, Mission City, British Columbia; *Literature East And West*, Austin Texas; and *The Journal Of Literary Translation*, Columbia University.

It is a pleasure to acknowledge my wife Viola's gallant assistance in ironing out rough spots in my translations. Thanks to my daughter, Susana, for again doing artwork for the cover.

Finally, my appreciation is extended to Zülâl Malm, who now lives in Izmir, for consultations on many finer points in Turkish only a native might know.

In conclusion, let me add a word on Turkish pronunciation and transliteration in the text. Turkish sounds generally approximate English ones represented by the Latin alphabet. However, the Turkish "c, ç, ş, ğ and ı" which sound closer to our "j, ch, sh, gh, and ı" as in joke, chance, shot, though, and habit have been thus transliterated even in proper nouns. Umlauts "ö and ü" which sound something like pert and put have been retained, but the circumflexed "â and û" have been omitted in favor of "a and u." May these simplifications promote your smooth, happy reading!

Joseph S. Jacobson
Professor Emeritus
Middle East Center
University of Utah

Istanbul Boy, Part III

Yokuşun Başi (The Climb)

Jobs for Tomorrow

"What happened to the advertisement? The fables and 'Today's Children' to be sent to Hasan Ali, The Soyut issues. Letter to Iran—Mail—I'm going to Orhan Apaydin's. Why did you give away the Harpagon notes? Get a watch for Meral. A table lamp for Ahmet's birthday."

Every night—well, if not every night, every second or third night—I list on a piece of paper the things I have to do the next day. At the top of the sheet, I write "Jobs for Tomorrow" or "Things to be Done" and draw a line underneath. While these sheets, scribbled with things to be done, should have been thrown, without remorse, into the wastebasket long ago, I just don't have the heart to do it. In some ways I'm extravagant to the point of being prodigal; in others, I'm stingy enough to be called tight-fisted—after all, these papers are used only on one side.

In addition to the jobs that I put off from day to day, I make monthly and annual project lists, under the headings "Work I Must Do" or "Things I Will Do This Year."

I used to tear these lists up and throw them away, but one day, somehow, I tucked a few away. Later, upon my finding these old work programs of years ago and reading the writing on the old tattered paper, they seemed very interesting and suddenly appeared valuable. In those writings, I saw my own past; I saw myself as I used to be.

So, from that day on, I no longer threw away my daily, monthly or annual "Jobs for Tomorrow," but collected them in a file. Upon occasion, as I thumb through, I find among the papers not only the past but also my future days. They are documents which tie my todays to my tomorrows. I look at the "Jobs for Tomorrow" and can't even recall most of them—I've forgotten. And many, many of those things to be done were put off until tomorrow, again and again, then never done at all. As I regard them, I feel regret.

So, for the tomorrows when I no longer exist—the tomorrows without me—written slips of paper will remain, a pile of old notes from me.

Now I am looking at files full of "Jobs for Tomorrow." On not one day have I been able to complete my work. Every day,

I've remained in debt to the day after—to tomorrow. This isn't due to idleness, it's my loading myself with more than I can carry. I've thought over why I loaded myself down so much. Perhaps it could be the result of a subconscious desire to live on: If I can't finish today's work, I'll be forced to do it tomorrow. Indeed, a person who has a job to do can't die... To remain in debt to the tomorrows, to always feel the debt, that means to try to live, to be forced to live in order to pay the debt. But this is a debt that can never be paid, one which grows ever larger upon being paid.

On that morning when I no longer exist, they will find on my table a piece of paper, used on one side, but with jobs for tomorrow listed on the other, which I jotted down but shall never be able to do. So, these full files will be the "leftover" from me; they will be the tomorrow's work that no one else can ever do.

Now I have in front of me a random paper from my "Jobs for Tomorrow" files:

> Shave, Breakfast, Addresses, Clean my desk, Telephone Hamdi, Jemal Süreyya, Agaoghlu, Ali, shoes, water flowers, Stamp album for Ahmet, mail, liver for the cats, Refik Halid's books, To Haldun Taner. Mengü and Mistik, money from Küflü, story to Akbaba, Zübük proofs, that one-act play.

Every tomorrow appeared so near that it couldn't be forgotten; and I gave such little value to these pieces of paper that I didn't even bother to date them.

We cannot determine, in the time we live them, which things that happen to us will be worthless in the future, and which ones might be valuable. We can't realize how an envelope with an address written on it (that we threw away as worthless), a note, or even a grocery slip, can become valuable with time.

Among the papers in the last two "Jobs for Tomorrow" files (most of which I'd put off until some other day, some vague tomorrow), there is one job: "To write the second volume of *That's How It Was But Not How It's Going To Be.*" Here's what I wrote:

In view of the second part of the first volume of *That's How It Was* . . . being finished 15 January 1965, I can begin the third part—the second volume—15 March 1965. Until then, I'll be finishing the 'Nasrettin Hoja,' 4/5 January 1965.

In the papers for "Tomorrow's Jobs," "Work To Be Done," there exist many such notes on *That's How It Was*... I've written myself, promised myself, and often tried to force or bind myself with such tricks as the above. But for naught... What with writing to make my daily bread, I simply haven't been able to begin this arduous task. Now, seven years have passed, and I've neither been able to finish the study of Nasrettin Hoja nor write the second volume of *That's How It Was*...

To me, the writing of *That's How It Was*... is much more a duty, a debt I owe, than just an author's being forced to write to establish his own existence. Even though seven years tardy, herein, I now try to pay a portion more of that debt.[*]

The Curse

I had started writing some of my memoirs, but all remained half-done. While one usually begins by writing about his childhood, I began with the day I sat down to write. I'll repeat that portion for you here:

"30 April 1971, Thursday, 20: 30 o'clock, Motel Örtur-Burhaniye.

"When he curses, it means that a man has arrived at the last degree of hopelessness. When he's crushed under the cruelest injustice, has no more strength to resist, is crowded into a corner, then a man can really curse, because there's nothing else he can do.

---

[*]tr. Although the second volume of *That's How It Was*... began to be serialized in the newspaper seven years after the publication of the first volume, it was only after ten years that it could be published as a book.

"During my life I've often fallen into such situations. But until today I've cursed no one, not those in power—who put me in these painful circumstances—nor the upper classes. I've fought on when my strength was exhausted. But today? As I write these lines, what a fearful situation I'm in... I'm as if drunk. My head spins. My blood pressure must be up again... I've been unable to use my eye drops because I've been traveling continuously by automobile and bus for the past thirteen hours. My eyes are hurting again. From this age on, I'll not be able to bear up well under these illnesses and fatigue, as I used to.

"My head is spinning so badly, that as soon as I entered this room at the Motel Örtur in Ören, I staggered as if on my last legs. I sat on the bed.

"'God damn it! God damn it to Hell!' I muttered.

"I was completely without hope. There was nothing I could do but curse."

For the present, I'll not reveal under what influence, why, I wrote these pessimistic words. Perhaps some day in the future I'll explain. For now, let's go back forty-eight years to my childhood days...

Mulberries, Figs, Birds

Mulberries and figs were the fruit my mother loved most. I'd overheard several times when she instructed my father: "Plant a mulberry tree at the head of my grave, a fig tree at the foot!"

There would be a period of silence in our room. Then Mother, as if repeating something very ordinary, would say, "The birds, especially those chattery sparrows, really love figs and mulberries; let them eat and chirp away above me..."

From some place in Istanbul my father had brought a young mulberry and a fig tree. Together, we'd gone to Mother's grave in the Heybeli Island cemetery. I carried the baby trees, my father the adze and shovel. With his skilled hands, Father planted the mulberry at the head and the fig tree at the foot of the grave. Using a can borrowed from the cemetery sexton, we carried water to soak the young saplings.

4

Father frequently went to water those two tree-starts he'd planted at Mother's grave. Sometimes he took me along too. He also gave money to the sexton to water the trees. Still they didn't take hold. A second time, Father planted starts he'd brought. They froze that winter. He planted mulberry and fig trees three or four times at the grave—and Father was very expert at this business too—yet, somehow or other, the starts wouldn't take root.

A person will die, return to the soil, and certainly won't hear the birds singing in the tree branches above. The important thing is not whether the deceased hears the birds singing. While we live, we should think about the birds which will sing above our graves, and be pleased while we're still alive... That's the thing that's beautiful.

I, too, at that last halt, want the birds to sing in the mulberry and fig branches above me. Of course I won't hear or know; I'll be unaware. But I can think now of the chirping, the beauty of that time, and be pleased; I can live now what will come after me.

A Greasy Black Disgrace

Mithat Jemal Kuntay[*] said this of Mehmet Akif: "He can disclose his entire life, from end to end, without needing to tell a lie."

To be able to reveal his life from beginning to end, with absolutely no necessity of lying, is important, but really not so difficult. Those who have smooth, uncomplicated lives (and there are practically none of them) can comfortably relate all their memoirs. What's much more difficult, much more important, is for a person to be able to reveal his life—in all its nakedness, from beginning to end—without feeling the necessity to lie when there are incidents in it which he objects to telling,

---

[*] tr. Mithat Jemal Kuntay (1885–1956) a nationalist poet and Kemalist. Mehmet Akif Ersoy (1873-1936) the great religious and patriotic poet who wrote the lyrics for the Turkish National Anthem.

which make him ashamed. In order for a person to relate his life's story—complete with embarrassing details—from beginning to end, without feeling the necessity to lie, he must have reached such a high plane that these disgraces and faults can't leap above him. This plane is the place from which Nesmi* proclaimed, "So I smashed the bottle of honest modesty on a rock! Who cares?"

I have neither a simple, straightforward life like Akif, nor have I reached that plane from where I'll feel no objections to revealing shameful incidents in my complicated life. But I have, after all, embarked upon the telling of my own life, and as long as harm doesn't touch others, I've decided to reveal my disgraces, secrets, and faults. I bear a disgrace which smears my memory like a greasy stain, one that I haven't been able to cleanse myself of for all these years.

Water is carried to many houses on the Island in wooden-crated cans, on the backs of donkeys. There was no water in our house, so my sister and I carried water from the fountain in jugs. Only one time did we get water by donkey—the day after my mother died... The waterman, Hafiz, brought three donkeyloads. In the two wooden crates, on the left and right of the donkey's back, were two cans of water each, totalling four. Water was priced at one hundred *para* per can, so a donkeyload cost ten *kurush*.

The kettle on the stove in the kitchen of our little house was boiling. The body-washer woman had made her preparations. Hafiz had brought water three times with his donkey. The first and last time that water came to our house by donkey was that day.

My father handed me thirty *kurush* to pay Hafiz for the three donkeyloads of water. But I didn't give the money to Hafiz. Why? Had I thought that on that sorrowful day, that in the confusion, no one would ask me for the money? Had I thought that Hafiz would be embarrassed and not ask for the money? Or had I bought something I'd long yearned for while I had thirty *kurush* in my pocket? I don't know. For whatever reason, I hadn't given Hafiz the money.

---

* tr. Nesmi (Imadeddin Nesimi, b. ?-1405) a mystic poet of the Hurufi sect.

Hafiz waited a week. Then he asked Father for the money. Father showed no surprise at all. He didn't say anything such as, "I gave your money to my son," or "I sent it with my son." He merely paid Hafiz the money.

One evening at home, my father (that hot-tempered man), asked me in his gentlest tones, "My boy, didn't you give Hafiz his money?"

Well, Hafiz could have received his money and forgotten it, and that's why Father was asking me. In his eyes I was the most trustworthy person in the world.

I said nothing. Father didn't say anything either.

As the years passed, this shame spread through me like a black, greasy smear and stained my memory. At the most unseemly times, I suddenly remember and relive that disgrace again.

The Island's watercarriers made good money. Three of those who delivered water to houses by donkey were our neighbors: Sherif Efendi, Ahmet Aga, and Hafiz...

Waterman Sherif Efendi, originally from the Black Sea, was one of the Heybeli Island oldtimers. Father had been acquainted with him a long long time. He was very industrious; day after day, with his two donkeys, he delivered water to houses on the hill. He lived on the hill too, in a house with a vegetable garden, which he cultivated himself. To the right of the government-owned house we lived in, he'd built another concrete two-story house, which he rented out. He had a son, Ihsan, the same age as I, and a daughter. Ihsan, who entered the military school, as I did, became a general.

On the slope above our single-level, one-room, government-owned house, Ahmet Aga owned three houses, lined up one behind the other. He lived in the front two-storied one with his wife, Fatma. Waterman Hafiz was a renter in the second, single-storied one. The two-story house furthest back was rented out by Ahmet Aga as a summer place.

Mulepiss For Beer

Compared with the other watermen, Hafiz wasn't considered well-off, because he'd started in the water business late. He was a renter. Since Hafiz had no place to stable his donkey, he used to put the animal in the stable behind our house. Father didn't charge him any stable rent. The Rumelian who abandoned this house and escaped to Greece, must have owned a donkey, because our house had a stable behind it. He'd either been a waterman or had sold rides to people on his donkey from the quay to the houses.

Hafiz was a small, short man with skin pasted on his bones—swarthy and skinny, like a can of nerves. He was as high-strung as a taut bow. His lips were thin and teeth pure white. Though his name was Tevfik (which he used to pronounce "Tawfik" in his Arabic accent), he didn't want to be called by it, just by Hafiz. He was from Erzinjan. Because he always tried to say a long sentence in the time you would say one word, and say a long word in the time of one syllable, he spoke in a great clatter, foaming and squirting like beer from a bottle with the cap just opened...

To be able to understand what he said, one had to become accustomed to his accent. He used to call my father "Shih Efendi" by expelling the letter "h" sound from some place deep down in his larynx, as if it would tear his throat. He was trying to say "Sheyh Efendi." Hafiz used to visit us often and tell about his war experiences. In World War I, he'd fought on the Eastern Front, and later on in the desert. I heard the names of places he'd fought, like Sinai, Gaza, Suez, and Kutülammare, for the first time from his lips. My father liked Hafiz because, like himself, he was a conservative and against Mustafa Kemal. In those times, because surnames hadn't yet been adopted, Ataturk was referred to as Mustafa Kemal Pasha or, more often, simply as the Gazi. Neither Father nor Hafiz ever let the words "Gazi" or "Mustafa Kemal" pass their lips. If they had to speak of Mustafa Kemal, they would say "the Blind" or "Salonica Convert." Among all the conservatives and reactionaries, Mustafa Kemal was referred to in those terms. Because his one eye seemed to have a slight cast, they claimed it was glass, so they called Mustafa "blind." And they considered him a Jewish convert to Islam because he was from Salonica.

In those times, I couldn't understand why Father was an enemy of the Gazi, because my father had left wife and family behind to voluntarily join the War of Liberation. Mulling this over later on, I discovered the reasons. Before the National War of Liberation began, in a communication to the people, Mustafa had asserted that he nourished the aim of preserving the "Office of the Caliphate from occupation by the enemy." Many men like my father had joined the war in order to protect the Caliph and preserve the Caliphate. After the war was over and the entire Caliphate, which they'd fought to save, was banished from the country, they reached the conclusion that they'd been deceived.

I listened with interest to Hafiz's war stories, which he punctuated frequently by swearing, "By God it's true!" to make his listeners believe him. But upon my realizing that one of the stories he told was a lie, I never listened to him again. Here is his anecdote that sounded like a lie to me.

Hafiz was an orderly in the service of young German officers on the Sinai front. In that desert heat, the German officers often had Hafiz fetch them cold beer from the ice box. Hafiz believed as Father did: principally wine, but drinking even one drop of any strong spirits was a sin. Hafiz was very angry at these "German unbelievers" who glugged down their iced beer. And the "German unbelievers" who glugged down their iced beer got mad at Hafiz if he failed to bring them cold beer whenever they wanted it. One day, when Hafiz saw that no beer remained in the icebox, he became flustered. There was no chance of going to get beer from anywhere. So he took the empty beer bottles and went to the pack mules. Whenever a mule made water, he'd hold a beer bottle underneath him. Thus he filled the bottles with mule piss and put them in the icebox. When the German officers asked for beer, Hafiz rushed in with the ice-cold mulepiss. From high above the mugs, so it would foam up well, he poured the mulepiss, and oh how it foamed! Those German officers drank it, and what's more, liked it so much that they said, "Ah-h!"

Hafiz knocked himself out laughing at this clever trick: "*Kih kih kih!*"

At that age, I'd never tasted beer, yet even I couldn't believe that German officers would think mulepiss was beer. Hafiz, who kept on swearing "By God it's true!" to make people believe his words, saying that beer resembled mulepiss, did so because he'd never drank nor known the taste of beer, and he'd fabricated this lie. Perhaps the other war stories he told were true, but from then on, I had no belief in him.

Hafiz had a year-old son named Jazip. Even when only a boy myself, I loved children very much. Because I liked Jazip a lot, I used to visit Hafiz's house.

We heard that Hafiz beat his wife, and on my account too. One noon, when he returned home for lunch, I was there. His wife was nursing Jazip and, evidently, I was looking at her breast. I don't remember such an incident at all. But Hafiz, so the story went, beat his wife because she showed me her breast while suckling her baby. After hearing this rumor, I never went to Hafiz's house again.

My father decided I should be away from the oppressive, worrisome atmosphere in our house for a time. I heard him discuss the matter with our acquaintances.

My Uncle Galip, after suffering unemployment year after year, finally obtained a job teaching in Gebze's Balchik Köyü. As far as I'm concerned, Uncle Galip was one of Turkey's most rare and learned men. (Today, I'm still of the same opinion.) Imagine that great Dervish, Galip, having to become a village teacher!

An Addition and Explanation

A few days after the above portion of my memoirs were published [as a newspaper serial], I learned from various people that I was being talked about at the mosque. Some preachers and imams were quoting my work and discussing me. I was at a loss to know in what connection my name had entered the mosques, because those who reported it hadn't given me any concrete facts. My sister told me about it first; but I didn't dwell long on the subject. Later, upon others mentioning it, my thought was that they were, at the most, saying in the mosque

10

that I was performing a good deed by establishing a charitable foundation.

Lawyer Burhan Apaydin threw light on the subject with an explanation: An acquaintance had telephoned him and asked, "How can Aziz Nesin write such things? He's giving the reactionaries an opportunity to use his writings..."

What's further, an imam, a client of his, informed Burhan Apaydin that this writing of mine was being read in the mosques in order to create enmity for Ataturk.

I thank Burhan Apaydin for giving me this opportunity to explain.

In this biography I'm trying to write my memoirs realistically, as I believe them to be true, as I lived them, as I witnessed every event, even though they may be turned against me. And the sentiments I wrote concerning Ataturk were not my own beliefs, they were my father's. In order to protect my father, I can't continue without explaining these things. There remains the fact that I didn't write them just to tell about Father; I wrote them because they are thoughts which are explanatory of this entire era, and because some people held that opinion.

The interesting thing here is this: the ideas the reactionaries discussed among themselves and propagated, in addition to those remarks against Ataturk (which *they* hadn't the courage to write), they found the means to spread through the medium of my writings. They are cowardly, without conscience and two-faced. They are opportunists who, in order to reach their destructive aims, will even utilize in the mosques the work of a writer who is their enemy.

If they should ask, let me explain briefly what my thoughts concerning Ataturk are: I have a very great respect for Ataturk. To dare to denigrate his great value in our history is either deception, ignorance or treachery. I am neither a Kemalist nor an Ataturkist. But I believe that in the society, and under the restrictions of present-day Turkey, even Ataturkism is extreme liberalism.

The existence of those so low that they would dare use parts of my writings, torn out of the whole context, in order to promote enmity against Ataturk, shows that the reaction, fanaticism, and conservatism of fifty years ago still continues today, moreover, in an organized way.

Gegbuze's Balchik Village

It had been, at most, two years since I'd seen Uncle Galip. But because the dimensions of people and places in childhood seem very big and the time very long, it was as if a century had passed since I'd seen him.

I was going to spend my holidays in Balchik Village with Uncle Galip. I can't remember the train journey at all. From the recollection of that journey, which has completely been erased from my memory, only a station sign is now before my eyes. It was the sign for the Gebze station, written in black paint on a white background. "Gegbuze" was written in Arabic script by using two *gef* letters with elongated tails, side by side. I learned then that Gegbuze, written with Arabic letters, was pronounced "Gebze." Perhaps Gebze's old name was Gegbuze.

There were phaetons that went from the station to Gebze. But we went on foot. There was no transportation between Gebze and Balchik Village. On that hot day, I walked all the way there. At every step, my feet were buried in the soft dust of the road.

One entered the village through the cemetery. A half-ruined mosque, whose minaret had long since fallen down, occupied the center of the village; it was obvious it hadn't been used for years. For as long as I stayed there, no prayers were performed at that mosque, nor were there any calls to prayer. The two-room house adjacent to the mosque was Uncle Galip's. He lived in the smaller of the rooms, and the other was the classroom. Inside, a few rows of old wooden benches... Everything lay under a thick layer of dust.

In his single-windowed room, Uncle Galip's dirty bed was spread out on the wooden bedstead. I was to sleep together with him on this bed. The window casement, used as a shelf, was filled with books.

Balchik was the first village I'd seen.

During the two years that I hadn't seen him, Uncle Galip had broken down and aged twenty years, his joy and hope finally lost. He'd started writing satiric poetry. I went to Gebze once or twice on bazaar days with Uncle Galip. We ate kebab at a place near that big mosque. Then, on low-legged rush chairs, we sat under the broad shade of a plane tree and drank tea. There were Gebze intellectuals, whom Uncle Galip knew, around him. I recall that one of them was a Dervish, employed as an officer-clerk at one of the Gebze courts. Another was either a poet, or had memorized a lot of poetry. Uncle Galip pulled a very cheap notebook from his pocket and read his poems aloud from it.

Only a few notebooks from Uncle Galip have, somehow or other, remained with me. I am now thumbing through them; in them I find some of those verses he read to his comrades forty-five years ago under the plane tree in Gebze:

Oh King of the universe,
Appear! Console!
No grace from Thee,
No one saves me;
Oh Master of this body,
Appear! Console!
My eyes turned upon Thee,
I see no other than Thee,
Everywhere my face toward Thee;
Appear! Console!
My every deed, revolt and sin,
My life gone; for Thee I long,
Father grant mercy
Appear! Console!
The world's end is death;
My path the saints' of God,
Your slave, Secret Galip.
Appear! Console!

In his poetry, he used the name of Galip Nihani [Secret Galip]. Beneath this poem is written 4/5 Teshrinievvel 340 [27 Sep 1922].

Among Uncle Galip's friends there, were other poets. One of them either wrote under the pseudonym of "Ishreti" [The Drinker] or recited poetry written by someone using the pseudonym. Uncle Galip copied those poems in his notebook, on the spot, because he admired them so much. I'm quoting Ishreti's poem from that notebook, which I still have:

> Think not that lovers pass on in death
> Impatient pilgrims renounce the earth.
> Strip crown and cloak, they don the shroud
> Ashamed to wear the robe of honor.
> See not only that rider's face they say
> Mount the velvet coffin up and away.
> Remains lie behind in grave repose,
> Weeping for you, Drinker, bitter and indisposed.

Uncle Galip's monthly pay as a village teacher was something like fifteen or sixteen *lira*, definitely less than twenty. His greatest concern was his mother, whom he spoke of as "Valide" [Ottoman: mother], who lived in a village in Gerede. He worried about living far from her, not being able to bring her to him, and his inability to send her any money. Year after year, he couldn't even go to see his aged mother because he had no decent clothes and no money to buy her a present.

Carrying on an old tradition, according to their turn as set up by the village headman, every household in Balchik Village sent meals to my Uncle Galip, just as they used to do for the village imam. Every day, a boy from the household whose turn it was, brought lunch and the evening meal on a tray or in a basket. Generally, together with two bowls of food, no-fat buttermilk and household bread was sent. During the time I spent at the village, no meat or food with meat in it, nor dessert came. Balchik Village, which I hear has become affluent because of the minibus which operates from Gebze now, at that time was a poverty-stricken village. Because the week's or ten-day's supply was baked at one time in the oven at each home in the village, the bread would become very hard, gritty, and difficult to eat. In addition, this stale, hard bread would get wormy after two or three days.

14

One day I went to a neighboring village with Uncle Galip. They had me ride a horse there. Why, I can't recall. Perhaps for me to enjoy myself, to pass the time... The horse had no riding saddle, just a packsaddle, and the wood on the packsaddle hurt my calves. It was the first time I'd been on a horse. I even made him run, or thought I did... The horse was taking me anywhere he wanted to go. He gradually went faster, until I thought I was flying along with the horse under me. When he came up to a gate in the village, he stopped. No matter what I did, I couldn't make him move. What's further, I couldn't get off the horse. A village kid passing by looked at me struggling in the packsaddle and laughed.

"He won't go," I said.

"Of course he won't."

"Why not?"

"He's come to where he was going, that's why..."

The gate where the horse had come and stopped was the gate to his stable. He didn't suppose I was a horseman, so as he approached the stable, he speeded up and stopped there. With the help of that kid, who was bigger than I, I got off the horse.

The packsaddle had galled my legs so badly, that the pain lasted several days and I walked bandy-legged.

Uncle Galip was not my old Uncle Galip. He wasn't interested in me and gave me no lessons. He'd become a pessimistic, withdrawn person. My father came and we returned home together.

Escape from School

I was frequently running away from school. Most of the time I told my father that school was in recess. Father, with his endless trust in me, believed this lie just as he did everything else I told him. Like those of every other truant school child, my relations with the school were gradually becoming strained. At the beginning, it was my intention to be absent for a single day; but upon not going that day, I couldn't go the next, nor the days following.

15

I would announce I was off to school, leave the house, then return a few hours later. When Father asked why, I invented lies, such as: "They said school was closed, but I hadn't heard about it."

I played truant because, due to my father's being alive, I felt guilty about going to the Orphan School, where only fatherless children were supposed to be educated. I was scared to death that one day it would be heard, or somehow learned, that Father was alive, then they'd throw me out of school in disgrace. Almost all the time, I was possessed of such fear that, in trying not to think about having a father, I thought about mine constantly. Repeatedly, and at the most unwarranted times, I would start talking to my friends about him: "My father said..." "My father suddenly came..." "At once, I saw my father..."

Then I would try to collect my wits and change my words. This was happening several times a day. The thought of my father, like a contrary notion one tries not to think about, had become stuck to my brain like a tick. I'd slowly begun talking more about my father, especially among my friends.

One day, when a remark about him escaped my lips, a classmate by the name of Fikret, his eyes wide, asked, "Do you have a father?"

I'd fallen into a mess that couldn't be explained away. I was confused as to what to say, what to do. The blood rushed to my face; I must have turned crimson. I faltered, stuttered.

What could be so painful, so agonizing for a boy as to deny his father, especially when he loved him greatly and adored him as I did?

What should I have said to Fikret? I'd rather have died than say I had a stepfather.

So it was with these anxieties, this unbearable discontent, that I was running away from school. But, at the same time, the words my mother spoke when she died were always in my ears: "With my son in boarding school, I can die happy!"

I wanted to study, and yet I wanted to run away from school. I was in a quandary and just couldn't find a way out. Thus the drama of my life had already begun at that age.

Father didn't suspect that I was sluffing school, because he trusted me and believed everything I said. The administrators

16

and my teachers at the Orphan School weren't suspicious of the forged excuses that I brought them either, because I was industrious and they liked me.

It was the month of Ramazan. That year, Ramazan came in the winter. I'd lived those amusing, traditional, unforgettable, beautiful nights at the Orphan School during the previous year's Ramazan.

It was the month in which the school administrators were most tolerant toward the students. We ran about and played until the *Sahur* [the meal before dawn] hour. After the *Sahur* meal, we went to bed and slept till noon. We were spared being awakened early on winter mornings before the sun even rose.

However, most of the nights of this Ramazan, I spent at home, a truant from school.

The only mosque on Heybeli* Island was at the Naval High School. Those living in houses on the hill found it difficult to go to the mosque at the quay to perform the special *teravih* prayer and then return to their houses on winter nights.

In our neighborhood, under the leadership of my father, they started performing the *teravih* prayers at waterman Ahmet Aga's house. Father would be the imam, who led the prayers; I would be muezzin and recite the call to prayer. I climbed the stairs to the high porch on the front of Ahmet Aga's house and recited the evening call to prayer from there.

Feyyaz, the Island mosque's muezzin, stuttered badly. He spoke with great difficulty. However, his voice was very melodious, and he didn't stutter at all when reciting the call to prayer or Muhammad's Birthday Poem.

While I was reciting the evening call to prayer from the high porch on front of Ahmet Aga's house, yelling so that the inhabitants of every house on the island would hear me, I used to fancy my voice was as beautiful as Muezzin Feyyaz's. In later years, after people kept mentioning it and shushing me when I was about to hum a ditty, it dawned on me that my voice actually was quite unattractive. As a matter of fact, in my childhood they did like my voice when I recited the call to prayer; but there's no doubt that they didn't like it because it

---

* tr. I have omitted Nesin's long explanation of why he spells this *Hegbeli* rather than *Heybeli*.

17

was nice, they liked hearing a little boy recite the call to prayer.

Fatma Anne

Waterman Ahmet Aga was a man of few words, unrefined in speech, a loutish egotist. But his wife, a negress, was a good-hearted, well-bred, extraordinarily clean, tidy woman. Everyone around there called her "Fatma Anne" [Mother Fatma]. She had in her the whole essence, the personality of motherhood, and thus, calling her Fatma Anne was most appropriate. She had no children, but she loved all the children around there as if they were her own. And she loved me most of all. Maybe the other children also thought Fatma Anne loved them best. Perhaps too, she showed more affection toward me than the rest because my mother had died recently. Long in advance of the holiday, she prepared the presents she planned to give the children. No matter how many children came to kiss her hand on the holiday, a present was found for each. She tried to help me forget my pain at the loss of my mother.

Three lines scarred each of her cheeks. Obviously, these lines had been scratched on her cheeks with something sharp by some tribe some place in Africa, when she was still a child, in order to make her pretty, for decoration. I likened those scars on her face to the splits in the center of bread loaves, fresh-baked out of the oven, like the split in the center of a black loaf... When she laughed, those lines on her plump cheeks, by widening and spreading, seemed to laugh too. Because of the lines which laughed on her cheeks, her own laugh was more joyful. Fatma Anne's tongue was the sweetest of any woman I knew; she spoke in the best Istanbul Turkish.

The edge of the snow-white headscarf, with which she always covered her head, reached over her shoulders, her back, and extended down to her breasts. The color white predominated in her house: pure white cambric curtains, cream-white curtain swags, corner cushions (the embroidery of which was called white work), the white linen scarfs, the

18

table cover of white voile, whitewashed walls, her white headscarf, the shiny white mother-of-pearl prayer beads in her hand, and her pure white sparkling teeth...Even her prayer rug was white. But in all this white, Fatma Anne had a light tint of blue. It was as if a pale blue cloud had drifted into the house through a window, and brushing everything with that delicate hue, had flown out the other window. The whiteness of her teeth and headscarf made the velvety blackness of her skin appear even darker.

In later years, I thought about why I'd loved Fatma Anne so very much. I loved her because she didn't treat me like a child, she acted as if I were her equal. Mother used to treat me the same way.

And today, whenever I eat muskmelon, I can't throw the seeds away. Even if I'm eating melon in a restaurant, I crack the seeds with my teeth and eat the inside. This habit originated with Fatma Anne. When she opened watermelons or muskmelons in her home, she didn't throw out the seeds, but separated, washed, drained them in a colander, and spread them on clean paper in front of the window to dry in the sun. On the second floor of her house, in the room with two windows looking on the sea, a raised platform ran the length of the wall. She would sit in front of one window, I the other... Sometimes my sister came too. We would munch on the sundried melon and cantelope seeds before us. We'd eat so many that finally the tips of our tongues would get sore and hurt.

We talked all the time. Now, I can't recall anything of what we talked about.

Sometimes I used to gaze at Fatma Anne's face and daydream, wondering from where in Africa, and how, she came here.

Fatma Anne's Thrift

Did she remember her father, mother, brothers and sisters? Was there a tree, a rock, a stream from her childhood that had left a trace on her memory? Did she see them in her dreams? How had she come to Istanbul; where had she been raised here;

19

by whom? From whom, and how, had she learned to cook such delicious food, learned this refined speech, her Istanbul manners, and this beautiful behavior? Above all, how had she come to marry Ahmet Aga? No one around there considered him Fatma Anne's equal. If he had three houses, it was because of her thrift, her business acumen. If in Ahmet Aga's circle there were friends and acquaintances, it was because of Fatma Anne's warm concern, her charm and her goodness.

While Fatma Anne was performing her prayers on her rug she'd spread, I would eat melon seeds and gaze at the steamers' wakes, which remained in lines—path after path—for hours in the calm sea.

One day, the white world of dark-skinned, pure-hearted Fatma Anne turned black. She wouldn't visit nor speak with anyone.

That summer, a couple had moved as summer renters into the big house behind Ahmet Aga's. The woman was all painted up, very fancy. Customarily, on the Island, summer rents were paid all at once, in advance. But somehow, for reasons clear only to himself, in spite of Ahmet Aga's being very tightfisted, he didn't take the rent from these tenants in advance. They paid no rent at all. What's further, summer passed and they didn't move out. Ahmet Aga often went there to ask for the rent. He'd begun staying for a long time. One day, Fatma Anne decided to visit too, not knowing Ahmet Aga was there. Had she known this, she'd never have gone. She was a proud woman.

She Was Deeply Offended

And they had left the door open. Fatma Anne saw her husband in bed with the renter woman. She returned home without saying a word. Her silence wasn't temporary; after this incident, Fatma Anne really never spoke with anyone again. From what I gathered, she just couldn't extricate herself from the shame of this situation she'd fallen into. She couldn't look anyone in the face. She couldn't tell anyone the ugly story. The ones who did tell were that woman and Ahmet Aga. If no one had heard, perhaps, in time, Fatma Anne could have regained her composure. But everyone had heard the story, and Fatma Anne didn't want to see nor talk with anybody. Even the white cambric curtains on her two windows facing the sea were always drawn. This dark-skinned, white-hearted woman, who had been uprooted and brought from who-knows-where in Africa at a very young age, who had no one hereabouts, but who generously gave her heart and soul to everyone—especially children, must have been so devastated, so buried in shame, that after this incident, she lived in indignation at the whole world.

When I saw Fatma Anne, whom I considered the closest woman to me, next to my mother, silenced in her deep dejection, it seemed to me that I was the guilty one, that I'd put her into this state. I could no longer go to Fatma Anne's house as I used to. I slowly broke off going there, and we became strangers.

Living Cheaply

We were living the years when the economic depression of the United States of America had spread over the whole world, years during which poverty-stricken Turkey—recently emerged from war—was also affected. Unemployment, poverty, and want penetrated everywhere. And one of the homes hit hardest by this depression was ours.

After my mother's death, it was very much harder for us to make a living. My father had no visible means of support. Actually, at no time had he ever had definite employment. That's why it is that I can't say what Father's occupation was. For a short period, in those days, he looked after the garden of a towered, white mansion. He was gardener at that place two days a week. But when winter came, that job was finished too.

I think that in the months just before her death, my father lavished everything he possessed on Mother, and had spared no effort to keep her from hearing of our financial distress.

Every morning, he used to leave the house early, as if he had a regular job, go to Istanbul on the steamer, always leaving at the same hour, and return home on the same steamer every evening with his bag, basket and big red kerchief, we called a bandana, filled with fruit and food. Because everything was cheaper in Istanbul than on the island, he bought the necessities there: big melons that had fallen and cracked, honeydews with one side squashed from being overripe, *chavush* grapes that had fallen off the bunch from being too mature, soft too-ripe tomatoes, every kind of vegetable... Most of the time, he used to even bring bread from the city. Stale bread was sold ten or twenty *para* or even a whole *kurush* cheaper in the Istanbul shops. Father used to say that stale bread was better for the health of our stomachs, and he never ate fresh bread himself. As for me, I loved fresh, hot, soft bread.

We didn't eat filberts, pistachios, chocolate, candy, and so on, but in their place, we had musk and watermelon seeds. My sister and I used to gather wild plants and vegetables from the meadows, such as mallow, chicory, dock, sheep's sorrel, and others whose names I've forgotten, for salad-makings. We were able to easily distinguish harmless mushrooms from the poisonous ones. Under the dense pines on the Priest School and Abbas Pasha hills, which were especially damp, beneath the span-long pine needles, we found and dug out mushrooms. We used to take a basketful home. I loved mushrooms grilled on the embers of a fire. Their juice would drip on the hot embers just like blood dripping from lamb cutlets on a charcoal fire. When a teacher of mine at school said there were the calories of only 250 grams of meat in five kilos of mushrooms, I was really disappointed.[*]

We also gathered our own fuel for the hearth and stove. How beautifully the dry pine branches burned, especially the cones with pitch that burned with crackly, popping sounds.

We used to raise chickens and turkeys. Father brought feed for the chickens from Istanbul. We had a feed for the turkeys which was my father's discovery: acorns. On the Island, there were many oaks among the pines. Even if they wanted to eat them, the acorns were too big to swallow. We would hold a turkey, open his beak, and force an acorn into his mouth by

---

[*] He was talking of wild mushrooms. I don't think that the cultivated ones could have so few calories.

hand, then watch the acorn's descent down his long neck. The turkey's craw would soon be filled with the acorns we fed him. This nutriment—my father's invention—made the turkeys very fat and big. The care of turkey poults was difficult. When they were chicks, their bottoms would crack in the heat because they had no feathers. That's why we used to grease their behinds.

We would sell our turkey and chicken eggs. There were many tuberculars who came to the Island for treatment and a change of air. Because daily fresh eggs were good nutrition for these TB victims, they sold for a high price.

Barges loaded with quince, walnuts, crabapples, and such fruit used to come from Yalova, Karamürsel, and other places, to the little bay, surrounded by a breakwater, below the olive groves. The crabapples were sold tied up in bunches. We bought fruit quite cheaply from those barges.

In short, we were forced to live cheaply, so we had to search and find ways to do so.

Most of the houses on the Island had a cistern, because there were no water sources. There was no cistern at our little house. In order not to spend money, we didn't buy from the man who delivered water by donkey. My sister and I—but more often just my sister—carried water home from the fountain at the landing in copper jugs. The road from the fountain to our house was extremely steep. But, to shorten the way, I chose an even steeper path, which was the best shortcut. The reason for my choice of this steep goat-trail that ran among the vineyards was not merely to take a shortcut, it was because I didn't want my friends to see me carrying those two jugs of water.

When these well-dressed and cared-for rich children, who were my friends and my age, grew thirsty, they wouldn't fill a glass with water and drink; they would ask the adopted children, the servant girls, the maids, or the boy servants for water; and if they weren't around, they'd ask their mothers. But they didn't say, as we did, "Gimme a drink!" because they were well-brought-up children. No matter whom they asked for water, they used to say "Would you get me some water?" This question, which didn't need an answer, was an order. If they wanted water from their mothers, they never failed to add a "please" to their demand.

23

Their fathers weren't like mine. They had a *Baybaa* [Mr. Father] or *Beybajim* [Mr. Papa]. I was amazed at how those boys could call their father "Mr. Father." Their affected speech, in which they called their own fathers "Mr. Father," as if he were a stranger, irked me. That's why I climbed up that steep goat path, carrying the two jugs full of water, staggering under the weight, so those kids wouldn't see me carrying water and make fun of me.

Father, I Thank You

I certainly didn't realize then what resolve, endurance, and strength poverty was developing in me. From that time on, life for me was a cruel battle, a pitiless contest. I didn't initiate this contest, I didn't want it; a struggle which was taking place outside of me enveloped and drew me into it. And in order not to be defeated in this battle, I was determined to win. In this contest—which I joined with two jugs full of water in my hands—I had to pass these well-dressed, well-raised boys, who even had to ask their mothers or servants for a glass of water. Thirty long years were to pass, after those days that I carried the full water jugs, before I was able to understand the superiority our poverty gave me over my friends, the rich boys. Only after thirty years did I become the writer who understood that the embarrassing situation of those days had developed in me the strength to resist, to endure, and I wrote an article in the Evening Gazette titled, "Father, I Thank You."

Father, it seems to me that I love you more than any other son could love his father.
Mine was another kind of love. What great catastrophes you saved me from by not being notable, important, or great. For that, I thank you.
And what if you had been rich! Then your name wouldn't have become mine.[*] Father, I thank you."
(From my book, *The Speech Machine*)

---

[*] tr. The author's given name was Nusret. Aziz Nesin was actually his father's name.

The Second Scar On My Forehead

It was before noon, a summer day. I was swimming alone in the sea from the rocky shore of a place called *Shafak* [dawn]. The children of those times didn't often wear swimsuits. Even some of the rich kids went swimming in the sea in their underwear. I'd gone swimming and gotten out. I was sunning myself and looking, from above, at the sea, which formed a small pool between two pointed rocks. A quiet, motionless sea...just as if the grains of sand, the pebbles on the bottom could be counted, one by one... Tiny fish swam in schools, then turning together the same instant, they traced zigzags in the water. Opposite was Büyük Ada [Big Island]... I heard footsteps coming from higher up. Our neighbors, a mother and daughter... The ends of bathing towels could be seen sticking out of the bags they carried. The girl was two or three years younger than I. Her big brother was my friend. She was a pretty girl with blonde wavy hair. They weren't well-to-do, but managed to make a good livelihood through their hard work.

When the mother and daughter appeared above, I acted as if I hadn't seen them and stood up so they could see me. Now, I'll dive head first off this high rock and amaze the two of them. "Bravo!" they'll say. They'll like my dive...

It seemed as if there was no sea below, but, rather, a flawless mirror, reflecting the clouds. I dived headfirst into this mirror. It shattered into pieces, the water splashed up.

I'd dived so fast, to show off for the girl, that my head hit a pebble or rock on the bottom. I got out of the water. Hot rivulets of fluid were spreading over my face. I put my hand to my forehead; it was bloody. My first act was to look out the corner of my eye at the mother and daughter on the path above to find out if they saw me in this awkward situation and were making fun of me. Hooey...they were long gone, and maybe they hadn't seen me at all. My forehead didn't stop bleeding. I went home and pressed salt, then tobacco, on it. The scar from that jackass trick of my childhood is still on my forehead.

I am climbing the hill with the two jugs full of water. When my arms grow tired, I set the jugs down and rest. Then, with new strength, I grasp the handles of the copper jugs. They bump my legs while I walk and water spills down into my shoes. As my shoes—patched sole-upon-sole—get wet, my feet slip out of them as I walk. When they strike stones or clods, I stumble. If I let my arms hang down, I can carry the jugs more comfortably, but then, the bottoms drag on the ground because I'm so short. When I try to bend my arms at the elbows and hold the jugs up to keep the bottoms from striking rocks, I get even more tired. I don't want it to be noticed that I'm tired either. As far as I'm concerned, I'm a big twelve-year-old boy.

I looked, and again it was that woman with her daughter. Upon seeing them, I became disconcerted. I set down the jugs. I must have put them on uneven ground, because one overturned. For some reason or other, I didn't right the upset jug; it seemed as if they might see and shame me... I could hear the dull gurgling of the water as it slowly poured out the jug's neck. I waited until it was gone. The hot, red soil instantly sucked up the water. The mother and daughter passed by without ever being aware of my presence. I went back to the fountain and filled the emptied jug again. All my enmity was against that jug, because it was the fat-bellied, skinny-necked symbol of the embarrassing situation I fell into.

The Fat Wallet

The summer people had left. It was the beginning of autumn. Hardly anyone who came to the Island for the summer remained. However, the summer renters of the three-story house on top of the hill, to the left of our house, hadn't yet gone back to Istanbul.

I was below the hanging trellis in front of our house. The renter of that three-story house was coming home, mounted on a donkey, as he was every evening. The donkey driver, a skinny old Greek, was trying to keep pace with the donkey, and every time he caught up, he poked him in the behind with his stick to speed him up.

I was very angry with people who rode donkeys up this hill (which we climbed four or five times every day), because they made the poor donkey man run after them on foot. It seemed nonsense to me for one person to ride a donkey so he wouldn't get tired, while another ran behind the donkey, and up a steep hill at that.

I think the man on the donkey was a grain merchant at Istanbul's Produce Dock; perhaps he wasn't a merchant, but I thought he fitted the role.

The Greek on the donkey arrived in front of his house and waited for the donkey man to catch up and help him dismount. With his help, he got off the animal. As he went up the steps to the front door, he rummaged in his pockets, perhaps looking for change... Evidently, he couldn't find any, for he pulled a wallet from his inside pocket. He gave the donkeyman a paper bill and took his change. Possibly because the donkey was tired, the donkeyman didn't mount, but left, prodding the donkey along with his stick. As the Greek merchant raised his hand to ring the bell, the wallet fell from inside his coat to the ground. He probably hadn't put it securely in his inside pocket. The door opened, and the man went inside.

The house was only about forty or fifty steps away. I'd seen everything that happened.

I jumped up, ran to the house, and rang the bell. The Greek merchant must still have been in the entry, because he opened the door himself. I pointed to the wallet on the ground. He leaned down and picked it up. It was a fat wallet. He opened the wallet and it was loaded with money. I didn't leave; I waited with the hope that he'd pay me. The merchant counted the money in his wallet. When he found that none was missing, he put it back in his pocket. Probably, he thanked me too. He closed the door.

Only God Is The Eternal One

One must wait for the earth in a grave to settle well before building a wall around it or setting a gravestone. If it's done before, as the body rots and the ground sinks, the wall will fall

27

and the gravestone lean. We waited a winter to fix up the grave for my mother. The first summer, Father bought bricks, sand and cement. He hired a mason and had a wall built around Mother's grave.

Explanation: As I read this memoir again, which I'd written previously, I find that I erred. Our memory makes its own selection from our impressions in consonance with our inner desires; it erases some and changes others. Our memory forces incidents, which belittle or degrade us, into an entirely different form in order to conform with our secret wishes. For example, here I wrote that my father had a mason build the wall. When I reread what I'd written, I thought and thought, then recalled that it wasn't that way. Because I had an inner desire for my father to have a mason lay it, so the wall around my mother's grave would be well-built, my memory changed that event. Actually, it wasn't like that. My father built the wall himself. This little recollection, which changed my memory to fit an inner desire, has made me think of my memoirs in general and thrown me into doubt. No matter how sincere we are, no matter how hard we try to write things as they are, to what extent have we told the truth when we relate our memoirs? Our memories change our recollections in order to exalt our egos, without our even being aware. While we sincerely think we're telling the truth, we tell what our memories have invented. Still, within my capabilities, while attempting to double-check my memory, I will try to write my memoirs truthfully.

Father bought iron fencing and two gravestones from the cemetery watchman. It was obvious they'd been torn up from an old grave with no owner. The watchman had sold them very cheap. The iron fencing was all bent and crooked. Father struggled for days to straighten the bars. One of the gravestones had only carved flowers on it, the other had writing. My father erased the writing in the stone with a steel chisel.

I was to write the inscription for my mother's headstone. I bound two lead pencils tightly together. Father and I got hold of the other necessary equipment and went to the cemetery. With the two pencils I'd tied together, I wrote on the surface of one of the marble stones, *"Ve Hüvelbaki"* in the *sünüs* script, and in Arabic letters; that's how Father wanted it. (The meaning of these words written on gravestones—"*Baki kalan O'dur*"—is "Only God is the eternal one.") And under this, still in Arabic letters, in the old *rik'a* script, I wrote Mother's name: "Hanife Havva." I wrote the dates of her birth and death, and at the extreme bottom, "*Ruhuna Fatiha*" [Bless Her Soul].

Father had brought with him chisel and hammer with which to carve in the stone where I'd drawn with the pencil. He began to engrave in the marble with a steel pencil, what I'd written on the outside with a lead one. This work continued for days. Of course, the result really wasn't professional, but it was satisfactory as far as we were concerned. It was good, we liked it. A headstone had to be made for Mother. This was the only gravestone and wall we could build, because we were forced to live so cheaply.

The Beggar's Daughter, Marusa

A very beautiful Greek girl, named Marusa, and her husband, Rejep, moved into the second house on the right side of ours. It was a tiny one-story house. One entered directly from the front door into the kitchen and passed through to the house's single small room. And an iron four-poster bed, with brass knobs, covered half of that room. There was a mirror in a brass frame between the posts at the head of the bed. The bed was enough, why would they need any other furniture?...

Rejep was from Marmara Island. Marmara Island was a barren place which raised only onions; but they fished there also. While Rejep was serving at the Heybeli Island Naval High School, he fell in love with the Island's beautiful Greek girl, Marusa. Upon his being discharged, they married and settled on Heybeli.

Rejep was a fisherman, a tall, swarthy, smiling young man. He seldom spoke, remaining silent as if he didn't know how to talk; he just smiled. And while smiling, rows of white teeth sparkled. He wore sailor's trousers of blue serge. He was a man who looked handsome in anything he wore.

There was a rather elderly Greek woman, with hair gone gray and ratty, who wandered barefoot, begging in front of the coffeehouses along the dock at the Heybeli Island wharf. Sometimes a sickly but quite beautiful girl-child of indeterminate age, perhaps ten or thirteen, rambled about with her while she begged. This unfortunate girl was also barefoot and dressed in rags.

Well, Marusa was this beggar woman's daughter and the little girl was her sister. It wasn't easy to believe that such an ugly beggar woman had a daughter as beautiful as Marusa because Marusa was fair-skinned, limpid and pure, like a husked almond with the skin peeled off. Her jet black hair extended past her waist. The purest Greek beauty: her smile charming, glance charming, posture charming—charming from head to toe. A sparkling Mediterranean girl... And Rejep was like a hard, silent rock from the island of Marmara, upon which that sparkling, dancing sea struck and broke into bubbles and foam...

Rejep and Marusa both loved me. They remained strangers to everyone around there but me, as if they were living a forbidden love.

Fisherman Rejep had forbidden Marusa to talk with her mother. Perhaps due to the old woman's being a beggar, or possibly for some other reason, he didn't want her coming to his house. This being the case, when fisherman Rejep wasn't home, Marusa used to take her mother and little sister in and give them food to fill their stomachs. She also cautioned me not to tell Rejep.

One day Rejep and Marusa moved away. Much later, we too had moved from that house on the Island to Istanbul. But because we couldn't move out all of our things at once, from time to time, I would go and stay at that house. On one of my trips to the Island, I heard from someone who knew him: Rejep was in jail. In a jealous rage he'd knifed Marusa and killed her.

In her every glance at Rejep, Marusa's jet black eyes used to sparkle with fire, she loved him so much.

The Fire Prayer

One day, before noon, first a little smoke started coming
from the third house to the right of ours, then flames spurted
forth. The house was on fire. All the neighborhood was
alarmed. The houses were of wood and built one next to the
other. Our neighbors were carrying their belongings from their
homes and piling them on a nearby slope. But we couldn't take
our belongings out of our house, because my father prevented it.
Though in control of his bad temper, still he was sternly
yelling: "Stop! Leave it alone! Don't touch it! Nothing will
happen! The fire won't harm us!"

He knelt down on the sheepskin. And, telling his beads,
prayed. He was reciting the fire prayer. Fire and flame
wouldn't touch the house of he who recited this prayer. Even if
every house burned, not one spark could fly onto our old, rotten,
wooden house with its dry, warped siding. When my sister
couldn't stand it and wanted to smuggle out one or two
belongings, my father saw her and yelled. Everyone else was
outside, but Father wouldn't leave the house. Hafez rushed in
and said, "Come on, Sheyh Efendi; outside!"

Waterman Ahmet Aga came and urged, "Come on, Sheyh
Efendi!"

Father, with the belittling smile of one who knows many
things, said, "Our house is insured, it won't burn!"

There was no telephone. It was difficult to inform them, so
the fire department was late in coming. It was hard, too, for
the fire-cart to climb the steep hill. But most difficult was
finding water on the Island to put out the fire.

The great, long foundation bolts of the house which was
burning grew white-hot, whined through the air like shells,
and flew far. It was feared that these fiery bolts would ignite
the other houses or the pine trees.

The firemen pumped water on the houses most likely to
catch fire. When the burning house collapsed and fell in the
flames burned even stronger, and the fire roared louder. But the
wind suddenly started to blow in the opposite direction and
fanned the flames away from us. Our house had been saved
from the fire. Near evening, the fire was completely

extinguished. However, the next day until evening, smoke and hot steam rose from the burned pile of rubble.

At the time of the fire, word spread of my father's not leaving the house. The rumor that our house didn't burn because of the prayer he recited, was on everyone's lips. Thus, my father's influence increased.

I would tell Father, "The wind shifted, and that's why our house didn't burn..."

And he would say, "True, but who shifted the wind, my son, and why did He shift it?"

An Epileptic Woman

Above the road that goes to Ayazma, behind the Navy High School, were two rows of look-alike wooden houses, called the *Beylik Evler* [G.I. quarters]. The Navy High School and Naval Academy teachers—those on duty there—and naval officers used to live in Beylik Evler.

On the first floor of one of these two-story houses lived one of my father's acquaintances, Hasan Usta [Hasan the Master Craftsman]. Hasan Usta was a master boilermaker at the Navy High School. Invariably, he wore dark-blue clothes, a white shirt, black tie and well-shined shoes, the same as worn by the administrators of the Navy High School. He came from Sivas. Short but broad-shouldered, he was a stoutly built man with a large head. Perhaps he appeared short due to the stoutness of his body. Hasan Usta's body was so husky that only if he were two meters tall would his height correspond. He had a son three or four years my senior. He'd given his son, who was uninterested in education and who, at that age, had only been able to finish elementary school with difficulty, to a Greek grocer as an apprentice. The son, like the father, was stout, husky and strong.

Upon the death of the boy's mother, Hasan Usta had married a second time. His second wife was young and beautiful. But the poor woman had epilepsy. At unexpected times, the woman would suffer epileptic seizures. Furthermore, these attacks would last a long time, sometimes even two or three hours. When having these fits, the woman would fall and suffer cuts and bruises. Every day, Hasan Usta went to his job, his son went to the grocery store where he was an apprentice, and no one stayed at home except the woman. Sometimes, upon Hasan Usta's return from work, he'd find his wife there, injured. He'd requested that Father let me stay at their house and visit with his wife during vacation, when I had free time. For this reason, I stayed days, and sometimes nights, at Hasan Usta's house.

My father used to recite prayers for this epileptic woman and try to make her well. Every two or three days, he came to pray over her. He'd also written an amulet for her. It must have been the power of suggestion, but Father's prayers had a positive effect. As the epileptic seizures occurred less frequently, Hasan Usta became filled with hope that his wife would recover. He felt that if my father would pray right at the time the fit came, the woman would be completely cured.

One day, the two of us—Hasan's wife and I—were at the house. I think she was nineteen or twenty years old. I'd never seen her when she had a seizure. That day, while I was talking with her, the woman suddenly threw herself to the floor. Her jaws were locked. Foamy saliva kept drooling from between her teeth. She clenched her fists. All her muscles were taut and she'd become stiff as a board. She lay on the floor in a completely rigid seizure.

I couldn't do a thing. There was no one to call. I couldn't leave the woman in this condition to go tell some one, anyway.

There was an add-on room at the entry of the house, and the woman had fallen down there. I was taking care to see that she didn't roll down the stairs. How long this went on, I don't remember, but it seemed like an awfully long time to me. Soon, the woman began to perspire. Sweat beaded on her forehead. Her hair became soaked in perspiration. Gradually, more foam spilled from her mouth. First she muttered, then began to make unintelligible noises and murmurings. For a time, she convulsed. She tore her smock and ripped her underthings, so that I was ashamed to look at the half-naked woman. I couldn't decide whether I should stay there or leave the house. While I was hesitating, she wet herself. Later, she commenced to weep. She sobbed and sobbed. I thought her weeping was because she had come to and was ashamed at my being with her when she fell into that state. Later on, her husband told my father that every time she came out of her epileptic seizure, she wet and cried.

Then the woman, who'd stopped weeping, got to her feet, and though her gaze was directed at the walls and ceiling, she actually was looking at some indistinguishable point in the distance. She started to talk to people who weren't there and, from time to time, to laugh or yell at them. So, the talk of her speaking with genies and fairies had grown from this. It was also rumored that the woman had married a male genie, or that one was in love with her. Therefore, when she married Hasan Usta, the jealous male genie had made the poor woman this way.

She spoke sweetly with some people who appeared to her and fought with others. I even got scared when she looked right through me and talked with those imaginary people... But much later on, I came to the conclusion that the woman only pretended to talk with so-called genies.

The woman spoke for a long time, then sat down, fatigued. To come to her senses took a considerable length of time. She pulled herself together and changed her clothes. She said very little to me and spoke as if in her sleep. Then in the evening, when Hasan Usta came, I left.

My father tried hard to get the woman to tell about those hallucinations, the people she saw and talked to when she had a seizure. It was Father's belief that if she could tell, when she was lucid, what had happened during the seizure, the woman would be saved, but she couldn't remember what she saw or said during the epileptic fit. Some time later, saying that she'd slowly recalled, the woman related a few things. She even spoke of the young man and such.

I listened to the woman a few times when she talked about these things. It seemed to me that there was nothing she remembered from her epileptic state, but due to my father's influence she'd made up a few things to tell. While on the way home with Father, I told him I didn't believe her, that she'd invented something because he insisted. He told me that whether or not she remembered what she said or saw in the seizure was not important, and that even if she did make it up, what she told us was very important.

Another day, while my father was at Hasan Usta's home, the woman had another seizure. He prayed over her while she was in that state, but still she didn't get well.

From the top floor of boilermaker Hasan Usta's house, either the noise of stamping and fighting was heard or (when those noises ceased) the sound of violin playing. The history teacher for the Navy High School and Academy lived on the top floor. This teacher was blind in both eyes. Guided by the arm of a seaman, he went back and forth between home and school. He was a famous historian who'd written history books, especially naval warfare histories. This distinguished historian had three sons. Due to a well-known dread affliction, the three sons, like their father, were going blind. The hereditary disease had been transmitted through the father to the sons. The children weren't blind at birth, but later on, slowly began going blind. Usually, by the twelfth to fifteenth year, blindness was complete. The oldest son had been blind for a long time; the second had become so just recently. The small brother was half-blind. In a few years, he too would be blind like his big brothers. I had never seen them. They didn't go out. All of them knew how to play the violin. In their home on the top floor, they either played the violin or made a rumpus. Probably they roughhoused and wrestled to pass the time. There was no woman in their house.

Hasan Usta's son had an amazing talent. One night, when I stayed at their house, I became acquainted with his "gift." That night, Hasan Usta and his wife had gone visiting. His son was at home, along with a number of his friends. Because I was three or four years younger than they (at that age, three years seems a great difference), they considered me small and unimportant. Hasan Usta's son was slapping his fat stomach with his hand, just like playing a drum, and making music by passing wind. His marching in time with the drum, as if he were in a parade, lasted several minutes. What's further, he could perform this ugly drum solo any time he wanted. His friends laughed themselves silly at his exhibition.

Sex Education

Like all of my generation, I was brought up without any sex education. We received no sex education either indirectly, through movies and books, or directly. My father was a dignified man who didn't make jokes on the subject of sex, even among his friends. I've never, even once, heard him tell a dirty story, nor has he let anyone tell one to him. As a matter of fact, other people told all kinds of those vulgar stories. And although I've heard and learned many anecdotes of this type, I just don't like to tell them myself. (However, among these obscene stories, there are some which are so effective as the shortest means of interpreting political events, that when told with that aim, they are no longer obscene...)

My father, who never spoke about the subject of sex, said a few words to me in this regard one day. This was the first and last bit of sex education I had in my childhood:

A retired naval-officer friend of my father's lived in one of the Beylik Evler houses. We were passing by his house on our return from some place, and were going to visit him because he'd suffered a stroke. At his age, a man should never have had a stroke! He was still young. But he hadn't known how to take care of himself. Intelligent people take care of their health. After lamenting his friend, Father mentioned that some men suffered paralytic strokes because they slept too frequently with women. A man should refrain from having excessive sexual relations.

While on the way, Father had explained these things to me, choosing his words and speaking easily, as if the conversation were natural and of no importance. As a matter of fact, in those times, a father's telling his son these things wouldn't be considered natural at all. I really enjoyed my father's indirect counseling. It meant that I'd reached the age where I would now be able to speak about such subjects. I was twelve years old, so my father would consider me a young man from now on, and bring up this subject. Yet I still couldn't talk with Father on this theme, I just listened to him, walking silently beside him...

War With The Greeks

It had been five years since our war with the Greeks ended. But the dregs of the struggle hadn't yet been cleaned up nor the ill effects exhausted. Even among us children that enmity dragged on. We didn't even like blue and white, the colors of the Greek flag. My father had bought me two T-shirts, one with blue and white, the other with red and white stripes. I couldn't wear the blue-white striped T-shirt a second time, because my classmates at the Orphan School had teased me for wearing it.

We had battles with the Greek boys on Heybeli Island. The war of five years ago was continued as a game among the kids. Who were my war buddies? There's only one of them I seem to recall. His name was something like Jenan, Janip, or Jenap. He was a boy from a rich home. Later on, he entered the Navy High School. I didn't join in the war against the Greek boys because it was fought with rocks. To tell the truth, I considered throwing rocks as underhanded, and I was afraid of rock fights too... Even much later on, I still avoided rock fights. I always felt that if there was going to be a fight, it should be face-to-face, with fists, not with rocks from a distance.

One day, when we either grew bored with playing at the wharf square, or ran out of games to play, at the insistence of that boy whose name began with "j," I too went along when he cried, "Off to the Greek quarter!"

Actually, there was no place where the Greeks lived as a group, they were scattered all over the island.

The boys filled their pockets with rocks, and I filled mine with rocks too. We walked toward Mill Point. Below the olive grove, we spied five or ten Greek kids.

We were imitating the war of five years before, and well knew who won.

When the Greek kids fled without defending themselves, I felt ashamed. I hadn't been able to throw one of the rocks from my pocket at them. I slipped the rocks out of my pocket, one by one, and dropped them on the ground without letting my comrades see.

The Greek boys weren't doing anything to us, so why should we fight with them? Should one start a fight without provocation? So that was why my relations with the boy, whose name began with "j," cooled.

Thirty-nine years would pass over this incident. *Coffee and Democracy* had been my first book translated into Greek. My Greek publisher would ask me for an introduction to this book of mine. And I would write up this incident—thirty-nine years later—with the wish for a future world of peace where Turkish children wouldn't hate the colors blue and white, and Greek children wouldn't hate the red and white; and the book would be published in Greece in 1965.

Malta Exiles

I am still burning with regret for not taking those pictures and saving them. But after all, at that time, I couldn't know their value and the worth of the writing on the backs of them... Only much later did I think that the pictures and writing could have any value.

Boilerman Hasan's son had piles of photographs in his possession, two or three hundred. They weren't thick photograph cards, but brown pictures printed on glossy paper. Piled in boxes in a cupboard, these pictures passed from hand to hand, were thrown here and there in the house, and ended up— one or two at a time—in the trashcan when the house was cleaned.

There were always men in these pictures, one person, two or a group together. Almost all of them were dressed in white. Most wore short pants, or shorts. Some carried a stick. On the heads of some were hats shaped like a bowl with cork inside for protection against the sun, which are worn in hot colonial countries and called sun helmets. They wore white rubber sport shoes on their feet. Some were bearded. Most had glasses. It was obvious from their dress that the pictures were taken in some hot place. In the autograph on the back of each picture was written "Malta" and under that, the date. They had penned long sentiments on the backs of the pictures and given them to one another as souvenirs.

At that age, I was of the opinion that Turks could easily be distinguished from other nationalities by looking at their faces and outside appearance. Turks had faces, facial lines, and movements peculiar to themselves; they could easily be distinguished from people of other countries. On the Island, there were people from a number of countries. I used to look at these people and classify them to myself, saying, "This is a Turk, this one isn't."

The men in the pictures weren't dressed like Turks, but if one looked at their faces, each was a Turk. And how beautifully they wrote on the backs of the photos—legible, pearl-like words. Only much later did I learn that these men in the pictures were Turkish intellectuals whom the English, who had occupied Istanbul, had exiled to the island of Malta. What valuable historical documents these pictures, with writing on the back, were, but they'd been thrown into the trash can! I think that they were taken, somehow, from the home of the history teacher upstairs to boilerman Hasan Usta's place.

My Son, Of Whom I Am Proud

Navy Commander Salim Bey and his wife, Süreyya Hanim—who adopted my mother at about age six and raised and then gave her in marriage to my father—were truly good people, whose equals are seldom found.

Salim Bey, who placed me in the Orphan School, thus providing the opportunity for my education, had opened a wholesale olive-oil and soap warehouse (long since in ruins) on one of the narrow, crooked streets at a place called Yaghkapani, between Unkapani and Eminönü. The storehouse, on the ground floor of an old stone building, had folding iron shutters. It was a small storehouse. Inside, in an office separated by a glass partition, Salim Bey used to sit at his desk, dressed immaculately as always. He employed a man to load, unload, and carry barrels and tins of oil and the sacks of soap.

Salim Bey certainly didn't know I played truant from school. I would go to this storehouse, kiss his hand, and stay there for awhile. If he wasn't there, his older son—my big brother Edip—would be.

In those days, I no longer went to their home because of the conspicuous manner in which everything I used at the table was separated from theirs, since my mother had died of tuberculosis. I was rather insulted at this display of fastidiousness, but couldn't call it entirely unjustified. Tuberculosis, which is communicable, was the biggest killer disease of that time. I couldn't show offense over it, break off, and stop going altogether, because every time I went, Salim Bey or my big brother Edip used to give me money. That I went to the store to get money is a fact, but my going to them wasn't merely for the money; I believed they loved me. I can't recall now how much they gave me, but it seemed like a lot of money then. Edip gave me more than Salim Bey did. I tried to go very seldom in order not to impose on their generosity and make them annoyed with me. I would kiss Salim Bey's hand and leave the store. So ashamed would I be of taking the money, that on the road I would be angry with myself and decide never to go again. I was as ashamed as if I'd gone there just to get money. As a matter of fact, this was true too; I was going in order to get money. I was in a quandary. I would resolve not to go again; then, two or three weeks later found me on my way once more. Upon entering the storehouse and sitting down, I realized I had the wish that they shouldn't give me money this time. But, you may be sure, if they hadn't given me any, I would've been even more hurt and offended. My dilemma was nothing other than the struggle of a poor boy who needed money to save his pride.

I will talk at greater length about Salim Bey and his wife, Süreyya Hanim, in sections further on. But, thinking that perhaps my life may not be long enough, that I may not find the opportunity to write my memoirs of those days, I wish, at this point, to present a letter that shows how Salim Bey truly loved me as a son, and feel once more inside me my unrepayable debt to such a benevolent man.

Fourteen years have passed since the days when Salim Bey gave me money at each visit to his store. I am a lieutenant in

Kars, and am married. I've sent a holiday greeting card from Kars to Salim Bey and Süreyya Hanim. In reply, Salim Bey wrote me this letter:[*]

My Son Of Whom I Am Proud:

We were worried and anxious at not knowing since you left—until today—that you had arrived and what your address was, so we received your greeting card with pleasure. Our thankfulness and pleasure are difficult to express. Your mother, who got the good news that our daughter is "on the way" (is pregnant), asked me to write to tell you. She also said, "I wonder if he has a youngster like his big-brother doctor." Yes! The doctor had a son, named Özkan. You know he is in Izmir. Your big brother Edip's is almost ready to come (his child is about to be born). Abdülkadir can't visit due to his situation being very tight the past two months. (It was the difficult period of World War II.) God willing, you're comfortable. If it's cold around there, why, you're young and not afraid of the cold. How is my prettier-than-an-angel daughter? We cherish her health and happiness in our prayers. God willing, in the beautiful future, you will live endowed with happiness. You brother, Kadri, has no intentions yet. They've extended the requirement to first lieutenant. (Those not promoted to first lieutenant couldn't marry.) We await a letter. Our best regards, with love.

Salim Ergin, Navy Retired

This letter, sent in answer to my greeting card, and his other letters, told me that Salim Bey truly loved me. As I read his letters, I felt in his sincerely written words, his heart beating with love.

---

[*] tr. Salim Bey's Ottoman language expressions are unintelligible to most modern Turkish readers. Nesin has translated these into modern Turkish and made comments in parentheses.

His wife, Süreyya Hanim, wanted so much for me to call her "Mother." And I wanted to call her that. But after my mother's death, it wasn't within my power to call anyone else "Mother." However, my not being able to call Süreyya Hanim "Mother" cast no shadow on my great love for her, because I knew that she loved me too.

Respect For Paper

Whether written on or not, printed or not, I feel a respect for every kind of writing paper. I can't stand the edges of notebooks being curled, or stacks of paper being out of order. After reading the newspaper, I can't leave it as it is, turned inside out, with pages out of order. For instance, if someone sitting opposite me on a public conveyance raggedly opens the pages of the magazine or book in his hand, with a rip of his finger or a comb, I become upset right then and there.

Why am I this way? I can give the answer to this question by going back forty-five years.

First, let me mention that in my childhood, whether he could read or write, whether villager or from the city, every Turk would immediately pick up two things from the ground and put them on top of a wall, between siding boards, in a hole in a tree, or some place high above the ground. One of these was bread, the other, printed paper. These two things were not to be stepped on. Bread was "God's gift" and the printed page was holy. That is to say, he who picked up the bread, first kissed it and touched it to his forehead, then put it in a high place where it couldn't be stepped on. It wouldn't even be thought that something evil might be printed on the paper. Among the letters printed on the paper, the letter "Elif" was special, the most holy. "Elif" was symbolic for Allah, since it was the first letter in that word.

But my feeling of respect for paper doesn't result from my being devoted to this beautiful tradition, now forgotten.

Among my father's friends was an elderly Cretian, whose name I can't recall. He was older than my father. I'd never seen him without a shave. Though old, his clothes were neat and pressed. His tie, especially around the knot, was very shiny from wear. The sleeves of his jacket and trouser cuffs were frayed. He worked as a petition scribe at the Justice Building—which was later razed—above the Sirkeji wharf. (The big Justice Building at Sultanahmet hadn't burned down as yet either.) In the top floor corridor of the Justice Building at the Sirkeji wharf, he had a rush chair and a small drawer which he used as a table. The Latin alphabet hadn't yet been adopted, and Turkish was written with Arabic letters. Typewriters weren't used, so petitions were written by hand.

Early one evening, I went with my father to the courthouse in Sirkeji. The Cretian petition scribe gathered up his chair and table and put them away. First, we all boarded the ferryboat and crossed over to Haydarpasha, caught the train there, then got off at Pendik. We were on our way to the Cretian petition scribe's home in Pendik to stay overnight. Who knew how poor this destitute scribe's house would be! How we would spend the night there...

From the Pendik train station, we went down to the seashore and walked a few hundred meters on the narrow road along the shore. We came to a beautiful three-story frame house, above the sea, with a large garden—a cross between a mansion and a seaside home. We entered. Obviously, this was the elderly petition scribe's home. He lived, together with his family, on the three floors. The furnishings weren't rich, but they were nice and clean. We slept that night in a comfortable bed, spread with sheets as white as snow. Imagine my surprise at that poorly dressed scribe's being the owner of this beautiful house.

The next day my father explained it. In Crete, the scribe had been very rich. When he came to Turkey as an immigrant, he'd left much property in Crete. To repay him for the property he had abandoned, the government gave him this house which was confiscated state property. The house was fine; however, because he was elderly, the man couldn't find employment here and was forced to work as a petition scribe at the courthouse.

The next day was the weekend. We were spending the day off at that house. I can't remember now in what connection, but I had haphazardly ripped a piece of paper (at that time called dossier paper, but now, legal-size bond) in half. The old scribe said, "That won't do, Nusret Efendi, my boy; that just won't do! That's no way to cut paper!"

Among the things he told me that day, he repeated, several times, the words: "One must feel respect for paper! Whoever has no respect for paper cannot become enlightened." I can still hear this advice he gave me forty-five years ago. After this advice, for practical education, he folded a piece of bond paper in two. He ran his two fingernails a few times along the crease, then folded the paper backwards along the fold line and pulled it again between his fingernails a few times. As he did so, he said, "Your hands must be clean so you won't smudge the paper." Then, starting from the end of that fold line, he tore the paper in two. The torn edge was without fray, absolutely straight.

"As for books..." He looked for and found a book on the shelf whose pages hadn't been separated. He took pains to open the pages of the book with a letter opener.

"This is how...one should feel respect for paper," he said.

My Uncle Shaban

One of the places I took shelter during my truancy from school was my Uncle Shaban's house.

The last time I'd visited Uncle Shaban, my father's older brother, I was four or five years old. While on a few days' visit with my mother at Uncle Shaban's house in Dereboy, Bebek, I had caught the measles. And Uncle Shaban didn't want to shelter my mother and her child, sick with measles, in his house, so he turned us out. In those days, my father wasn't around. He'd caught the fever and gone off to hunt buried treasure—where, we didn't know—leaving us once again. We were waiting for a streetcar at the Bebek streetcar stop. I was in my mother's arms, wrapped in a blanket. I'll never forget the way the snowflakes softly fell on my cheeks, burning with fever from the measles, nor my mother's tears which also dripped on my face.

So, after that day that we left his house, I hadn't seen my uncle.

As my father saw it, a good person must have two qualities: one, he must have compassion; another, generosity... Father never liked selfishness. He loved and respected his big brother because he was his big brother, but he didn't like him at all, because he found him to be selfish, irresponsible and lacking in compassion.

A few months after my mother's death, I went to my uncle's house with Father. My father had finally started to visit with his big brother, but infrequently. And always, it was my father who looked him up. It never happened, even once, that my uncle looked up my father.

The house of my uncle, who had long since moved from Bebek, was in the courtyard of the Arab Mosque. Upon passing under the arch which opens on the mosque courtyard, you came face-to-face with my uncle's house. It was a little two-story wooden house. It was obvious from the remnants on the boards, from which the paint had blistered and peeled, that the wooden siding once was painted red. He lived in this house with his wife (my aunt-in-law), son (Muhittin), and his daughter. He was the night watchman at a tobacco warehouse. The tobacco warehouse was very close to his house; it was a big building on a dead-end street on one of the hills that extend from Tünel to Bank Street.

As to character, my father and uncle were complete opposites. Father was a generous person who felt all the weight of his responsibilities, was compassionate, and rushed to help... And my uncle? You know, there are men who, good or bad, no matter what circumstances they live under, live like kings, who were born to be kings. Well, my uncle was of that breed of men who live like kings. He loved living, dressing up, and ridiculing, but didn't know how to feel sad, to frown, or to think. Whether at home, at work, or anywhere else, everyone must accept his kingship—and they did! This kingly behavior wasn't feigned, it was spontaneous; for this reason, like it or not, it was taken seriously in his social circle. Though my uncle was the nightwatchman at the tobacco warehouse, I don't think he worked at it, because, when he returned in the mornings, he didn't sleep much during the daytime. I was even

45

witness a number of times to his joking with the director—perhaps he was the owner too—of the warehouse (who wasn't a Turk), and his saying, "Hey, boss!"

Uncle was rather tall and thin. He used to wear boots in the winter, *yemenis* [light slip-on shoes] in summer. He wore high-heeled, pointed-toe, black patent-leather shoes (called "egg-heels") with his heels crushing the backs. He took pains to wear expensive socks. In summer he used to wear riding breeches of thin wool, and in winter, of dark-colored homespun wool. A silver cigarette box was tucked in his cherry-red cummerbund. His vest and jacket were of a dark fabric. A five-strand silver watch chain passed through the top buttonhole and hung between the two vest pockets. On the end of the silver chain, in his vest pocket, was a big silver watch with a cover. His shirt, which didn't have a high collar, was buttoned all the way to the top button. In the back pocket of his breeches he carried a heavy brass shoehorn. This brass shoehorn's end was shaped like a bird and, when necessary, could be used as a blackjack. Upon the rare occasions he wanted to raise the back of his patent leather shoes, which he wore with his heels out, he would use this shoehorn. He never let go of his large amber prayerbeads with the silk tassel which smelled of attar of roses. The tip of his silver cigarette holder was also of amber. On his ring finger was a large gold ring with a big stone. (My father never wore a ring.) In wintertime, Uncle wore a sheepskin coat of homespun wool, or a short coat with a fur collar. If the weather was good, rather than wear his coat, he carried it over his shoulder.

According to what my father said, Uncle Shaban in his youth was quarrelsome, drank, and was on good terms with loose women. When I knew him, none of these habits remained. But he was a man who commanded respect in his circle of society and was esteemed. It was as if he were not the night watchman at the tobacco warehouse, but, instead, the owner. Everyone—where he worked, at the coffeehouse, on the street, and his wife at home—called him Mister Shaban.

At that time, his son Muhittin, whom I loved very much, was only four years old. Every day, my uncle gave Muhittin an amount of money that I had difficulty in getting my hands on in a whole week. And one of his biggest pleasures was his four-year-old son's swearing like a trooper about this and that.

"Swear at this dolt, my boy...now then, swear, my lion..."

Muhittin would repeat his most resounding oath and my uncle would laugh with pleasure.

In the morning, breakfast was held at home. If Muhittin tipped over his glass, my uncle would yell: "Throw it, my son! Break it! Strike, my boy!..."

If Muhittin picked up something as if he were going to throw it, whether it was valuable or not, and his mother dared to say, "Please...easy!... Don't throw it, my son!" my uncle would call: "Don't get used to being a coward, my boy...throw it! Break it on the floor, my lion!"

A couple of times a week the window panes, which Muhittin had broken by throwing something, were repaired.

A very surprising thing was that my uncle, without being obvious about it, was afraid of my father, who was considerably smaller than he. Perhaps he was like this because he wasn't literate like Father. As a matter of fact, my father was always respectful of him. Still, my uncle couldn't behave that way in front of Father. Once, my father criticized his big brother for giving Muhittin so much money: "Big brother," he said, "giving a boy this age so much money isn't good..."

My uncle laughed, with his usual ease, but he didn't say anything.

The Magnificent Lie

I kept on running away from school and going to my uncle's house. I was staying at his house two or three days in a row, and sometimes even a week. It was comfortable to live at his house.

Occasionally, I ran into my father at Uncle's house or at the home of someone else we knew. My father, who thought I was at school, would be surprised at seeing me in an unexpected place. I told him the lie that school was in recess. It was either a holiday, an official recess, or we had been vaccinated, or because of a contagious disease, that school was closed for a week or ten days. Father believed it, because in his view, I never told lies; I was a boy whose every word was to be believed. Because of my father's having such faith in me, after every lie I was crushed and felt an indescribable ache. Within myself, I made a decision to do something—I didn't know what. I must do something, must win such a success that I could be saved from this disgraceful situation with my father. I had to do something, but what? I just didn't know what it was. In order to find this unknown job which I had to do, I began buying the newspaper. Whenever I got hold of any money, I would buy the *Köroghlu* paper and also a daily. From that daily newspaper, I hoped to find some kind of help—what, in particular, I couldn't determine. I would search the school and employment ads in the paper. Which of the advertised schools could I enter, and for which of the jobs might they hire me? Wasn't there a free boarding school one could enter by examination? Or couldn't a job be found for a boy my age? Certainly I would find, one day, in the newspaper ads a job or a school suitable for me. There were ads in the paper for courses, schools, and jobs, but none of them were for a twelve-year-old boy who was a runaway from the fifth grade.

I could never, ever, forget my mother's last words: "My son is in a boarding school, so I won't die disappointed..." As for me, I was playing truant, and on top of that, lying to my father, who believed every word I said. I felt myself very degraded. While I was looking for ways to save myself from this ugly situation, I did something much more evil. I found the means of salvation in a lie. In order to conceal my lack of success and make my father happy with a false success, I told the biggest, the most magnificent lie: In school I was so successful, such a successful student, that my teachers found me deserving of a higher grade, and without an examination, had promoted me. Right while I was a school truant from the fifth grade, I'd told my father that I had been promoted to the sixth. Still, Father believed me. Only he didn't stop at just believing, he found that even the sixth grade wasn't sufficient for my knowledge and intelligence, and said, "If you wanted, you could even be promoted to the seventh grade..."

With this outlook of my father's, one could think him a very naive man. In reality, he was extraordinarily intelligent. I just don't know whether his innocence where I was concerned was due to his loving me a lot, or whether he possessed endless faith. It seemed to me that he appeared to believe some of my lies without actually believing them, and wouldn't throw my lies in my face and embarrass me.

Father was proud of my being promoted a grade. And he told others about it. It had been said so much, that I'd been promoted a grade, and I had repeated it so many times myself, that I began to believe my own lie. I acted as if I were a student in the sixth grade.

In our class there were one or two of our comrades who were promoted a grade, due to their superior knowledge. One of these was my friend, Faris, who was an artist after he completed law school and who, after being imprisoned for years for some political reason, died from bleeding stomach ulcers.

It's been ever in my mind: has my father's unwavering belief in every word I said been good for me or bad? The last time I took an account of myself, I reached the opinion that Father's belief in me produced a very good effect. His belief—even in my lies—made me so ashamed, that I tried to save myself from this disgraceful situation and really become a person to be believed and trusted. As a matter of fact, after becoming older, my deciding not to lie, regardless of consequences, and my sticking with that decision, was the result of my father's belief in me.

Would my father's procedure, if applied as a principle in the education of every child, have positive results? If the education of our children could have been tied to such models, how much easier it would have been for us! I think this procedure, which produced quite positive results for me, could have very negative results in another child.

First Relation With The Press

No newspaper came to our house nor to my uncle's. Only after Father was seventy-five years old did he get interested in newspapers and start to take two each day.

My first contact with the press had been with a journal named "Children's Voice," published, I think, by Faruk Gurtunja. When I had a little money, I used to buy this magazine and enter its contests. As a result of joining in some contest or questionnaire (the subject of which I can't recall now), colored postcards were sent to my home a number of times from the magazine. From time to time, I bought another magazine, whose name I've forgotten. It had horror stories in it. I used to read the stories in that journal to my father.

I was also reading *Köroghlu*, which Burhan Jahit (Morkaya), the famous writer, published. His novels were best-sellers at that time, but his name and fame are completely forgotten today. The year I passed from the third to the fourth grade (or the fourth to the fifth), *Köroghlu* was publishing pictures of students, who had no "incompletes" and were straight promotions, in addition to little pieces on what they thought about the future. My first publication was that piece published in *Köroghlu*. I'm truly very curious now as to what I wrote...

The Cock Fight

My uncle had a few chickens and a rooster. The neighbors had chickens too. They all used to wander together around the mosque courtyard. The neighbor's rooster beat my uncle's rooster, pecked him wherever he saw him, and chased him off. One day, when he saw his rooster taking a beating from another, my uncle became very upset. How could Mister Shaban's rooster take a beating from someone else's!

"This rooster will be butchered!" he said.

Pleading, with things like, "Pity, uncle! Please don't... I'll find a way out for him," I prevented the poor rooster's being butchered.

50

That day, I immediately went to Heybeli Island. In the
lean-to stable on our house, whose door opened out, we kept
hens and a swashbuckling rooster. One of the hens had become
so tame that she would fly up on top of the zinc-covered terrace
above the stable and call us by pecking with her beak on the
window pane there. Sometimes she'd awaken us early in the
morning. We would open the window and take her in. She
wandered about in our room and flew up on our shoulders or into
our laps. When it was time for her to lay an egg, she started
singing a song. Then we opened the window and let her out.
She would go to nest in the stable. The cleaning up of the tracks
this hen left in the room fell to my sister.

Our rooster was something to see! All of the ostentation,
all valor, all the audacity and spirit of roosterhood had been
concentrated in him. He wasn't a fighting cock, he was a show
rooster. But he was so well-kept, so well-fed, that he thrashed
all the roosters in the neighborhood and chased them off. The
one big obstacle to his being a fighter was that beautiful, that
great, comb of his which opened out in layers like a double rose.
His bright red comb, which burned like flames, was so large
that the tip of it rested well over his left eye. Just as the
rowdies wore their caps on one side in order to appear tough, our
rooster's comb leaning to the left made him more of a rooster
and added to his cockiness. In his plumage there were all the
shades of color from yellow to brown. His tail feathers turned
navy-blue, black, and poured out in profusion. When the sun
struck, his neck feathers would burn and change to all the tones
of color of red, yellow and henna; they shimmered and shone.
He was only two years old.

When I hurriedly came back to the Island, so my uncle
wouldn't kill his rooster who'd been beaten, Father wasn't
home. As I always did when I fed the chickens, I entered the
stable, swinging the feed pan in my hand. Thinking I was going
to feed them, the hens and rooster followed into the stable
after me. I closed the door. Due to the windowless stable's
being dark, it was easy for me to catch the rooster. In my hands,
he was making defiant sounds and plucking up courage.

On the ferryboat, a man praised me for not carrying the
rooster upside down, tied by his legs, as others did. I hadn't

even bound my rooster's legs. Holding him on my lap, I continually loved and petted him.

The man asked, "Where are you taking this beautiful rooster?"

I explained to him. Upon this, the man informed me that my rooster wasn't a fighting cock... Whether he's a fighting cock or not, still he'll fight the other rooster. He whips all the roosters in our neighborhood...

The man gave me some advice: Even if he were a fighting cock, if I turned him loose without his becoming accustomed to the place, he'd be beaten by the rooster who was... As they say, "Every rooster scratches in his own barnyard..." First, he must stay a few days in the coop with the hens, to get used to the place; after that, I could release him to fight. The things that man said stayed in my mind: "Why does a rooster fight another rooster? In order to defend his hens, his coop and himself..." So why, for whom, would a cock—who had no place, no country, no hens nor coop—fight?

Despite what the man said, I believed that my rooster would definitely fight the other rooster. But his words cast a doubt into my heart. If my rooster gets beaten, what then!...

Upon going to my uncle's house, I took the man's advice. I put the rooster in the coop. He stayed there a few days with the hens. He gave a couple of blows to the old rooster of the coop, as if in training, and quickly defeated him. From then on, he was king of the roost. One morning, I let my rooster and the hens out into the courtyard. The other rooster was nowhere in sight. Our fine bird—strutting, preening his feathers and making rooster-clucking noises—was acting the rooster for his hens. Immediately, the other rooster appeared. As soon as he saw our fine bird, he started to come up sideways on him, arrogantly. First he ran, but as he approached, he slowed down. My cock took up position against him too, but showed no boldness at all. I wondered if he was afraid or something!

The two of them faced off; they were circling each other with their backs half-turned away, their neck feathers ruffled and heads bowed to the ground. Though their heads were bowed, their eyes were on each other, and both were on "hair-trigger." The other rooster was tall, white-feathered and short-combed. When the two cocks came face-to-face, the other's superiority was clearly evident. My fancy rooster looked big because of his fluffy feathers. Upon seeing the other rooster's physical advantage, a shrewd idea occurred to me: as soon as my rooster seemed to lose, I was going to chase the other one off.

The roosters flung themselves at each other once, then backed right off. The second attack was something like a test of strength. Again, they leaped and came claw-to-claw. Right away, spectators started to collect around the fighting cocks. The crowd piled up and their numbers steadily grew, so that soon the mosque courtyard was going to be filled. With these spectators completely surrounding the cocks, when my rooster was beaten there'd be no chance for me to chase the other one off.

Either someone called him or he came on his own, but anyway the owner of the white rooster had arrived. He was one of the prayer-callers of the Arab Mosque. I had thought that the prayer-caller would be angry with me for getting his rooster into a fight. Actually, as if his rooster could understand his words, he kept on trying to incite and encourage him, saying, "Come, my lion, come on!...Good boy, good...Get him, lad!..."

The fight picked up momentum. I too grew very enthusiastic. Already, I'd regretted putting my rooster into the fight, but it was too late now. The white cock's height provided him with an advantage. In addition, he had a rosette comb—that is, a very short comb. My rooster couldn't peck that tiny comb, but the white cock, at every peck, opened up a wound in my rooster's big red comb, that blossomed like a double flower. My rooster was covered with blood. The blood didn't show much on his feathers because they were red, brown, and yellow, but at every clash with the white cock, his blood could be found on the other's white feathers.

Among those dozens of people, I was expecting one compassionate or reasonable person to step up and say, "That's it...That's enough! Have pity on the birds!" But where *was* that person?... I kept searching in vain for a reasonable man in that exuberant crowd.

The two fighting cocks leaped upon each other, withdrew, got up speed and leaped again. Beak-to-beak, talon-to-talon, a merciless fight... My rooster was receiving more blows, but he wasn't licked... And neither of the two was about to retreat.

I felt heartbroken and started to implore my rooster to give up trying to defeat the other, saying to myself, "What's the difference; if only he'd run away and be saved from the blows..."

My rooster, being shorter than the other, was forced to jump more. As weapons in the fight, their beaks, claws and talons didn't suffice, and they started using their spurs. (The spur is the hard, pointed nail, in the form of a little horn, that extends back from the inside of the rooster's legs.) At one point, the white cock clung with his beak to my rooster's meaty comb so hard that he couldn't let go, and he staggered and shook him. He was trying to climb on top of him. Blood spurted from my rooster's comb. Fighting for his life, with a swagger he freed himself, but he was badly shaken. He staggered a few times and drew back... "Ah, if he would only run away and be saved!" I begged.

Upon pulling back, my rooster, pretending to pick up some feed from the ground, once again made brave rooster noises. Obviously, he was resting and catching his breath. This time, my rooster attacked the other one first. He attacked,...then again... They collided in midair. The white cock's snow-white neck-feathers began to get plucked out and fluttered in the air like butterflies. There were red spots on the butterflies' fluttering white wings because my rooster's blood had smeared them.

A fearful thing happened. At the roosters' last leap and mid-air collision, my rooster's spur passed through the white cock's neck, hooked his craw, ripped and opened it up. The poor white cock collapsed to the ground and commenced to flop around. The greenish, dirtied corn, barley and plants, which flowed onto the earth from his craw, were steaming.

My rooster, the victor of this merciless battle, attacked the poor white cock struggling on the ground (now smeared with his own blood) a last time, like the Angel of Death. His strength, too, had become exhausted. He collapsed on top of his enemy and lay there.

The prayer-caller picked up his wounded cock from the ground and left. Most certainly, he intended to butcher the poor thing.

I picked up my rooster too, wiped the blood from his big comb, and put him in the coop.

What had my big worry been? To save my uncle's slovenly rooster from being butchered. But now, the prayer-caller was going to kill his beautiful cock, who'd fought bravely and was defeated, because his craw was torn open. All this effort of mine was not producing any good results whatsoever. And thus, with that dejection, I walked to Beyoghlu.

After that, a week—perhaps two weeks—passed. Again, one day when I cut school, I came to my uncle's house. My rooster wasn't around. I asked my aunt about it.

"Your uncle butchered him," she said.

"Why?"

"He was sick—it was so he wouldn't die unclean."

Raw Spirits

In those days, our enthusiasm over our War of Liberation and our newly founded Republic hadn't yet been lost. Everywhere in the country there were national and idealistic activities from the impetus of war. At this time, folk schools had been opened in many places in order to make the population literate. Citizens of every age who were not literate, by going to these folk schools outside of working hours, were getting an education, then later, after entering the examinations, were winning their diplomas.

In these folk schools, not only reading and writing were taught, but also subjects such as mathematics and geometry. The folk school teachers were people who were enthusiastic about the idealism movement of that period. The administrators truly wanted the people to read. If the folk schools of that period had continued, the people of Turkey would have been saved from the disgraceful situation in which, even today, sixty percent are illiterate.

My sister, who was illiterate because she couldn't go to school, began to attend the folk school that had opened on Heybeli Island. With that passionate selfishness in all children, I felt her going to the folk school unnecessary—so she *did* read, so what?...I must have found her undeserving to read and write. Only *I* could go to school, because...well, *I* was intelligent, *I* was bright. Perhaps it was because I was a school runaway that I couldn't abide my sister's going to school and felt a secret jealousy. But I didn't reveal this wicked feeling of mine in any way.

As a matter of fact, my sister possessed a quality, a peculiarity, a "thing" that one can't obtain through schooling, education nor a diploma. What was it, that "thing"? Must it be called maturity, common sense, aesthetics? My father, like his comrades in the Dervish lodges, still called those who had no share of that intangible "thing"—even though they had a diploma, money and a high position— *"Ham Ervah"* (Ham Ervah means raw spirits). As the great Yunus[*] [Emre] said in this quatrain:

> In worship of Thee
> He served in Thy house;
> Wretched Yunus was raw
> Praise God he is cooked.

And they called any member of the lodge who was the exact opposite of those "raw spirits," "The Perfect Man."

Later on, I saw and understood that common sense was much more important than being in high positions of power or being a "raw spirit" with a diploma. I've felt very sorry for people who have common sense and are unable to find the opportunity for an education, for they are the ones who have met with the greatest social injustice. My sister was a person who had common sense. Her lack of education was a great pity.

I don't know from where, or how, it came to our house, but there was a used jacket of gray and green-speckled wool fabric with ridged stripes. My sister unstitched. picked apart, turned

---

[*] tr. Yunus Emre (14th Century) the greatest and most popular Turkish mystic and folk poet; widely known in Turkey today.

that grown-up's jacket inside out, and made a jacket to fit me on the sewing machine left her by my mother.

"Let it be hunter's style!" I told her.

I don't know why that jacket had to be just like a hunter's. Perhaps I'd seen that style jacket being worn by one of the rich kids on the Island and taken a liking to it. This jacket I called "hunter" style, had tails, four pockets (two up and two down), accordion pockets with pleats in the middle, and a belt around the waist, with a buckle too. It must have been very funny to see a short boy, twelve years old, wearing such a jacket.

The secret, but real, reason for wanting my sister to sew me a jacket from an old, worn-out one, was my truancy from the Orphan School. I no longer wanted to wear the Orphan School jacket—with its name prominently displayed on the collar—and go to that school.

What small, detailed incidents of that age remain in my memory!

A black woman teacher on the Island had a daughter and a son. Her son was a handsome boy; her daughter, on the contrary, was homely. And the two of them were light chocolate-colored.

Early one evening—it was at the hour the shadows were deepening—I was running, for some reason I can't recall now. Five or ten paces ahead of me, I saw that girl. And the girl started running in front of me. I went my own way and didn't even look at her... A rumor grew that I chased that girl at night. Though my sister knew nothing of this incident, she defended me. I'd never mentioned the subject. It's obvious the poor girl, in her heart, wanted me to chase her, or maybe she really had thought I was chasing her. Even among children of the same age, boy-girl relations were not that commonplace.

The Furry Velvet Hat

I was supposed to return to school on the evening of the weekend holiday. But when I left the house to go to school, my feet dragged back. It wasn't because I loved home or wanted to stay there, I just didn't want to go to school... I made up excuses not to go back to school in the evening, deciding, instead, to go the following morning—the first of the new school week. I used to leave home with the intention of going to school. One morning, I had boarded the ferry from Heybeli Island with the best of intentions. The ferry stopped at Burgaz Island. I wonder if I should get off at Burgaz?... Until the ferry pulled away from the dock, I had a hard time to keep myself from getting off at Burgaz. But when the ferry neared Kinali Island, I could no longer restrain myself, and disembarked. It was my first visit to Kinali Island. Why had I gotten off at this place? There was no "why" to it... I just didn't want to go to school... I didn't know where I was going or what I was going to do. I was aimless. Since the summer people had all moved out, Kinali Island was practically deserted. Very few people were seen, since it was one of the first days of winter.

I was walking aimlessly from the dock along the shore, when I saw something black that the waves were washing against the beach. I approached and looked more closely; a hat was bumping on the sand. With a branch, I fished it out of the water. It was a furry, black velvet hat with a brim, rather new. It didn't seem to be a hat that had become old and been thrown away.

Father, like many people who believed as he did in those times, didn't want to wear hats, because—due to the ban on fezzes and turbans, in the name of the so-called "clothes revolution"—they were forced to wear them; in short, because he considered wearing a hat an infidel act, my father wore a horrible shapeless one... Maybe he would wear this hat I'd found in the sea. It would look good on him too. But if he wore it, it wouldn't be to look good, it would be because it was free.

I returned to Heybeli Island on a ferry that came from Istanbul and stopped at Kinali Island.

With that gentleness that my father always reserved just for me, he said, "What happened? Why did you come back, my boy?"

"Three-day school recess...'cause there's some contagious disease..."

We dried the hat I'd found in the sea. It fitted Father's head, and he wore it for some time.

The Girl Whose Skin Bred Lice

Some among my father's acquaintances took an interest in me—that is, those who liked me—and on days that I ran away from school, I would go to their homes and stay with them. I stayed at each acquaintance's house one, two, or at the most, three nights. It seemed as if I hit these homes in turn, about once every fifteen or twenty days between visits. I think they not only liked me but felt sorry for me, because I was a little boy whose mother had died. And I, with the shrewdness of a child, exploited this feeling of love mixed with pity.

Every night, I went to bed with the intention of going to school the next morning, come what may. But when it was morning I just couldn't go to school. The whole psychology of the child who runs away from school is that once the links of the chain of continuity are broken, no possibility remains, from then on, to fasten those broken links together and repair the chain.

One house I went to on the days that I ran away from school was that of Ismail Efendi, the dockman. It was an old, two-story wooden house on a narrow street behind the marketplace in Kasimpasha. his wife was Fatma'nim [Fatma Hanim]. From her former husband Fatma'nim had a son, who was a young man, and a daughter.

The thick wooden wings of the street door to this house were very old and crooked. In order to raise the iron tongue inside the door's latch and open it, a cord, tied to the latch tongue, had been hung outside through a hole in the door. A heavy knot was tied in the end of the cord to keep it from slipping inside. Due to its long use, the rope had acquired a dirty dark-brown color comprised of sweat, grease, dirt and filth. There were knockers on the two door-wings also. Whenever someone knocked, Fatma'nim would call from her top-floor room above the street, "Who-o's there?" and her voice resounded throughout the emptiness of the house and courtyard.

Since Istanbul life passed from the old style houses to big-city apartments, the question, "Who's there?" echoing from the inside out to the street, directed at one who had knocked on the front door, is no longer asked.

At that time, this question seemed so difficult for me, that it couldn't be answered.

"Who's there?"

What can you say? After all, you're not going to read your identity card from outside the door, to some person whose voice you can hear but whose face you don't see... The usual answer to this stereotyped question went something like this:

"Open up, it's me!... It's me, I've come!..."

If it were a casual acquaintance, the caller would say, from outside, "I'm no stranger, sister!" in answer to the woman's voice inside. If the one knocking were a stranger, she would say, "May I see you for a moment, lady?..."

The knocker on Fatma'nim's door wasn't used often. And the door-latch rope wasn't pulled frequently either. Usually, by grasping the brass handle of the crooked door, they would shoulder and lift up, and it would open. Hung on the wall behind the door, as was customary in houses of this type, was a thick iron bar almost a meter long.

At night the hook on the iron bar was fastened to the iron ring behind the door.

Upon entering this street door, one crossed a dirt floor (hard from being walked on), then sandstone (which was broken here and there), and saw, on the left, a long-handled pump.

In this dark place with the dirt floor, a girl wandered about like a ghost. On her back was a plain, dirty, wet gown. Saliva flowed, unceasingly, from her mouth and trickled down the front of her gown. She was barefoot, her hair tangled. She held her hands in a crooked fashion over her chest. She didn't know how to talk, but she wandered until evening in that dark place below the house, continually murmuring unintelligible sounds as if she were talking to someone. Her age was indeterminate—perhaps fifteen, maybe twenty-five. She was aware of neither thirst nor hunger. This poor thing was the daughter of dockman Ismail Efendi's wife, Fatma'nim, and her former husband.

Lice are not something that children of today see and know, but in those days, lice were one of the great curses of our people. It was extremely difficult to avoid lice and keep from becoming lousy. For this reason, those who couldn't avoid lice consoled themselves with the following myth: Some people's bodies make lice from themselves, and the skin of some people breed lice.

Whenever I ran away from school and spent the night at Fatma'nim's house, I became lousy and started to scratch. It never crossed my mind that I got the lice from the bed there.

Biting lice give a person a very pleasant type of itch. Lice don't inflict a sudden sting like that of a flea, bedbug or mosquito—the bite's not felt immediately. The place where a louse bites itches pleasurably and for a long time. This good aspect is recompense, perhaps, for their being so fat and oily, for their dirty vulgarity; they make you sick, they're loathsome! Neither flies, fleas, nor even those foul-smelling bloated bedbugs are as revolting as lice. The louse is so disgusting that, in comparison, the bedbug, mosquito and flea seem charming.

Fatma'nim, her husband the dockman Ismail Efendi, and that mute daughter of theirs, lived in a single large room. Fatma'nim's son, a sailor, used to come home once a month—or, a year. A mother, from Erzinjan, and her young daughter were living in a small room across from theirs. And the two of them were lively, cheerful and beautiful. They liked me very much. I used to read folk books to this Erzinjan girl, and she listened with interest. One day, that girl told me that Fatma'nim's psychotic daughter couldn't be cleansed of lice because the poor thing's skin bred them. Fatma'nim would wash and scrub her daughter and dress her in clean underwear, but shortly thereafter, the body of this drooling girl (who spoke only to fairies and demons) would swarm again with lice.

Thus, by concocting an explanation that they couldn't save themselves from lice, they consoled themselves.

The Fortune Success Brings

Even years later, I can't forget his pleasure and happiness when dockman Ismail Efendi was telling of a triumph in his work. Ismail Efendi was a master construction man in the building of steamship docks. He boasted a lot about his expertise at his work. According to him, there was no one who knew his work or could do it as well as he. He was the only master in his occupation, to which he'd devoted his whole life since boyhood.

He used to come home once every three or four weeks because his work was some distance from Istanbul, on the shores of the Marmara and Aegean Seas. I can't forget his enjoyment and happiness upon one of his returns home. He was enjoying himself immensely by telling of his victory, a success he'd won on his job.

They were repairing the Karabiga dock. An engineer was in charge. Master Ismail suggested that the large tree poles, to be driven into the seabed as piles, be placed without having the bark scaled off. The engineer protested, "You've been a master all these years; have you ever seen a dock pile driven in with the bark remaining on it?"

And Master Ismail replied, "My recommendation results from long experience. I've spent years in this business. I've observed that unpeeled dock piles last longer than squared and peeled piles."

The engineer said, "Such a thing is impossible. It's just the opposite of what you say. If the tree stays in the sea with its bark, all kinds of bugs, sea animals, clams and fish make their homes in the cracks and crevices. Therefore, the tree rots faster. On the other hand, sea creatures can't find a place to make their nests on piles when the bark is peeled off, and, as a result, they're longer lasting."

"True," said Master Ismail, "fish, shellfish, bugs, these and those, do make their homes on piles with bark. But it's *because* they make their homes there that the unpeeled piles stay sturdier in the sea. In time, that perforated bark calcifies and petrifies. The very thing that you claim rots the tree preserves it with a protective layer, making it last longer. As a matter of fact, where there is no such protection on the piles, they are damaged more easily by the elements, deteriorate quickly and become unsound."

Due to this argument, his relations with the engineer were strained. Of course, in the end, things were done as the engineer desired.

A long time passed... Then one day, that engineer who'd been upset with Ismail Efendi came up to him and said, "You were right, Master; I didn't know, I was wrong. At an old dock at such-and-such a place, I saw dock piles—some with bark, some not—driven into the sea at the same time, years ago. All these years have passed and those with bark are still very strong, but the barkless ones have rotted. As you said, the sea animals nesting in the bark, protected the wood!"

Of course, Ismail Efendi hadn't related the conversation with the engineer exactly like this, word for word. Since he was past fifty when he told of the incident, Master Ismail has long ago rotted and returned to the earth, transformed into another of Nature's forms. But, although forty-eight years have now passed, the things he told, in all their detail, have remained in my memory.

That night, with pleasure, Ismail Efendi recounted the story of his victory several times. He was filled with the joy of success; he was happy. Only a scientist who had made a great discovery, an artist who'd created a great work, could have been that elated.

My play, entitled "Please Come Here" [*Biraz Gelir misiniz?*] (which I wrote thirty years after the date I listened attentively to those words of Master Ismail, the dock construction man), begins with this dialogue between master Mateh and his apprentice, Bornok:

MASTER MATEH—You will have a job in this world, Bornok, but whatever job it is...

BORNOK—Whatever job it is...

MASTER MATEH—Let's say you whistle. Everybody whistles.

BORNOK—They whistle, Master.

MASTER MATEH—But when you whistle, they will say, "My word, how he whistles!"

This was the lesson dock-builder Master Ismail gave me: not everyone can be the man for a big job; but everyone can be a big man for his own job. If you're going to whistle, whistle! But when you whistle, the listeners will be amazed at how well you whistle. You will be a dock builder, but as with Master Ismail, they will say, "He really knows his business..."

Fatma'nim's son, Sailor Ismail, came to the house on leave. The ship, on which he worked as a winch operator, lay alongside the quay between Sirkeji and Eminönü. He said we'd go together to his ship, and we did. It was a tiny ship. Ismail went to work at the ship's winch machine, unloading the goods from the hold onto the quay. I watched him with interest until evening.

I enjoyed seeing Winchman Ismail control the great winch by pulling its iron lever a little, pushing it a little. As Ismail pulled the iron lever, while hot steam spouted from the winch, the machine's iron wheels and cogs turned noisily; the long arm of the winch, which carried a sling, went back and forth from the ship's hold to the dock, transporting bales, loaded baskets, and steel-banded crates. The chains of the sling tied to the winch's derrick were making a clatter. It seemed as if not only the levers of the winch, but the whole world, were at Ismail's command. From the two holes in the ship's prow, two anchors hung into the sea, like mucus flowing from the nose holes of an iron giant. After discharging its cargo, the ship would pull its intestines, made of chainlinks, inside its belly and depart. The dropping and raising of the ship's anchors were also among Ismail's duties.

From time to time, I did go to school. One day at school, in the mess hall, I encountered the mother from Erzinjan and her daughter, working there as servants. They were pleased to see me. But I wasn't pleased at all, possibly due to an idiotic embarrassment at someone I knew being a servant, or maybe, from the fear they might tell my father that I ran away from school...

Either school was really in recess, or I'd again fooled my father be saying it was. With his permission, I had gone to Karabiga to see Master Ismail. His wife, Fatma'nim, was there too; they'd rented a house. (Fatma'nim's son from her first husband is also named Ismail.) I stayed as a guest in their house for some time. But I simply can't remember how I went there and how I returned. The only thing that stays in my memory is Master Ismail's working as head of the workers on the dock they built. The driving of the piles into the sea bottom with that huge pile driver greatly intrigued me. With a rope tied to the pile driver's monstrous iron hammerhead, two workers slowly raised it up, then right from the top of the pile driver, together with the cry of "Hip, hip," they suddenly dropped that iron weight on the pile being driven. At each drop of the iron hammer onto its head, the pile was pounded, centimeter by centimeter, into the sea bed, and this appeared to me as a lot of work for nothing.

But what attracted my attention more than the hammering of the piles by the pile driver, was the exactly square, smooth form given the tree trunks by sharp axes. What great dexterity, what skill that took! Each workman who did this job was so in command of his big sharp axe that he used it as if it were a pocketknife, whittling on the tree, which he held with one foot, as if sharpening a lead pencil.

Lousy Boy

In the first part of my memoirs, I talked about Aunt Zeynep Hanim. This woman, after her husband had been knifed and killed, made her fourth marriage with an Albanian who cultivated his garden on the Feriköy Ridge. I concluded that writing, which told about Aunt Zeynep Hanim, as follows: "After my mother's death, Zeynep Hanim was destined to be of great assistance and goodness to me..."

In my escapes from school, one of the houses I took shelter in was Zeynep Hanim's house. She was living in a house in a garden that was back of the Feriköy cemetery. This house was a single-story ramshackle building of old wood, covered with rusty tin. I went there seldom because it was distant. At every visit, Aunt Zeynep Hanim would greet me lovingly in memory of my mother, who'd been her friend. Her Albanian husband, who knew very little Turkish and was a homely but good-hearted man, also treated me warmly.

One went to Zeynep Hanim's house by passing through the gypsy quarter on top of a steep hill in Kasimpasha. On both sides of that hill, paved with broken stone, there were tiny houses, all one-story, wooden, most of them faced with rusty tin, old, ramshackle and leaning on one another. That hill, all the way to the top, every hour of the day, was as crowded as if it were a marketplace. The majority of the crowd were children—a herd of barefoot, raggedly-dressed children, every age, every size, girls and boys, who kept sniffing back their runny noses... Groups of fifteen or twenty kids were in front of every house. They were so numerous that I puzzled over how, when night came, these children, who just about overflowed the streets, could fit into the tiny houses... Probably some of them *couldn't* fit in the houses, so they stayed in the streets. It seemed as if some of the children's arms and legs would flow out the windows and doors of the houses which couldn't hold them, like clippings overflowing from a sack full of rags.

I feared that one day, when I was passing through there, those playing, swearing, fighting kids on the hill would attack me—gang together and beat me up. There were so many that I couldn't fight with them, yet I couldn't stand the idea of running away either, so what was I to do?... Every time I went up or down that hill, I always felt this fear. So I tried to pass through them silently, like a shadow, gazing straight ahead. But on none of my excursions through there did my fears materialize; they neither harassed nor attacked me...

Who could have known, who could have foretold that, years later, I would make prison friends with some of the gypsies who lived in the little houses on that hill; that with these comrades (whom I jokingly referred to as our "swarthy citizens"), I would share my troubles and would have many sweet and bitter memories...

Most of those who lived in the tiny houses along both sides of that hill were migrant tobacco workers from Kavala. And when they migrated to Istanbul, they brought their crafts with them and continued their work here. They'd brought something else here too: a working-class consciousness...

During the past forty-five years, whenever or wherever there was a working-class organization, action, lawsuit or trial, these swarthy citizens took a stand and participated in all of them. The reason for this—from my view—were the social traditions they'd accumulated in this direction in the places they'd emigrated from. I never begrudged the comradeship that I shared with them in the prison barracks, cells or dungeons. Perhaps some of those children whom I passed among in fear, while going up and down that hill, were among those prison comrades who left me so many memories. In future sections of my memoirs, these comrades will also take a place.

Because of this fear I mentioned, I took another route to Zeynep Hanim's house. This wasn't a road, it was a goat trail over the ridge called Baruthane [Powderhouse]. On these moderately steep, rough hills in the countryside, there were round, stone, whitewashed towers, which resembled the trunks of windmills. A sailor guarded every tower. I think those towers were powder magazines. In winter, I used to go to Zeynep Hanim's house by way of the hill where the gypsies lived; in summer, on the country path where the powder magazine towers were.

After a two-night stay in the house of Fatma'nim, I was walking again, one day, on that back path to Zeynep Hanim's house. It was the evening of a hot day. Even while walking along the path, I couldn't resist scratching. I could scratch without embarrassment because, out in the countryside, no one would see I was scratching. It was such an endless itch, that upon scratching, I felt compelled to scratch even more, and couldn't hold back. With my fingernails, I kept on scratching away at my back, flanks, waist, wherever my hands could reach. I thought I itched because I'd gotten dirty. At one point, a round, slippery, live thing rolled between my fingers and skin. I picked it up and saw that it was a louse... I put my hand in again, and another louse came from my armpit.

In the countryside, there was no one to see me. I entered the shelter of a hollow and undressed. Help!... My T-shirt teemed with sticky lice. Big, fat, greasy, plump lice were swarming lazily—the armpits of my T-shirt, the neck, the seams, the crotch of my underpants, the waist, were full of nits (louse eggs). While wearing them, there was no way of cleaning my underwear, so I stripped. I threw my T-shirt and shorts down, stepped back, and gazed at the lice-filled clothes. Perhaps the lice clustered on top of my underwear because the ground was damp and cool—what a lot of them there were! I picked the lice off my T-shirt and underwear and put them on again. Then I put on my shirt, jacket and pants. I thought I was clean and free from the lice.

I'd scratched before that time, but due to my going home and bathing, and changing my underwear more often, I either didn't get lousy or hadn't been aware that I was.

That day, when I took off my underwear and threw it down, I became so disgusted with lice, that I never again went to the house of Fatma'nim, the mother of that girl whose skin supposedly bred lice. It was evening when I arrived at Zeynep Hanim's house. I recall our eating soup with plenty of red pepper and a cheese omelette, fried in oil with more red pepper.

After dinner, I must have been scratching enough to attract attention from where I was sitting, because Aunt Zeynep Hanim brought me in front of her by saying,

"Nusret, come here; let's have a look!"

After inspecting my collar and neck, she said, "Undress, right now!"

Trying not to let me see, she wiped her tears on the corner of her headscarf (beaded on the edges) with which she bound her hair. She felt sorry for me: the son of that fastidious, immaculate mother shouldn't get lousy!... She must have thought I'd gotten lousy due to neglect at home and at school. Actually, the only one responsible for my getting lousy was me.

Until a late hour that night, Zeynep Hanim—greatly troubled—boiled my underwear in the laundry tub on the stove, washed and then dried them at the fire. When I went to bed, she was still working at ironing my underwear and clothes.

I stayed as a guest two or three days at Aunt Zeynep Hanim's house. Her husband was the youngest of three Albanian brothers. The houses of the three of them, and their garden, were adjacent to each other. The garden, which they planted with every kind of vegetable—things like onions and corn, descended in a pleasant curve, in the form of a rectangle, and reached a small hill opposite there. In the area on the hill across from the garden, there were fig trees.

Boy and girl elementary-school pupils had come on a country outing with their woman teacher to the hill across the way. The weather was fine. While the students were running about and playing, they entered the garden, climbed the fig trees, started picking the figs and eating them. They were doing all this right in front of their teacher's eyes, but she didn't say a word.

Although Zeynep Hanim's husband called from a distance not to do that, to stop it, the children not only paid him no heed but found his Albanian accent funny and began to mock him. Zeynep Hanim, though very upset, couldn't say anything. I was seized with a feeling that I must interfere in this situation. Why? I was wearing the Orphan School clothing, which is, after all, an official uniform. If one considers how grown-ups, police, watchmen, and even the trashmen, dress in an official uniform and pretend to be heroes, perhaps it's understandable why I, too, had become childishly brave by trust in my Orphan School clothes. Perhaps too, I so believed the lie I'd kept repeating to my father ("They promoted me to the sixth grade without examination,") that I thought myself bigger than the children who were stealing figs and could make them listen to me.

I walked up the hill. A squad of children had grouped around where the woman teacher sat. While I was walking toward them, I felt bold, but when I came up to them, I didn't know what to say. They were my age. All at once, I burst out with remarks such as, "You're supposed to be students... Shame on you! And there's a so-called teacher with you!" But none of them paid any attention to what I said! Even the teacher didn't care... I was humiliated. While I was returning in that heavy atmosphere of defeat, I started to cry. I kept repeating to myself, "I'll show you, I'll show you!" What was I going to show them, what could I do? I was going to write up this ugly incident—which seemed to me the worst scandal in the world— and send it to the *Köroghlu* paper. After all, my two- or three-line piece, with my picture, had been published in *Köroghlu*, so from then on I considered it to be my own newspaper. I was a writer, such a writer, that I would show them!

I gradually grew angry and wept even more. Zeynep Hanim's husband, whom I'd supposedly been trying to help, smilingly tried to comfort me with sweet words.

I was going to write the newspaper; I'd show them... But I neither knew the children's grade, which school they went to, nor who that teacher was. It didn't matter... I would write: "On a certain day, at such-and-such a place, students stole figs, and right in front of their teacher..." When the piece appeared in the paper, all hell would break loose! No doubt as a school truant, I must have understood inside that I was bidding farewell to my school days, which I valued highly, so it was with this pain that I kept on saying, "And they're supposed to be students too!..." If they weren't students, they shouldn't steal, they *mustn't* steal...

I left Aunt Zeynep Hanim's house. As the hours passed, that anger of mine slowly cooled. As the days passed, the incident lost its importance in my eyes.

The Karagöz Show That Didn't Materialize

I was in a turmoil, I couldn't contain myself. I wanted to do something, without knowing what it was... The month of Ramazan was coming. I thought of putting on a Karagöz show [shadow theater]. I don't know who inspired or influenced me to put it on, or whom I was imitating. But I intended to have a show in our stable, adjoining the house. If I swept, dusted and cleaned the stable, I could stage it there. I was going to invite an audience. They would fill the place. Definitely not free, but by ticket...

My first chore was to cut paper and make tickets in my own handwriting. As I remember, five *kurush* would be the admission. I began by making tickets for the show and even drew up a list of those I would invite. Out of thin cardboard, I cut the characters for the Karagöz play and painted them. I oiled the pictures with olive oil so they would be transparent and let the light through. The play, I'd write myself. But when I tried to write, the work went on and on... The Karagöz play was one of my many childish plans that didn't materialize.

Puberty

A warm summer afternoon... Or, perhaps, the afternoon of a left-over summer day in the middle of winter. But again, perhaps the afternoon of one of those beautiful autumn days that drags summer along with it. No matter what season or what kind of day, it was a day that the vapor from the grasses, plants and moist earth rose to the skies in the heat, and the colors of nature melted, one into the other, like an impressionist painting.

I lay as if loose and melting, with my arms and legs extending and spreading out into the distance. I was rolling on the border of being asleep or awake, crossing now to this side, now to that. Both asleep and awake, I was neither sleeping nor waking.

I spread one of the quilts, piled on top of each other in the corner, on the floor in the middle of the room. Then I spread the sheet, which gives the feeling of coolness, and crawled in under the blanket. The blanket-sheet, soft from many washings, wraps and envelops my hot skin like an enormous warm hand.

Do I really see the two windows of our room, or is it a dream? The light, passing through the tiny parallelograms of the screen, has perched on the cambric curtains, like white-winged butterflies. Shadows from the leaves on the trellis outside reach for these sunlight-butterflies, like hands which strive to catch them. When the curtains move in the breeze, everything moves, everything dances. Not only the sunlight-butterflies, not only the shadows, but the ceiling too, also the floor and the soft bed under me... I'm as if stretched out, lying in a boat on an undulating sea.

The warmth from my skin warms the blanket-sheet, and the warmed sheet gives heat to my skin. I put my hands and arms in the cool places in the sheets, as if I'm putting them out of the boat into the cool sea. I must be in a dream, but perhaps I'm seeing this dream without being asleep... Anyway, I'm crossing back and forth over the border between being asleep and awake.

Softly, softly... I raise the edge of the blanket. What a soft thing she is... Don't waken her! If she awakens and sees I've been looking at her naked legs, she'll cover them and I'll be

71

very ashamed. Who is this girl in bed? It's not important. As the blanket edge slowly lifts, the bed fills with light. The girl's two legs, bare clear above the calves, are shining a lively pink. More, more... I can see her panties too.

A warm melting, a relaxation—like one feels while descending in a swing, or like that inner fainting sensation when an airplane falls through empty air, an evacuation.

I am conscious that something secret has happened to me, something so secret that no one can be told about it, yet it's something everyone knows about, everyone had had... Although nothing had been explained to me on this subject, I somehow knew that's how it was.

Sweet dreams, off to sleep...

The Horseshoer Who Pulled Teeth

I don't know which event came first and which came after, because I can't put them in their order.

In those truant days of mine, when I was frequently running away from the Orphan School and couldn't go home, I'd gone to Kemerburgaz once or, perhaps, twice. In Kemerburgaz, my father had an acquaintance. This man raised vegetables and took them to a market, then called "*Meyve Hosh*," and sold them wholesale to the middlemen. He carried the vegetables in his own horsecart. Because I've seen him, once or twice, with his cart loaded with celery, these many years since, wherever I see celery, whenever I eat celery, or at some place where celery is even mentioned, I immediately recall Kemerburgaz. These two words, in which some of the same letters are found— *kereviz* [celery] and Kemerburgaz—seem to me as if they're bound together...

I can't even remember now how, by what route, from where, or by what means I went to Kemerburgaz. I probably went by Alibey Village. The man, whom my father knew, was one of the rich men of Kemerburgaz. He had some grown daughters and a son. The son was bigger than I. On one of the two or three nights I put myself up at their house, the son took me to the Kemerburgaz coffeehouse. The elders had gathered inside the building, the young men, outside. The older men had slowly left, and only the young men remained. They were talking indecently. I sat alone at one side, and they ignored me. They were, at the most, boys of seventeen or eighteen years. One of them, a little more vulgar than the others, told at length of his visit to a brothel and of laying with a woman. Those gathered around him—laughing and asking for all the details with avid curiosity—listened to everything that was being told. The one who was telling about it "poured on the honey" and dressed up the story. It was the first time I heard about such a thing.

The brother of the man I stayed with was a horseshoer. During the day, I would go to his blacksmith shop and watch how he worked the bellows to fan the fire in the forge, how the shoes were formed by beating on the anvil the redhot iron he'd heated in the fire, and how he shoed the oxen. The binding of the animals' feet, the way they were thrown to the ground, and their shoeing was most interesting. When shoeing horses, they didn't put them down. Before shoeing, the blacksmith's trimming—with his special round, sharp knife—of the hooves of the animal to be shod, seemed like an extremely difficult operation to me. I was amazed as to how he could make the decision to trim the hoof, and worried that he might cut off more than necessary.

Kemerburgaz made a deep impression in my memory, because one night while I stayed there, one of my lower right molars ached so much that the man at whose house I stayed took me to the coffeehouse and had my aching tooth pulled under the light of a gasoline lantern. And the one who pulled my tooth was his brother, the blacksmith. He twisted my molar with the pincers he'd stuck into my mouth, pulled it out, and dropped it in my hand.

At that age, how was I able to go to the houses of my father's acquaintances and stay? What I know is this: The didn't treat me like a child. They acted as if I were a big man. Perhaps this was due to their respect for my father, and maybe I was a boy who couldn't be considered a child.

I Had To Invent My Crime

Father had learned that I ran away from school. Had I told him? I don't think so. Had a note come from school? I don't think that either. Today's tradition of the school's showing interest and writing a letter home, saying, "Your son isn't coming to school..." didn't exist in those times.

However it happened, my father had learned I wasn't attending school.

"Why aren't you going to school, my son?"

He didn't yell, didn't scold, didn't appear angry; he was only asking: "Why aren't you going to school, my son?"

Upon my remaining silent with head bowed, Father persisted in asking, with that ever-present gentleness: "Why aren't you going to school, my son?"

When he wished to gentle his voice even more, he said "my little boy," not "my son."

Father's questions were boring into my brain like a corkscrew. If he'd only get angry and yell, perhaps I wouldn't be so touched and crushed!

"Tell me, my little boy, why aren't you going to school?"

He was being very careful not to say, "Why are you running away?"

I had to give an answer to his question. But what could I say? After all, I just couldn't tell my father, whom I loved so and who loved me that much, "I'm running away from school because of you!"... If I were to say such a thing, his whole world of love would have collapsed. "All of these things happened to me because of you... I'm running away from school because you're alive, because you exist. While you're alive, how can I go to that school where only fatherless children can study?"

Could I have said these things to him? To hear these things from the lips of his only son—his sole support and love— would be worse than death.

Father, who didn't know why I ran away from school, was still insistently asking: "My dear son, please tell me, why aren't you going to school?"

I wasn't even searching for an answer to his question, because I'd rather have died than answer what he was asking me.

He insisted so hard that finally, in the end, I abruptly blurted out something that I hadn't even thought of before: "They expelled me! They threw me out of school!"

With this answer, my chance of going to school was being stopped for good.

Father was stunned. I couldn't look him in the face; yet without looking, it was as if I saw: Nusret, his son—how could he be expelled from school! How could they do this? For Father, my being expelled from school was much more important, much more painful, than my not being able to be educated. I was terribly sorry that such a lie had suddenly slipped from my mouth in my despair at not being able to find an answer to the question he insistently asked.

After Father had remained silent for a long while, he asked in an even gentler, even sweeter tone: "Why, my son?"

In order to comprehend why so gentle a question crushed me so much, one must know Father's personality. Whenever he grew angry, at anyone, he was a very hard, aggressive, yelling, ill-tempered man. Only with me did he conquer himself and become mild.

Because this expulsion from school was not at all to be expected of me, he didn't ask, "Why did they expel you?" Without even saying the word "expel" he simply asked, "Why?"

My head was bowed.

"Why? Why, my boy?"

I've taken many tests, have gone through many police interrogations, prosecutors' inquiries, judges' questionings, but I don't think I ever experienced the difficulty in any of them that I did in facing my father's question "Why?" that day.

"Why, my son?"

I realize quite clearly that my father was insistently asking, "Why? Why? Why?" to place the blame on those who expelled me from school, to accuse them and to clear me.

That lie was going to give birth to another big one. There was no other way out: I was forced to invent another lie to answer my father's question, "Why?" to cover my other fib,

"They threw me out of school." Again, without thinking ahead, on the spur-of-the-moment, I blurted out another one that was on the tip of my tongue: "The day school was out, I evidently put on a classmate's trousers by mistake, thinking they were mine. They expelled me from school for stealing trousers..."

Father turned chalk-white; all the blood had drained from his face. He didn't ask me anything more. It was all over. I think that, had he known this was what he was going to hear, he wouldn't have pressed me so hard and kept on asking. As for me, no matter how strongly I was accused, no matter how guilty I seemed, I had been saved from being crushed under my father's seemingly soft pressure; after all, he wouldn't be asking me about this subject again...

No, no; I wasn't saved at all. I *thought* I was saved.

The Boy Who Mocks

I'll not venture into a scholarly explanation of humor, but I will present you with an observation. Consider, in general, people who ridicule: they are people who mock and joke in order to cover up and hide their imperfections from their associates. Making fun of others is, in one sense, a defense of the one who does it. As for jokes and humor, they comprise one of the ways of making a fault disappear and hiding it from others.

In the theater, at rehearsals, players who cannot play the role they're assigned as well as they would like to, make fun of it, belittle, and get silly about it. Students at school who ridicule, are generally those who can't succeed in their lessons.

The newspaper and publishing house owner, Halil Lütfi Dördünjü, although he had three or four million *lira* in wealth, property and capital, was the stingiest person I've known. And he was very witty too. By making jokes, Halil Lütfi Dördünjü defended himself indirectly, and tried to cover up and hide his unlikable stinginess with the enjoyment of his wit.

Why was I running away from the Orphan School? It was not merely because, under false pretenses, I studied at a school where only fatherless boys were supposed to study. While this was the first reason, the second one was my classmates' continually making fun of me.

One of my sons, who now attends school outside the country, wanted to leave the dormitory of the school where he studied and live in a boarding house. I was insistent that he stay in the dormitory. He still insisted that he must live in a boarding house while going to school, so I tried to find out why. Out of a number of reasons, the most important was this: He was a bright student, studied until late hours in the night, and bought and read many books. Some of his friends, in order to defend their own laziness and failures, claimed that he was being pretentious by showing an excessive fondness for books. In order to be spared their teasing, my son wanted to move out of the dormitory.

Relating my own experience to him, in a letter dated 30 December 1974, I gave the following directions as to what he must do: "It was very nice that you wrote me an account of the *Seince* journals. It's good also, that you wrote me you were being gossiped about for collecting books as an affectation. Thus I was able to understand why you wanted to move to a boarding house. Son, since you wrote to me, I'll say, 'Ignore them!' However, there's a distinction to make: don't just appear to ignore them, but actually ignore them. There's a big difference between these two things. If you really don't care, you'll be at ease. But if you merely try to act like you don't, you'll be even more troubled. Hit the problem with ridicule.

"You wrote me, saying, 'Put yourself in my place!' Certainly I *am* putting myself in your place. A lot worse has happened to me. Why did I run away from the Orphan School? Well, this is the reason: I was diligent and knew a lot more than my classmates. The teachers often had me recite in class and liked me. My friends reached the conclusion that, at that age, one couldn't know so much, and thought I was a lot older than they. I was the shortest. So they looked on me as if I were a dwarf who was older, and tacked the nickname of '*Kart*' [past its prime] on me. In their envy, they always mocked me with 'Kart! Kart!' Naturally I was angry, but I couldn't pretend not to care, because I was only eleven years old. At that age, children are very selfish, pitiless and cruel. And my friends mocked me without mercy, relentlessly. I tried to appear as if I didn't care but, intuitively, they understood that I did. Their ridicule bothered me so much that I purposely didn't study in some classes and knowingly wouldn't answer my teachers' questions just so they wouldn't mock me. But I still wasn't able to save myself from their calling me 'Kart' and their vengeful jeering. Thus, one reason for my running away from the Orphan School was my having a father, but another was the ridicule by my friends.

"Did you know, my son, that later on, this ridicule proved very useful in my work and made me a writer of humor. The principal reason for my becoming a humorist was my classmates' making fun of me, calling 'Kart! Kart!' when I was eleven years old. As a result, when I ran away from the Orphan School and went to other schools later—especially the military boarding school, which was a social jungle—I looked for ways of avoiding the same situation, where I wouldn't be ridiculed again. I found the best way to defend myself, almost unconsciously, with an instinct for survival, just as an animal survives, and that was by these two paths:

1. I wouldn't appear to ignore those who ridiculed me, I really would ignore them.

2. And more important than this, I would ridicule everyone first. That is, I would steal their weapon.

"And that's what I did. I made fun of all, every one of my comrades. I attached nicknames to all of them. They are still known by those nicknames I bestowed on them. I gave myself a nickname too. And they called me by that name. They thought my nickname, 'Hairy,' was their discovery. Actually, I called myself 'Hairy,' because one way of being saved from ridicule is for a person to make fun of himself before someone else has the chance. A person's ridiculing himself, and getting accustomed to it, wins for him a maturity later on.

"I mocked them sharply, frightening and making them dread my derision. From then on, not one had the courage to make fun of me. Thus, with this joking that I started in my boyhood to protect myself, and my derisiveness (which continued and gradually developed), I gained a capacity for humor and finally created a job, which provides the wherewithal to educate you today in foreign lands, and secures a living for all of us. So even though this isn't the day for my humorous writing, this is the story of how it came to be."

The Lie Came Out

Father couldn't believe my reason for being expelled from school. He couldn't believe it because he just couldn't swallow this ugly insult to his great self-respect. "My son? My own son? My son would do this? No, impossible; it couldn't be possible!"

I don't know in what way it happened, but apparently he continued to ask and eventually learned that that ugly lie I told him hadn't happened, that I hadn't been expelled from school. Upon learning this fact, his discomfiture was gone. After all, I hadn't stolen anyone's pants, so Father didn't consider my not going to school important.

The director of the Orphan School was Ali Kami Akyüz, who had translated some of the classical literature from French into our language.

Ismail Safa,[*] Ahmet Vefa, and Ali Kami were three brothers who were raised in the Orphan School. The poet Ismail Safa is Peyami Safa's father. And our director, Ali Kami Bey, is Peyami Safa's uncle.

As a student at the Orphan School, I'd been able to see Ali Kami Bey once or twice, from a long distance. He used to live with his family on the top floor of his house in the section of the school which was called the "*Tali kismi*" [the high school division].

Salim Bey had also learned that I had run away from school but had committed no other offense. He was looking for ways to get me reinstated again. He didn't say anything concerning my being thrown out of school either. I had run away so often that I was no longer going to school at all.

Salim Bey who'd been at one time director of the Naval Academy, had a host of friends. Among his friends whom I can recall now, are one or two admirals, and names like the ear,

---

[*] tr. Ismail Safa (1866–1901) a poet of the late Ottoman period.

nose and throat specialist, Dr. Sami Yaver, and Vahit Bey (Moran), known for his English dictionary. Among his friends, he'd found an acquaintance of Ali Kami Bey. So it was this friend of his who had written a letter to Ali Kami Bey, requesting that I be taken back into school and be excused for my truancy.

Letter of Reference

I took that letter of reference and went to the Orphan School. I was twelve years old, but it seemed that I hadn't gone there since more years than I had lived. The way to school was strange, the school gate was strange, the gray-bearded gatekeeper was strange—everything, everybody, had become strange. When I went to school it must have been class-time, for there wasn't the slightest sound.

My heart was palpitating as if there were no heart, but, rather, a time bomb ticking in my chest. Oh, if only Ali Kami Bey would take me back in school again... If only he took me, I would never run away from school again, but really *never*... And I would study so hard, so hard, so very hard...

I was crossing the schoolyard. There, to the right, was the field where the big boys played soccer. Further to the right, the gymnasium, where first the dentist, Kemal Bey, then later on, our physical education teacher, the boxer Zeynel Bey, had us do gymnastics... I am entering the door to the high school division. This is my first entry through this door, and it will also be my last. I am climbing the stairs. I am holding the letter in my hand, taking care not to wrinkle or fold it. I am passing down the hall. There, I'm in front of the door to Ali Kami Bey's room.

For years and years afterward, I would see in my dreams this short path from the outside door to Ali Kami Bey's room, those stair steps I climbed, those corridors I went through. What fearful, stupifying, depressing dreams they are... Dreams, dreams... Either the letter—tight in my hand—disappears, or it changes in my hand and becomes something entirely different... Or I climb and climb the stairway steps, and they never end... I walk and walk through those corridors and the end never comes... No matter what I do, I can't reach the director's room, I can't give him the letter of reference... I wake up troubled and scared.

I tap on the Director Bey's door. A voice comes from inside. I enter. There I am, facing Ali Kami Bey, with his finely lined, handsome face, who gave me such a fearful feeling of respect. He is at his desk... The room I am in is so big, as if even bigger than the school...

I hand him the envelope. He takes it. He tears open the envelope, takes out the letter and reads.

They had evidently told him about me previously. He knew my situation. He didn't even consider it necessary to call some responsible person from the school and ask about my case. I hadn't come to school for a very long time. It was now impossible; I couldn't be accepted back in school.

He was going to write a personal answer to the one who had sent the letter by me.

I am returning. The corridor, stairs, yard... The outside gate...

For years, they would enter my dreams: doors, doors...enormous doors of heavy timber... Upon passing through one, and escaping, even bigger ones appeared before me... Then thick, high walls, precipices...places I can neither enter nor leave, where I can't escape, no matter what I do...

Years later, I thought about it a great deal: had Ali Kami Bey wanted, he could have avoided expelling me from the Orphan School—that's what I think. Were I permitted to go again to the Orphan School, I'd been saying to myself, I would never run away from school again. But was I really never going truant? Could I have been able not to run away? No! I still would have run away... The not going truant was out of my hands, because the fear that it would be found that I had a father had become so deeply rooted inside me. I was deceiving myself that I wouldn't run away from school...

However, this failure, like all the failures in my life, has stimulated me and fired my ambition. There was not only the failure in being thrown out of the Orphan School; afterwards, many more failures awaited me. After all of those non-successes—which came, one on top of the other—I was destined to leap into the race of life with a passion to surpass, to surmount all obstacles in my path. It's good that I met with many failures, because every vain attempt spurred me on more and set fire to my ambition.

First Runaway

The schools had started the big recess. My classmates had finished primary school and been promoted to the middle school. And me? I was a runaway student whose grade, even, was in question.

In my ears, I could hear my mother's last words: "My son is in a boarding school, so now I won't die disappointed!"

My mother's words gave my life direction. It's a good thing I heard these words she said to Father while I eavesdropped behind the door as she lay on her death bed. Otherwise, I couldn't have forced myself to go to school and study so hard.

Since I was a runaway from school, I was in disgrace for having broken faith with my mother; and I was also very ashamed of that terrible lie I told Father.

I had to do something, but what?

I decided to run away from home. I would go to some place in Anatolia, it didn't matter where... I would walk into one of the eating establishments in the place where I went, and ask for a job. I would tell the cook: "Uncle, I want to work. I'll do any job there is." If the cook says "Nope, don't need anyone," I'd go on to someone else. If I couldn't find work in that city, that town, I'd go to still another city, another town. If there was no job with restaurants, a grocery was okay; if no grocery, a blacksmith—any old job would do. "You need an apprentice? Just try me once... If you like me, put me to work." And if that didn't work, as a last resort, I planned to say, "I don't want any money, I'll work for my keep." Who wouldn't want someone who would be an apprentice for his keep?... Somehow or other, I'd find a job, no matter what job it was. Once I had that job, I was going to work so well, become so useful to them, curry their favor so much, that they wouldn't expect a boy as useful as I was to work just for his keep, and would start giving me a little wage. My goal was to go to school in the place where I found work. Either I would both work and go to school, or I would work a year, then go to school the next year on the money I saved. In any case, I didn't want my mother's last wish and my father's enduring trust in me to come to naught.

Very early one morning, I secretly took two-and-a-half *lira* from my father's pocket. Two-and-a-half *lira* of that time would be worth at least fifty of today's *lira*.

My first trip outside of Istanbul had been the one to Tekerdagh with my Uncle Galip. The second time was when I had gone to Balchik village, where Uncle Galip taught school. The third time, I had gone to stay at dockman Ismail Usta's house in Karabiga. This was my fourth time outside of Istanbul. I was taking off for some place—where, I didn't know.

I went to the Haydarpasha railroad station and bought a ticket. I don't know now where the ticket was for. While riding on the train, I figured on getting off at just any place that caught my eye.

Why had I bought my ticket at Haydarpasha, rather than one from the Sirkeji train station—for any place in Thrace, or gone to some place or other by ferryboat? A person can't even think about something he doesn't know or has never tried. Before then, in order to go to Gebze, on my way to Balchik village where Uncle Galip taught, I'd bought my ticket at the Haydarpasha railway station; so this time, I hadn't been able to plan differently.

The train I got on departed. I'm finally free... I'm happy in my dreams of great success. The train is speedily taking me into the unknown, where I will win success. No matter what happens, I'll never return without succeeding. I'm going to show my father just how right he was by trusting in me.

I don't know if I'd gotten the train ticket to Izmit or for a more distant place, but anyway, when the train stopped at the Izmit station, I liked the place and got off. It was my first trip to Izmit. Walking from the station, I came to the main street of town, through the center of which the railroad passed.

I look at the eating houses on the two sides of the main street. Then I choose the left side of Main and walk past the eating places along there.

Which one of these will take me as a waiter, a dishwasher, or a helper? Aha, that restaurant! Unh-uh, that's very fancy; they won't hire someone like me, a boy my age. How about this one?... That one's very small; why should they hire a helper? I was wandering around the cafes and shish-kebab places.

Finally, a restaurant caught my eye. But it was difficult for me to go in and ask for a job. Actually, I had decided to myself how easy it would be... I'll go inside and ask... After all, what could happen?... They wouldn't kill you, would they?... Is it a disgrace to ask for a job? If I could just take a step inside, the rest would be easy... After going in, somehow, I would be compelled to tell the owner that I wanted work.

As if forcing my feet—pushing myself—I entered the restaurant. There was no turning back now. Upon my going in, one of the waiters intercepted me, and saying, "Come in, come in, please!" he showed me to a vacant table.

There really was no necessity for the waiter to show such courtesy, because the restaurant was full of empty tables.

"Please sit down!"

Well, I just hadn't anticipated this. I sat down at the table the waiter showed me. He handed me the menu. My whole plan had failed, I was beaten. I looked at the menu and ordered a cheap meal. After all, I had become hungry.

Ice Cream After The Movies

I filled my stomach and slipped out. Leaving the Istanbul Restaurant behind, I walked along the left side of the street and came upon a movie theater. A double feature was playing. I hadn't seen a film for such a long time... I'll just go into this movie, and after seeing the film I'll think about what I'm going to do, I said. When I went in, the film was playing. After seeing only one feature, I left the theater. I took five or ten steps and stopped before a little ice cream store with an open front. I really loved ice cream. With the last of my money, I bought an ice cream cone and ate it.

84

I had no money left. With no more money in my pocket, I could now go into any old grocery, fruit store or eating-house and tell them I wanted to work. There was no other way out but to look for a job. I'd been forced to spend my last bit of money in order to reach that last ounce of hopelessness where I must ask for a job, just as Tarik burned all his ships to cut off any way to retreat. [Tarik Bin Ziyad at the battle for Gibraltar, 711 A.D.]

I had made a trip by train, filled my stomach, gone to a movie, eaten ice cream... After an interlude of unaccustomed luxury for me, I was on the streets of Izmit without a cent. What would happen now?

I walked to Izmit's seashore and found a park some place around there. Years later, on my trips to Izmit, I looked all over for that park but couldn't locate it. Either buildings had been erected on the park site, or I was mistaken as to where it was.

I went into the park, sat on a bench, and started thinking about what I should do. It was almost evening. What was I going to do when night fell? Where would I sleep?

A little beyond me, a young man and a girl were sitting on a wooden park bench. It was apparent from the way they treated each other that they were lovers. Since they were near me, I could see their every act. The youth was stroking the girl's hair, and the girl was playing with the fingers of the boy's other hand and the buttons on his jacket. From time to time, they laughed together. The girl's laugh, which suddenly burst out, then stopped, echoed like a dropped glass shattering on stone. I'd fallen into a reverie, watching them, and forgotten all about myself and my problems.

I can't remember now how I got acquainted and started talking with them there. But, for certain, I couldn't have said the first word to open the conversation.

During the days when I ran away from the Orphan School, the Arabic script had been abolished, and Latin letters adopted in its place as the Turkish alphabet. This conversion was a very significant event in Turkey; the custom of centuries was being changed. In the beginning, it was thought that this change in the alphabet would create very great difficulties.

I knew the Latin letters because both French and calligraphy (beautiful handwriting) were among our lessons at the Orphan School. For this reason, it had been easy for me to read in the new Turkish alphabet and to write it.

I learned that the girl and young man I talked with in the park were teachers in schools at separate villages. And the two of them were from Istanbul.

In that month of school vacation, teachers from Izmit and surrounding villages had assembled in Izmit. They were being taught to read and write the newly adopted Latin alphabet. Thus the girl and boy had come to this course. They became interested in me upon finding out that I knew, at my age, how to read and write the new letters which they were trying to learn. Then, upon their learning from our conversation that I had other knowledge beyond my years, they became even more interested in me. I don't know now the details of our conversation, but it's possible that I could have made quite an effort to amaze them with my learning. Perhaps I played the acrobat with my knowledge, and evidently made a show of my Arabic also.

When evening fell and they left the park, they took me with them. I couldn't have told them I was broke and had no place to sleep. Because, well, you know how they say: I know myself. Since childhood, it hasn't been my personality to reveal a sad situation just to get people feeling sorry for me. But even though I didn't openly tell them of my pathetic plight, I didn't want to make them aware of it in a roundabout way either. Still, they'd taken me to the place they were staying. And where were they staying? The Akchakoja Elementary School.

In my life there have been such amazing, inexplicable coincidences. It's been as if a heavenly hand—over the wishes of all men—prepared these coincidences especially for me. In the most difficult times, it seemed as if a divine power rushed to my aid, and with unbelievable strength, created more favorable circumstances, thus saving me. Through these coincidences, which cannot be explained, the belief that a supernatural force directs man—along with environmental influence—has become well-rooted in me. Therefore, my escape from blind faith, my arrival at free thinking, and my cogitative development occurred very late.

What hand prepared these coincidences for me? I'd gone to a park in a strange town, a place I least expected to find help, where I met two teachers, in love with one another, who journeyed there to take a course. They took me to the school where they were staying. But the coincidence didn't stop at that point; the most amazing thing of all was about to happen. I will tell you about it...

The Akchakoja Elementary School was a large stone building (according to my perception at that time) of two or three floors. When we entered the school, darkness had fallen. First, we went into a classroom. There were other teachers there also. The girl and youth who'd brought me, introduced me to the teachers, praising me highly. They, too, subjected me to a torrent of questions and were surprised at the answers I gave. The things I wrote on the classroom blackboard in the Latin alphabet astonished them. I knew the very thing they'd come to the course to study. At that time, all of the letters of the new Turkish alphabet had not been definitely determined. Many new proposals were being made. It was very difficult to give the sounds of the letters *"Ayin," "Hi,"* and *"Hemze elif,"* which were Arabic pronunciations, with these new letters. For the *"Hi"* sound, which comes from the larynx, the two-letter combination"kh" was being used. The soft "g" (gh) hadn't yet been found; and the letter "â," which would produce the sound between "e" and "a," and the "ü" and "ö" letters must still be debated.

I believe, that night, I wanted to present a demonstration and show off my whole knowledge and, like a circus acrobat, completely astound those teachers gathered there. Not being satisfied with my skill at writing, I drew caricatures on the blackboard, with chalk, of Ismet Pasha, Tevfik Rüshtü Aras, and other men in the government whom I can't recall now. I'd learned to draw these by looking at the caricatures in the *Köroghlu* newspaper, and drawing them—over and over—in imitation. The easiest caricature to draw was Ismet Pasha, the prime minister at that time. In his caricature, his face was presented from the side: a head in the form of a melon, or one called "double-head," mounded back of the forehead and depressed in the middle... a very open forehead, rounded nose... (While writing this page, I decided to test my self as to whether I could still draw Ismet Pasha's caricature. Yes, the caricature I drew still resembles Ismet Pasha, but not the Inönü* [Ismet Inönü] of recent days, the Ismet Pasha of forty-five years ago...)

The village teachers watched as if beholding a miracle, a wonderboy.

Time came for supper. We went down to the dining hall on the first floor. They gave me a place at the table too. Women and men teachers sat at separate tables. There were as many teachers as students in a school, perhaps two or three hundred people...

Well, the really great coincidence occurred in that dining hall. I had eaten my meal and was climbing the stairs along with the teachers. Suddenly before me!... Who? My Uncle Galip! This wasn't possible, at least, it seemed so to me... The two of us kept staring at each other in amazement.

"Nusret? Why are you here?"

"I came to see you, Uncle Galip."

How had I suddenly, on the spot, come up with that lie? How could I have come to see my Uncle Galip when I hadn't even known he was there?

The Conceited Rich Boy

Daytime, I was walking about Izmit and wandering on the seashore. There was a dock from where I watched the loading of things, like flour sacks and lumber, onto the barges, motor boats and small steamers. Extending from that dock to the railroad, were row upon row of grain, flour, and lumber warehouses. In two lumber warehouses, side by side, were two spoiled boys, very well-dressed and older than I. One of them could have been twenty or so, the other, perhaps a year or two older than I. When I passed by these two boys, somehow, they enjoyed making fun of me. I don't know if they were making fun of my old clothes or if there was something to be mocked in the

---

* tr. Ismet Inönü (1884–1973) Ataturk's successor as president of Turkey.

way I walked. Were I to take offense at their remarks and talk back to them, they would fight and beat me up. And maybe that's what they wanted, especially that small guy who wasn't much bigger than I. It was obvious he acted so smart because the big kid at the neighboring warehouse would back him. I think I passed by them without looking their way, as if their teasing wasn't directed at me; but if I did look, I'm sure I continued on as if they weren't worth looking at, in complete disdain. And it was because I ignored them that they couldn't progress from taunting remarks to using their hands.

I could have avoided passing by those warehouses, or changed my route and reached the dock by a back road. But any time I tried to change my route, it seemed as if I weren't in command of my feet. I felt compelled to walk past them, but as if I were unconcerned about their teasing. I was afraid that they were going to beat me, but still I couldn't change my way. I was very angry, especially at that small, conceited, rich kid. I was so angry that, as I walked along the road, I kept beating him up in my imagination. And the trousers of both of them were always pressed. They were wearing suits. They had ties. Their shoes were shined. Every two or three days, they changed their clothes. Who knows how many suits they owned! Inside me was a feeling of mixed fear and rage.

For some time, I continued to walk by them, and they made fun of me. And later on? It wasn't that I grew bored and tired of walking past them—they grew tired of teasing me. The little one—the biggest tease, the most conceited—when I went past, began to act like he didn't see *me*. Then, later on, when he saw me in the distance, he would go inside. In my fear, I wouldn't turn my head to look, and most of the times, with my hands clasped behind me like a grown man, I walked slowly by them—in my obstinacy, even more slowly. By paying no attention to their teasing, I had defeated them. I'd been able to do to them what I hadn't been able to do to those who angered me at the Orphan School by calling me "Kart."

A Special Examination

Had I told my Uncle Galip the lies I'd told my father, that they considered me ahead of my classmates and "by examination, promoted me to a higher grade—I'm in the sixth grade; I'm in the seventh grade"? Or had my father informed Uncle Galip of my lies (which he believed) in order to boast about me? I don't know. But it is clear that he knew I was in a depression and, understanding that I was in trouble, was searching for a way to help me out. What could he do for me? One night, Uncle Galip and I climbed and climbed a narrow path, with broken paving, winding up the Izmit hills. We passed among single-story, two-story, little old frame houses. Uncle Galip knocked on the door of a house in front of which we'd stopped. This was the home of the Izmit Director of Education (*Maarif Müdürü*). The Director of Education was a friend of his. In his way of saying it, Uncle Galip was a *Dervishan*, an *Eren* [one who had arrived at divine truth], an *Ihvan* [brother], an *Ehl-i dil* [a man of God].

We entered a small room on the second floor of the old two-story house. Upon looking from the window, the lights of Izmit appeared below, as if at the bottom of a well.

I perceived, from the way the conversation went, that Uncle Galip had told the Education Director a great deal about me. He was going to look into ways for me to be able to attend school. First, the Education Director, trying not to appear to examine me, asked questions. I didn't know anything he asked me. Upon my not being able to answer his questions, he gradually began asking easier questions from lower grades. Still I didn't know. The man took out a thick book, a history book: "You read this book, didn't you?"

Of course I hadn't read it, because it was the sixth grade history book. In those days, every subject had a single book for each grade. (E. A. had written the middle and high school history books. I couldn't have known that the day would come when I would become acquainted with E. A., the writer of the history book that the Izmit Director of Education showed me...)

If I answered the Education Director's question, "No, we didn't read it," it would be understood that I had previously lied. If I said, "Yes, we read it," I would have patently lied.

To lie was nothing, but he was going to ask questions from that book, and I still wouldn't know. My eyes straight ahead, head bowed, I shook my head in such a way that it could be understood both as "yes" and "no."

The director asked about Egyptian history, the pharaohs, and so on. Upon getting no replies, he passed on to the history of Rome. I well recall that he asked about Romulus and Remus, the founders of Rome. Perhaps a stone would speak, but I had no voice... I felt like my face was on fire; I was burning in flames. Inside me, that unheard voice was yelling, "I don't know, I just can't know... Why keep on asking more?...

I was confused, depressed, tense. My level of knowledge—more truthfully, my level of ignorance—had been determined.

In Filth

My Uncle Galip, who was the Balchik village teacher, like the other teachers, had come to the Akchakoja Elementary School to take the course and learn the new Turkish alphabet. Someone had told him that a mere boy knew how to write these new letters and, furthermore, had drawn caricatures of our important people. So Uncle Galip, in order to see this boy he was curious about, had come down to the dining hall and found me facing him.

"Was it you who drew those caricatures on the classroom blackboard?"

"Yes..."

He appeared neither to like nor dislike it. Yet, although he didn't want to make his feelings apparent, I could tell he liked what I'd done. Uncle Galip didn't know that I drew cartoons, because it was while I was separated from him that I'd started reading the *Köroghlu* newspaper and began copying the caricatures from it.

I don't know in what way, but I'd told Uncle Galip that I wasn't attending school and, even, that I had run away.

The top-floor classrooms had been made into dormitories for the teachers. They gave me a bunk beside Uncle Galip's. I had begun living together with the teachers who were taking the course. But I was much more comfortable than they because they went to class every day, just like students, but I picked up and wandered around by myself. I wasn't completely idle, however; outside of class hours, I was instructing some of the teachers in the Turkish alphabet.

That girl teacher and her sweetheart were my friends. They were always together, both in school and out. I was thinking that they met and became friends at this course. The young man played the violin. Many times, outside of class hours, upon opening the door to a supposedly empty classroom, I found them inside. I would silently close the door and leave. The youth was playing the violin for the girl in that empty classroom.

Uncle Galip wasn't attending classes here because his obvious superiority to these village teachers had been quickly discovered. He knew French. Not only the teachers who were students in the course, but the course teachers and the directors showed my Uncle Galip great respect. What's more, he was well-dressed, fashionable. When I'd seen him at Balchik village, his clothes were old and shabby. Now, he had a beautiful brown suit with light stripes, was shaving every day, and wearing a tie. I had never seen him this dapper before. He'd found his place, his knowledge was being respected, his words listened to. Perhaps for this reason, Uncle Galip had even become young... I was proud of him...

Every morning, breakfast; noon, lunch; evening, supper... How nice! There was a fresh, clean bed too. Oh, everything was in order!... I had only one great need: to bathe, to change underwear...

There was no bathroom, bathhouse or shower at the school. I think the teachers went to the public bath. I couldn't tell my Uncle Galip that I was dirty, because my going to the public bath wouldn't suffice. I had to get fresh underwear too. I couldn't ask him for those.

I'd become so filthy that my pillow had turned dark. In the dormitory when no one was around, I had turned the pillowslip inside-out on my pillow so it wouldn't appear dirty compared with the pillows on the other beds...

One evening, I was approaching the Akchakoja Elementary School from among the wooden houses. I kept scratching my head. My fingernails had grown long too. I couldn't cut them because there was no scissors. My head was so filthy and I scratched so hard, that every time I scratched, the under part of my fingernails was filled with black dirt. While on my way to the school, among the houses, I chanced upon a fountain with a broad marble face and a great yellow faucet. That day, unable to endure scratching my head any longer, I lowered it under this fountain and washed it in the cold water, without soap.

A Unique Intellectual From a Previous Generation

E.A., who wrote the history book from which I was asked questions, was an intellectual from the generation before mine. There were 20–25 years between us. Therefore, we definitely didn't become friends, but were acquainted. Because E.A. was an intellectual and a unique type from the generation before us, there is some value in discussing him a little in order to understand the previous generation.

Yusuf Ziya Ortach* made me acquainted with E.A. They reminisced about their youth when they'd been together. As far as I could see, among his friends E.A. was the only one for whom Yusuf Ziya Ortach felt respect. Therefore, even if E.A. came when he was working in his room, Yusuf Ziya would never have him told that he was out or that he was busy.

In his youth, historian E.A. was the friend of Yusuf Ziya, Orhan Zeyfi, Nazim Hikmet, Vala Nurettin, and Faruk Nafiz. They were a group of friends. E.A. was a few years older than the others. He dwelt in an old wooden two-story house, between Laleli and Sarachhanebashi, left him by his father. He lived very untidily by himself in this house, but his friends

---

* tr. Yusuf Ziya Ortach (1896–1967) a modern satirist and publisher. Faruk Nafiz Chamlibel (1896–) a teacher of literature and one time delegate to the National Asembly. Nazim Hikmet (1902–1963) a great international poet who, like Aziz Nesin, spent much time in prison and exile.

didn't leave him to his solitary life. Every week, they spent many nights in this house. Even in the late hours, toward morning, if they couldn't find a place to go, if they had no money in their pockets, or if they couldn't endure the winter cold, the snow, they'd drop in at E.A.'s house. It happened that Halit Fahri, and others, joined him too. They didn't knock on the street door. It was easy to enter this house; one merely took hold of the latch on the street door, shouldered it a bit, and it opened. The one who opened it would barge right in. Those who were hungry would eat whatever they found, would clean out all the food there was. And they used to enter the house when E.A. wasn't there. Sometimes, if E.A. was late in coming home and couldn't find an empty bed to sleep in, he would curl up some place and pull a cover or an overcoat over himself. To his friends, who came and went from his home with more freedom than they had in their own homes, E.A. couldn't even say a word. What's more, as if this weren't enough, his friends who spent the night at his house also borrowed money from E.A. the next morning—which they never paid back.

One snowy winter night—perhaps he was finally fed up or something—as he was rushing out of the house in a huff, they asked him where he was going. E.A. replied that "their kind" of men had all the luck, whereas his kind didn't, so tonight he intended to take care of his own desires in order that luck might smile on him, and he was on his way to try this out.

The gulf is great between the literati of our generation and the generation preceding us. They may have facets superior to ours, but, in general, they can't be considered serious. To them, wit was very important. As recounted above, for wit, for the beauty of wit, they could expend their friends, their loved ones, and even themselves.

Later on, in the middle school, we read E.A.'s history books. They introduced him to us as a great historian. He had gone to the University of Kabul, Afghanistan, as a professor of history, had taught there many years, and finally returned home with one eye missing as the result of a disease he'd caught. He had a fixation about exposing purported errors in "known" historical dates in use. Perhaps his corrections were valid and not merely products of his obsession. He used to engage in prolonged research, claiming that such-and-such a battle, mistakenly said to have taken place on such-and-such a date, really happened on another date; that that man didn't die in this year but, rather, during that year. Probably, from his view, most of history was in error. The birth dates of many of us are three or four weeks, or a couple of months, in error. There were those who felt his historical corrections were important; I couldn't understand this importance.

He married a beautiful lady, considerably younger than himself. (Later on, there was a lot of talk when he married this wife off to another man of more suitable age. In his last years, when he lived alone, I visited him at his home in the "Airplane Society" apartments in Laleli.)

One night, I was in the garden of the Municipal Casino (where the Sheraton Hotel is now) in Taksim. Two tables away, E.A. sat with his young wife. A foreign singer on the stage was singing songs in Spanish. E.A. suddenly jumped to his feet and yelled that this was Turkey, and that in Turkey only Turkish songs must be sung. The crowd filling the casino stared in amazement at this tall old man, with one eye missing like a one-eyed pirate, and with his flying white hair flowing down to his neck. A wave of silence swept through the crowd. E.A. and his wife picked up and left.

Well, there's a man of science, a type from the generation before us... I couldn't continue without writing about him.

Diploma From The Akchakoja Elementary School

What was going to happen to me? Uncle Galip told me what was going to happen to me: the Akchakoja Elementary School teachers planned to give me an examination. If I passed the test, they would award me my elementary school diploma. This decision must have been made by the Izmit Director of Education, who examined me at his home.

Akchakoja was a famous Seljuk commander who took Izmit and its environs from the Byzantines. In addition to Commander Akchakoja's name, some places he'd taken were called Kajeli [the hand of the great]. But I was to take my examination at the school which had been given his name.

I was waiting at the door to the room on the second floor of the school, where the examination would be given. They called me in. Inside, there were four or five teachers. The examination began. As always, I alternated back and forth between outstanding success and failure. Turkish, spelling, reading, grammar, arithmetic—very bright; but natural science—unh-uh... geography, history, so-so... I left the examination room. I'd really been in a sweat. My diploma was awarded that very day. I'd passed the examination with a "very good." What joy! What a joy! I simply flew with joy. I wouldn't be staying behind my classmates. Like them, I had finished elementary school. Whatever I attempted from now on, I could do!

Uncle Galip gave me money for my return. The next day, I went back to Istanbul by train.

The Return Home

I came to our house on Heybeli Island. Father wasn't a calm person, he was excitable. But he always behaved calmly and gently with me. Upon seeing me, as if I hadn't been lost for days, as though I'd left the house shortly before but was a little late getting back (and furthermore, smiling), he said, "Welcome, my son; whereabouts have you been?"

This wasn't a question which required an answer, just a remark to make conversation.

Those who don't know my father's personality could mistake his superficial question for disinterest or lack of anxiety about his son, as if he were unconcerned. That day, I understood my father very well, but today I understand him much much better, because today I too have become a father. My father—that angry man—had been eating his heart out during the days I was gone. He worried as much as any human being could worry. But he didn't reveal his feelings to anyone else. He didn't tell everyone he met that I had run away from home; he tried to keep from disclosing it to others. If there were those who knew I ran away, I know what he told them as if I heard him myself: "What's there to worry about, friend? That Nusret—nothing will happen to him. Let him wander a bit and have a good time; he'll come back when he feels like it..." However, his heart wasn't saying that. It was aching, what with my mother's death, and now, most particularly, at my being lost after leaving school. Father must have been exceedingly grieved.

Just as he didn't reveal his grief, he also didn't show his joy at my return. Only, with sparks in his eyes, he scolded my sister sharply: "Girl! Why do you keep on wasting time? The boy's hungry; hurry and fix some food..."

"I'm full, Father," I was murmuring...

"Look, we're hungry too, as a matter of fact." (To my sister) "You're still loitering... I said, set the table, girl. Hurry up!"

I was slowly becoming accustomed to the atmosphere at our house. Greatly magnifying my success, I told Father that I'd received my elementary school diploma. (I didn't mention that I hadn't known the natural science and geometry questions, but because of Uncle Galip the teachers had passed me.) I had made such a brilliant showing at the examination that the teachers were just amazed...

But even this exaggerated success didn't please Father enough: "What does that mean? You deserved being promoted to the sixth grade. You could even do the examinations for the seventh, the eighth grades..."

I Couldn't Enter The Trade School

Salim Bey was interested in which school I should attend. Considering my running away from the Orphan School and my failure there, he must have come to the conclusion that I wasn't going to be able to pursue a classical high school education, so he thought of sending me to the Trade School.

It was decided I'd enter the Trade School at Sultanahmet. I was to learn everything taught there. At that school there were sections in carpentry, iron work, lathe operating, surveying, and electricity. None of these were jobs that I liked, wanted to do, or was going to be able to do, because my hands were not accustomed to practical work. I didn't like it... But whether I liked it or not, in view of my having no other way, come what may, I was going to the Trade School—if I could get in... Of the students who finished elementary school, only those who took the competitive examinations, and won, could enter the school. And if I got in, what would I be? An electrician... Why an electrician?... Not because I liked it—perhaps because I found it a little more refined than the other trades.

Years would pass. After high school and the Military Academy, I would take classes in theoretic and practical electricity at the Science School, in a fine electrical laboratory, and get good grades on the exams for this course. But come see me now; if the power goes off in the house, I can't even fix the fuse!...

Well, that's what I'm like, and I was slated to go to the Trade School and become an electrician.

I took all my documents required by the Sultanahmet Trade School and was enrolled. They had posted the announcement of the examination subjects, and the days they'd be given, on the inside door of the school.

Every two or three days, we took examinations in four or five subjects. One of the problems they asked in geometry was to find the diameter of a cone whose volume and height were known. This question became fixed in my memory because I was unable to answer it. I was thinking, however, that this was the only problem I couldn't do. When the results of the examination were announced, I learned I could do neither this nor the rest of the geometry problems, nor did I achieve success in the other subjects.

I couldn't pass the examination. I couldn't enter the Sultanahmet Trade School. But I was so pleased that I couldn't become an electrician...

The Vefa Middle School

I, too, had an elementary school diploma. Like my classmates and peers, I, too, had finished primary school.

The school year was beginning; the schools had opened. Those who had finished elementary school were enrolling in middle school. What would happen to me? After my failure in the entrance exam for the Sultanahmet Trade School, there was no longer anyone who fought for me. And perhaps, other than my father, everyone had lost faith in me. I know my father's opinion; he figured that, some way or other, I would find a way out. He always had faith in me.

The high school in Vefa had burned down, and, for a period, the school had been moved to a building in Jaghalolu (which is the present-day girls' trade school). Since this building proved unsuitable for the Vefa High School, it was, at this particular time, being used for the Vefa Middle School.

I can't recall how I was enrolled at the Vefa Middle School; there is no trace at all in my memory.

I was a student of the Vefa Middle School's first class. I was firmly resolved to work with all my power to make up for my failures. I was very, very determined. But neither determination nor firm resolve, by themselves, were sufficient—other things were needed.

Metod Alge [The Alge Method]

First, one needed the means, the materials for school: texts, notebooks, pencils, this and that...

Almost all of the teachers, in their first class session—from the physical education, music, history teachers to the teacher of citizenship—explained that their course was the most important, much more important than all the other courses, and then said, "You will get these books, and this many notebooks of this thickness." They didn't stop to think of where, how, we could get them. To worry about this wasn't their responsibility.

My going back and forth from Heybeli Island to school cost a lot of transportation money: first, the steamer money from the Island to the Bridge, then streetcar fare from the Bridge to Sultanahmet; then there was the return trip too. In order to reduce the travel cost, I was going and coming on foot between Karakoy and school, but, after all, I couldn't swim from the Island to the Bridge...

At the second or third class, the teacher asks: "How about your book?"

"I haven't been able to buy it yet, sir."

"All right now; go get your book, *then* come back. We can't have a student without a book!"

Of course the teacher is right.

Embarrassed in front of my classmates, I leave the classroom.

What will I do now, after being sent from class for not having my book? I can't return home early and tell my father, "They won't keep me in school, because I don't have a book!" I can't distress my father by throwing his poverty in his face. I know that I have no right to force him to give me more money than he already does.

As I couldn't return home that day, I wandered the streets until the hour for students to leave school in the evening.

No matter how firm my resolve, how determined I wanted to be in order to cover my failures, what was the use?

The next day, when I went to school, the teacher of another class, chastising me because I had no book, didn't send me out, but said, "Don't let me see you in the next class without a book!"

If I couldn't get that book by the next class, I'd be forced to sluff school that day. When the weather was bad, I went to the places where acquaintances of my father worked, and killed time there.

One day, my father ran into me in the company of one of those acquaintances. He didn't say anything concerning why I was there and not at school. We left the place together. On the road, he made the following remarks: "My dear son, you've noticed that everywhere you go people are pleasant and welcome you. But don't think their respectful behavior is for you; they act that way because you are my son."

Years and years later, in like situations, I want to repeat to my children these words that Father told me, but I just can't say them...

If I get two of the text books, I'll be short one; if I buy the notebooks, I'll be lacking the compass. Little by little, I'm losing my enthusiasm for school.

One or one-and-a-half months after my starting school, I'd finally gotten all my texts, except the English book: *Metod Alge*... the book was hard-bound, thick, an expensive book for that time. Our English teacher was Muhittin Raif. (At that age, from where—how—could we students have known of Muhittin Raif Bey's worth?...)

"The gentlemen who have no books may leave!"

In the school's first opening days, three or four of us went out. Divided among three or four, it was easier for us to endure the embarrassment; but, later on, there was no one left in the class who didn't have *Metod Alge* but me.

"The gentleman who has no book!..."

I stood up.

"You again? Didn't I say not to come to class if you don't have a book?"

I left the classroom...

I didn't like that English teacher *at all*.

Four years later, I would be his student at the Military High School. I would see Muhittin Raif Bey on the stand as my English teacher. Only then would I realize that he was an excellent teacher. He wouldn't attempt to teach English to 60–70 students in one class, because it was impossible for an English teacher to give lessons for four or five hours a week to 60–70 students. I think it must have been for this reason that he tried to limit his classes to only five or six students who were diligent and interested. As a matter of fact, from among those students, a number completed English philology at the university and became English teachers.

Years later, after leaving the military, I would establish a friendship with my teacher, Muhittin Raif, whom I didn't like while in middle school, but greatly liked in high school. I would join with him, at Riza Tevfik's[*] home, in conversations on literature. Only during this period of our friendship was I able to understand my teacher Muhittin Raif's value, this Muhittin Raif they called the last representative of Divan Literature, the last expert in the *rübai* [quatrain] meter.

"Where is the *Metod Alge*? Get the book and bring it to class, sir!"

No matter how firm my resolve, how determined I want to be in order to cover my failures, what's the use?...

The Trick Rider At The Astoria Cinema

In those times, at the top of Yüksekkaldirim, old book peddlers were situated at a number of places. As it is with shops which sell old used books, some had the books spread out on the sidewalk. Most of the books displayed there used to be in foreign tongues. So it was with these book dealers that a used *Metod Alge* could be found. Some of my classmates had bought used *Metod Alge*s from there, cheaply.

It was a day for the English lesson. Upon getting off the ferry, I went to Yüksekkaldirim, not to school. I asked the old book peddlers at the top of the hill:

"Do you have a *Metod Alge*?"

"There was—someone just bought it. Drop in again tomorrow, or the next day..."

I ask another book dealer:

"*Metod Alge*?..."

"There were two, but they're sold. Come back tomorrow..."

On the Yüksekkaldirim hill, where the old book sellers are, as you climb the hill, there is a cinema on the left. Its name of that time was the Astoria. The tickets were cheap. There used to be two films, one good, the other a swindle. The place I could spend my time the best, the cheapest, was this Astoria Cinema.

---

[*] Riza Tevfik Bolukbashi (1870–1951) medical doctor, philosopher, and poet, exiled for unwise political activities.

Frequently I went to the old Yüksekkaldirim book peddlers to search for the *Metod Alge* book, and not being able to find it, entered the Astoria theater. I saw Greta Garbo for the first time in that theater, in the film *Mata Hari*. Sinebar, Yedi Bela, Eddi Polo, these were heroes of the adventure films which we called *hafiye* [detective] at that time. Among those heroes was one named Masist. Seven or eight of his adversaries would line up, and he would lay such a fist on the front one that, from the force of his fist, the seven or eight would be knocked over on the ground like playing cards. And this was not a comic scene either.

The viewers gave Turkish names to most of the heroes of these adventure films. Every boy chose his own movie hero. The one I liked was a hero called *"Zipzip Suvari "*[Trick Rider]. Zip zip Suvari used to swing his fists and shoot like the others but he wasn't a big, overgrown person, he was rather slim, an agile man. Especially in chasing after the train, where they kidnapped his girl, his sweetheart, he leaped from the horse's back onto the locomotive as if he were flying. That's why I was crazy about him. His horse, like a faithful dog, would run behind the train. At the most critical moment, Zipzip Suvari would let out a whistle, and his horse would suddenly appear, as if descended from the sky or sprouted from the earth.

There are three famous comics whose names remain in my memory from comedies of those days. We didn't know their real names. Names had been invented for them: Zigoto, Malek, Lui. The real name of Lui, who wore thick-rimmed glasses, was Harold Lloyd. Somehow, only years later would I learn that the real name of the comic, who'd been called Malek, was Buster Keaton. His expression—a frown—never varied, as if he were wearing a mask. He never smiled. There was a great contrast between his face and the hilarious situations he fell into, and from this he derived a subtle, sad comedy. Later on, Buster Keaton's star dimmed, and he disappeared from pictures for years. In his film, *City Lights*, Sharlo [Charlie Chaplin] gave this great old comic a role.

I don't know, to this day, Zigoto's real name nor who he was.

103

Among these three comics, I used to love Malek the best. As a matter of fact though, Malek's pictures weren't as popular as Zigoto's and Lui's. Because Zigoto and Lui's films were based on action comedy, they made the viewer laugh more quickly, more easily, and more often. Actually, in Malek's pictures, situation comedy also existed, and some of the humor came from the contrast. I found that action comedy was a work that depended more on the technique, rather than on the art or artist. Action comedy seemed nonsensical and childish to me. Therefore, I really didn't like some of Sharlo's films, which were based on action comedy, because I couldn't understand what was implicit in them.

There was always a market in front of the Astoria Cinema where clippings of old films, cut into squares, were sold. At this market, both the buyers and sellers were children. There were children who collected the film squares in notebooks, like stamp albums. The most valuable, those which were most expensive were frames that showed bust or head shots of the *hafiye*s, the adventure films' heroes. Closeups of the *hafiye*'s girl or sweetheart were also considered valuable. Most sought after were the film square closeups of the *hafiye* and his girl, kissing. Action shots of the *hafiye*, swinging his fists or drawing two guns, were also high-priced. But squares of scenes showing crowds came cheap. Those who had no money, or who'd already spent it, weren't idle either; they were trading by way of *ayni mübadele*—straight barter. For example, they were trading ten frames of crowd scenes for one frame of the *hafiye*'s head.

Not having any money, I couldn't enter this trading, and I had no interest in these film clippings anyway. But the trading at the market place intrigued me. Being shy, I couldn't go inside that market, and watched what went on from a little distance.

At that Astoria Cinema, on the way to Yüksekkaldirim, I spent the money not for one, but for enough to buy ten or fifteen *Metod Alge*s. However, this much money was not spent at one time; I was spending it in small sums. In the end, I found and bought a very old *Metod Alge* from one of the used-book displays in the area. The binding of the book was frayed and the covers ripped off. The book's previous owner had drawn pictures on the pages with a copy pencil. One of these was of a fairy-tale witch who was flying, mounted on a long-handle broom. The old owner of this book either drew excellent pictures, or else he'd copied it from some place.

Well, anyway, finally I had a *Metod Alge* too. But, as a matter of fact, going to the Astoria Cinema had become a habit with me. On top of this, my classmates had progressed too far in English for me to catch up with them. There was no possibility of my catching up to them, of closing the gap. This falling way back of my classmates in English taught me a truth that would be very useful to me in my subsequent school years: some subjects—such as English and mathematics—develop like links of a chain, joined one to the other. If a number of these links are broken, the ends of the chain cannot be joined. Therefore, these subjects must be pursued without an interruption.

My Living Mannequins

I didn't own a school bag until I passed to the second class in high school.

And while attending the Vefa Middle School, I was ashamed of not having a school bag because, in addition to such things as books and notebooks, I was forced to carry my school lunch in a crude newspaper-wrapped package. Nowadays, even the children of the rich scorn going to school with a bag. They prefer carrying a few untidy books and notebooks in their hands.

Usually my lunch was a slice of fried bonito fish between two thick slices of bread. I also used to take things like boiled eggs or meatballs. I ate in the school dining hall. Many of the children ate lunch at the school canteen. It was run by a young man whose hair was cut to the roots, but who wore a long beard. Occasionally, I had a bowl of *ashure* [a sweet dish of cereals, sugar, raisins, and so forth] at this canteen.

Our teachers and elders often used to tell us: "It's not shameful to wear old clothes, it's shameful to wear them dirty; it's not shameful to wear patches, it's shameful to wear tatters!" Then there were these words which our mothers used to say, more often, at meals: "Eat bread with it! Eat bread with it!" This was like a slogan characterizing Turkey's economic situation of that time.

My clothes weren't tattered and dirty; other than my socks, I didn't even have anything that was patched. But everything I wore was old. My shoes had been resoled three or four times. One time, my father even bought the leather and soled our shoes himself to do it more cheaply. To wear shoes not obviously resoled (called "secret soles"—a term first heard at that time) was something I really longed for, even more than wearing new shoes. The soles on my shoes, one on top of the other, were crude, thick. Hobnails were tacked on the soles, and iron plates on the heels, so they would last even longer.

If the children in my circle, and my peers, had been under the same restrictions I was, then I certainly wouldn't have minded my own clothing, my not being able to buy my text books on time, or my made-over clothes. But many of the children from the Island who went to school were rich kids. They were all well-dressed. And they all carried beautiful school bags. Their hair wasn't cut short like mine; it was combed and well-kept. As for the children of those who weren't rich, they accepted defeat in this unspoken war with the rich, and didn't insist on going to school.

On the ferry, the streetcar, the streets, I used to look at the clothes of well-dressed students, and of those my own age, and think to myself, "Did they earn the right to wear such beautiful clothes? How can they deserve to wear such nice things?" This concept of "right," this "to deserve" notion, has continued to develop in me. I've asked of myself, more often than others, the question of whether or not something is deserved. I've become so accustomed to this, that even today, I ask myself concerning little things I own, "Do I deserve this?" because I am of the opinion that a person can't be the real owner of something he doesn't deserve.

I used to look at what the boys wore, and select from among them clothes I liked for myself: "Say, that's nice... If I wore

that, who knows how I'd be?... How well that becomes me!...
No, this boy's clothes are nicer. If only I had clothes like
that..."

I looked at the clothes the boys wore on the streets, in
streetcars and ferries, and chose and set apart in a dream world
the ones I liked. It was as if those nicely dressed boys, in their
suits and trousers pressed with knife crease, were my living
mannequins; they were passing before me in order to show me,
and make me like, the clothes they were wearing.

The Orphan School Jacket

The round-trip fare to school every day was costing a lot of
money. We had to find a way out. And we found it... The ferry
was free for Orphan School students; they weren't asked for
tickets. My Orphan School trousers were worn, but my jacket
was still good. Every morning, when going to school, I wrapped
that hunter's jacket my sister had sewn for me (by turning a big
jacket inside out and cutting it down) in newspaper and took it
with me. Wearing the Orphan School jacket, I got on the
steamer without a ticket, and when I got off, the ticket-taker
didn't ask me for one. On the way from the Bridge to school, I
would change my jacket. Then I made a package of my Orphan
School jacket and took it along. In my hands—my books,
notebooks, lunch, and also the wrapped jacket package...

The hardest ferryboat trip for me was the return to Heybeli
Island on Thursday afternoons, because the boarding school
students who lived on the Islands got on that steamer too. (The
weekly holiday used to start at the end of Thursday afternoon
and continue Friday. In place of the present Sunday holiday,
Friday was the weekly day off.) Their noise and hubbub filled
the ferry as if it were heavy enough to sink it. It was a good
thing they stayed in the steamer's first class, as I was always a
second class passenger. But still, as a false Orphan School
student, with my old Orphan School jacket on my back, my
other jacket packaged under my arm, I shrank from having
them see me. I used to go to the bottom salon of second class and
sit in isolation, so one of those I knew wouldn't see me.

One day on the steamer, while going down to the bottom salon, wearing that old Orphan School jacket, I ran into a friend from the Island who knew I attended the Vefa Middle School. He hadn't seen me yet. And he mustn't see me either! I was so confused and hurried so fast to avoid his seeing me, that in slamming the salon door, I caught the end of the middle finger of my right hand between the door and the jamb. That big thick door smashed the first joint of my finger. What an indescribable pain! I went down to the bottom salon to be by myself. I was really hurting. Tears flowed from my eyes with the pain; I was crying. There was blood under my fingernail. The pain and throbbing kept me awake all night. When Father asked about it, I told him someone had closed the door on my hand in the steamer. Father kept saying, "Oh, my little boy, you should be more careful! Tch tch!..." Some time later, the fingernail with the blood under it fell off. The new nail grew.

Ever since I've known myself, I've felt with a pain that goes to the marrow, a deepening of the inequality between rich and poor. The reason for my unaggressiveness, my living for years locked up in myself, perhaps was due to those shy, bitter days of my childhood.

Icebergs Came To Istanbul

At school we had six hours of classes—four in the morning and two in the afternoon. And Wednesdays weren't halfdays like the present schools, they were all day.

The first class started at eight. As it took half an hour to walk to school from the Bridge, where the steamers from the island came alongside, I had to get off the boat at seven-thirty. In those times, the steamers came from Heybeli Island to the Bridge in two hours or, possibly, an hour and forty-five minutes. In order to be at the Bridge by seven-thirty, I had to board the steamer at five-thirty in the morning. In order to board the boat at five-thirty, I had to awaken and arise at five.

Three hours going, three hours coming—I was spending six hours of my day in transit.

That year in Istanbul, there was a terrible winter, one such as seen, they say, only once in thirty or forty years... At four-thirty or five in the morning, when I leave the house, it is still dark. Snow covering that steep hill which descends to the dock has turned to ice, like glass... My shoes (with the hobnails tacked on so they will last longer) slip; I fall, and the packages in my hand, my books, fly one way, I another. And in the evenings I return home—which I left in the morning darkness—after darkness has fallen again. After eating supper I get sleepy. My eyes close; I can't study my lessons.

Yes, after so many failures, I had definitely resolved to redeem myself; I was very determined, but what was the use?...

Report cards were given three times a year. We had received the first ones. Only my English was weak; my other subjects were all good. On my first report card I was among the three or four students who got the highest grades in class.

A most difficult day of that fearful winter—there was a foot of snow on the ground. When I left school a blizzard was blowing. My shoes were taking in water. It was like ice outside. My hand holding the package froze. Walking, I came to the Bridge. I couldn't change my jacket along the way. Descending to the bottom deck of the ferry, I changed jackets and put on my Orphan School one.

That day, ice covered the Bosphorus. Ice which had broken up was flowing from the Danube into the Black Sea, from the Black Sea into the Bosphorus and Marmara Sea. The Istanbul harbor was dotted with icebergs and was gradually filling with ice. Each iceberg was the size of a two- or three-story apartment house. If one thinks of one-third of the ice projecting out of the sea with two-thirds remaining underneath, he will understand how large these icebergs from the Black Sea were.

For a time, we watched the ice from the steamer windows; then it slowly grew dark. The steamer's hour of departure had long since passed, but the ferry was not leaving. No steamer was going to operate. The passengers, who'd lost hope that the vessel would depart, started providing for themselves. Some of them were trying to fill their stomachs with olives, cheese, helva, bread, and bread-rings. Some left the boat and were going to some place of shelter—to acquaintances or hotels.

What was I going to do? Certainly they wouldn't put us off the boat in such weather.

But what was I going to eat?

On Heybeli Island there's a Mustafendi, one of Father's acquaintances. He was a servant at the Archeological Museum. Every day, he came and went from the Island to his job. This poor man had a compelling reason to live on Heybeli Island. Mustafendi and his wife were taking care of—for as long as she lived—an old, fat, bedridden woman who had means but no relatives. In return for this, when the old lady died, her house would be left to Mustafendi. So this was why they were living in her house on the Island. One Ramazan night, I'd gone to their place with my father for *iftar* [the sundown meal]. The fat, bedridden woman they called "Hanimefendi" [madam], couldn't get out of bed nor walk. Hanimefendi was cheerful—in appearance, a good-hearted woman. She loved Mustafendi's small child like her own grandson.

That evening, when the Istanbul harbor to the mouth of the Marmara was covered with icebergs from the Black Sea, while I was waiting and thinking in the smoke-filled second-class salon, Mustafendi saw me and called me to him. He was wearing a navy-blue suit, tailored especially for museum servants, with insignia on the collar and front of his cap. We sat there for awhile. Someone remarked that such a winter had never been seen before, but another claimed that there'd been a winter like this forty years previous. Still another said that, according to history, on a date long ago, even the Golden Horn froze over, and when a man, who boasted he could cross on the ice, got out in the middle, the ice collapsed and he drowned. Other similar things were discussed also.

Mustafendi took me with him and we left the ship. At Eminönü, we got on the Eminönü-Edirnekapi streetcar, and got off at Shehzadebashi. Behind the Shehzadebashi main street, and running parallel to it, was a dead-end road. Above this road were situated nice-looking old Istanbul houses, resembling one another, whose lower levels were brick and the higher, frame. Leading to the doors were stairs with marble steps. Middle-class people lived there.

Mustafendi and I went to one of those houses. Relatives of his lived there—a very pleasant husband and wife with their two beautiful, grown daughters... Considering the beauty of the furnishings and the three-story house, a family whose money situation was good.

Mustafendi explained what had happened to us. Immediately, they invited us to the dinner table. Laughter echoed and resounded from the walls and windowpanes of the house. The girls sided with the Galatasaray Club, the father with the Fenerbahches, so they continually made jokes and kidded one another. The girls were freely telling of how they liked the Galatasaray soccer players and the young men they'd made friends with. And they bragged about the playing of the soccer players and their good looks in front of their father. In these joking arguments, with a pretended naughtiness like little children, the girls sat in their father's lap, and he kissed them on the cheek. Until then, in a home, I'd seen neither such an argument over soccer teams nor such a father-daughter relationship. I was simply amazed. Having been raised in a puritanical fashion, I couldn't cheerfully countenance this family's free lifestyle, especially in front of guests. How was it possible for a young girl, as if she were a baby, to wiggle about in her father's lap, laugh out loud before visitors, and indulge in all kinds of naughtiness? And that father! If you want the truth, nothing I saw in the family that night was really bad or unbecoming, but even today, I don't like such a family lifestyle; I can't enjoy it.

I'm thinking now, too, of how surprising it is that there exists no trace in my memory of the woman of the family in whose home we spent that night. What kind of woman was she? Perhaps, like many many mothers of that era, she was one of those who, without showing herself, remaining completely inconspicuous, radiated warmth and affection on the family hearth... whereas her daughters displayed all the healthy, and unhealthy, symptoms of the opening of women's liberation in that first period of the Republic.

Due to the icebergs, the steamer to the Islands didn't operate for two nights and three days. The schools recessed due to the severity of the winter.

The Black Pencil Picture

One day, when I came to school, I saw that our class had
been moved to another room. This was a classroom in the form
of an amphitheater. With the timidity of students who didn't
study their lessons, I wanted to sit in the back row and not be
seen by the teacher. Since the classroom was an amphitheater,
the last row was the furthest from the teacher, but it was also
the highest. On this back row, my row mate (whose name I
can't remember) was a well-dressed, handsome student, a year
or two older than I, obviously a rich boy. Regularly, at every
class time, he sat in his seat, took from his bag drawing paper
of various textures, writing pads, a number of drawing pencils of
different hardnesses, an eraser, solid colors, ground colors, and
other like materials, then painstakingly drew pictures. In
whatever class, whoever the teacher was and whatever subject
he was teaching, that student still drew pictures. He was
interested in nothing but pictures. He copied the photographs
of film stars, printed in movie magazines and journals, on
drawing paper, enlarging them. Some, he copied directly;
others, he divided into squares, and by using larger squares he'd
drawn on the drawing paper, reproduced the printed picture
proportionately larger. He drew so well that his copies were
more beautiful, more lifelike, than the printed pictures of those
women's faces. He shaded the pictures with ground and hard
colors, then pressed the colors spread on the drawing paper
with blotting paper or the pointed end of heavy paper, rolled
up in the form of a thick pencil, which he called a "stop," and
worked the color according to the tone of the shading. When
necessary, he used an eraser to make the shading appear
lighter. Thus, through light and dark shading, the picture
took on depth. He delineated every hair of the stars he
portrayed, clearly and distinctly, showing the waves in all
their detail. By careful shading of the cheeks of those who
were smiling, their faces gained depth, became three-
dimensional, and appeared as if alive.

Most of the pictures he copied were from old issues of
foreign magazines, of which he had many. And he knew all

the names of those movie stars whose pictures he copied. I was respectful of his knowledge, his expertise, in copying pictures. Though I used to draw good pictures in the old times too, I could never make them as nice as my row mate. Under his influence, I also began to copy pictures by using squares. I didn't have as many drawing supplies as he. All I had was a lead pencil and some drawing paper.

At times, I didn't go to school for a week or ten days. In bad weather during the winter, in foggy and stormy weather, if the steamers didn't operate to the Islands, my father knew I stayed with some acquaintance of his in Istanbul, and due to his trust in me, didn't worry. We had a lot of acquaintances with whom I could stay overnight. But if the ferries were running, I had to return home every night.

Thoughts of sluffing school didn't occur to me until the Island steamer came alongside the Bridge dock. Upon getting off the boat, I didn't want to go to school at all. One such day, I got on the streetcar and went to Bebek. In an old house along the creek in Bebek, my Uncle Shaban's grown son, Uncle Yusuf, lived. Uncle Yusuf was a lean and wiry young man—tall, slender, a "wheat brunette," and handsome. His age would be thirty or thirty-five... For some reason or other, his relations with his father hadn't been good for a long time. But many of his habits resembled his father's. He was a watchman in Bebek. In order to support his large household, he must have had some income other than his watchman's wage. Perhaps he arranged a separate income from the rich houses in Bebek. Uncle Yusuf had two wives and children. Since he was a stern husband, like all the men in our family, quarrels between his wives didn't often surface.

This was my first visit to Uncle Yusuf's house. And I never went again.

Before I arrived at Bebek, while on the streetcar, snow had begun to fall in large flakes. And it snowed the whole day. Then a real blizzard developed. In such weather, I couldn't return home that evening, so I stayed the night in Uncle Yusuf's house. I had spent that whole day, until bedtime, drawing a woman's face on paper. I had sketched a woman's face freehand, because there was no printed picture in a magazine to copy. Like my row mate, I wanted to make every hair distinct and give depth to the convolutions of the cheeks. Scraping the point of my pencil with a pocket knife, spreading the dust on the picture and working it with paper, I tried to shade it. But it didn't turn out well. I consoled myself with the excuse that, other than a No. 3 Crocodile lead pencil and drawing paper, I had no art supplies, therefore the picture I'd drawn wasn't very good. As a matter of fact, I simply couldn't draw as nice a picture as that friend of mine.

That night, we ate black-eyed beans at Uncle Yusuf's house. There I heard that one must put more onions into food as a substitute for ground meat, that plenty of onions would give the food the flavor of ground meat: "Peel two or three more onions, girl; it takes the place of hamburger!"

We circled the round dining board on the floor—with children and adults, seven people. A large pan of black-eyed beans appeared. The lid was opened and it was steaming. Outside, the blizzard roared. The woodburning sheetiron stove in the room had become bright red.

After eating, Uncle Yusuf, being a watchman, strapped on his cartridge belt and pistol and went out to patrol his beat until morning.

Shortly after, Uncle Yusuf got sick and died at a rather young age.

It was becoming very hard for me to go back and forth to Istanbul for school every day. The worst of my difficulties was carrying the jacket I wore, wrapped in paper, while going to school and back on the steamer. Six hours of the day was being spent on the way. I was increasingly tired and couldn't study my lessons. A lot of transportation money was spent too.

For one of these difficulties, Father found a solution: I was to leave the jacket I wore on the way to school with an acquaintance of his in Istanbul. The place I was to leave the jacket was a room in the Tanburaji Inn at Tahtakale. Bashchi Ibrahim, whom my father knew, lived in that room.

Upon getting off the steamer at the Bridge dock, I was to go to the Tanburaji Inn in Tahtakale, put on my jacket that I'd left in Ibrahim's room the day before, and leave the Orphan School jacket I took off there. Then I would go to school. On my return from school in the evening, again the same procedure... From school to Tahtakale, from Tahtakale to the Islands steamer dock at the Bridge...

So this is the way I began doing it. My going and coming from school, which had taken five or six hours, now totalled six or seven hours. But, at least, I was saved from the embarrassment of carrying the package with my jacket to and from school.

A student who spent seven hours every day on the way to school... However, I had firmly resolved to study very hard to cover my failures.

For another of the problems, we also found a solution. Some nights I could sleep at the Tanburaji Inn in Bashchi Ibrahim's room. Thus I'd not lose time commuting to school and get so tired.

Istanbul evils such as gambling dens, dens of thieves, flophouses, every kind of underhanded devious low-down business, vice, infamy, smuggling, mugging, murder, robbery, fighting, bullying, drug trafficking, and heroin trade thrive in two places: Galata and Tahtakale...

Tahtakale rates much lower than Galata. Galata is worse than Tahtakale only in houses of prostitution and white slavery. In Tahtakale, women were not openly sold but, with that exception, anything else you could name was for sale. On the day the atom bomb was invented you could have found one in the Tahtakale blackmarket—if not the bomb itself, definitely, a fake one.

In this new life of mine, which began with the intervention of Bashchi Ibrahim, who occupied a dark, damp room in the Tanburaji Inn, I was becoming acquainted in Tahtakale circles. You know, with the term "University of Life," one tries to explain that he has gone through the rougher experiences of life, that he has matured; well, whatever is understood by that term, I lived and experienced it all in this Tahtakale district, where the Tanburaji Inn was located, when I was thirteen and received my entire University of Life education. There I was, gaining very rich, very colorful experiences. But the reward was such, that I had to keep my balance, just like an acrobat on a tightrope—if I lost my balance, I would fall into the morass of degeneracy and be buried.

115

Tanburaji Inn

It is said that some of the *hans* [inns] in Tahtakale were works of Architect Sinan.[*]

One entered the Tanburaji Inn through a vaulted stone gateway. On either side of that stone arch, an iron chain with heavy links hung like a watchchain. Those two heavy-linked iron chains were hung, as if for decoration, from the sides of the stone arch. One entered the inn's courtyard by stepping down one step from this gateway. Thus the dirt and rubbish of the inn courtyard didn't pass into the narrow street, and the street's trash didn't overflow into the inn courtyard. Upon entering the gateway, Bashchi Ibrahim's room led off directly from the left. And this room was entered by stepping down one step from the level of the courtyard. The room's dimensions were only 3x4 meters. Its floor, well-hardened by being walked on, was petrified black earth. Adjacent to the room's wooden door was a small window. Due to both the window's opening onto the dim passageway and the windowpane's transparency being obscured by cigarette smoke, coal soot, and fly specks, no light passed into the room from outside. A naked light bulb swung from the end of a cord hanging from the ceiling. If the light wasn't turned on, it was dark inside. In front of the window was a table resembling a workbench (or a workbench which resembled a table); inside, two crooked old wooden chairs, a brazier stove, a wooden bench; and opposite the door, against the wall, on a frame slapped together haphazardly from sugar crates, was a filthy bed.

As soon as a person entered Bashchi Ibrahim's room a stench comprised of rancid oil, dirt, soot, smoke, sweat, and stale breath hit him in the face. This confusion of smells struck a person in the face like gauze, as if tangible.

Next to Bashchi Ibrahim's room, a young man had a storeroom. This man sat every day, till evening, in the big

---

[*] tr. Mimar Sinan (1489–1588) The great architect and builder of mosques during the time of Suleyman the Magnificent.

coffeehouse below the Fourth Foundation Inn, ceaselessly twitching his eyebrows, eyes, ears, nose and mouth because of nerves; puffing away at his cigarettes; and making some kind of market deals (what, I still don't know) in which it was said he lost lots of money. The fingers of his right hand were stained dark yellow with cigarette smoke, and his teeth were capped with moss. Perhaps, like the visible parts of his body, his invisible organs, under his clothing, were also twitching away. It was said that he had finished the university. He knew French. The young man who used this room for storage was from Ayvalik. He stacked this storage room with tins of olive oil. Even many years later, I used to see him at that big coffeehouse below the Fourth Foundation Inn. When the coffeehouse was closed, he could be found in front of the inn doorway. His shaking had become even worse. Like a mackerel dries and becomes dried mackerel, he had turned into dried man.

Opposite the market player's room, up two steps, the man in charge of the Tanburaji Inn rooms, Dursun Efendi, had his room. This was the inn's best looked-after, cleanest room, and its furnishings were clean too. Dursun Efendi, from Eastern Anatolia, always wore a navy-blue suit, a white shirt, and a tie. He was a thin man, with rings on his fingers, and gold teeth. Two people looked after the cleaning of the inn. Those who lived at the Tanburaji Inn were reserved with Dursun Efendi, and outsiders also treated him with respect. I don't know who owned the inn, but Dursun Efendi handled all of its business. He didn't let evil people frequent the inn, nor allow persons he didn't trust to rent rooms.

Those who worked with their hands, highly skilled workmen, and peddlers of everything you could conceive—from fruits and vegetables to combs, knives, and mirrors—lived at the Tanburaji Inn. At every hour of the day there were workers at the inn. In the rooms on the top floor, men who made almondcake, sweets, and pastries worked at night, preparing their trays. They made their way to the bakery after midnight, and early in the morning brought their goods from its ovens. In the small hours of the morning, in other rooms, the yarn-, piecegoods-, silk thread-, and button-peddlers had started work. Before daybreak, the peddlers descended to the courtyard and arranged wares they were going to sell—the fruit, vegetables, this-and-that—in their baskets, handcarts, trays, or cases. They continually drew water from the well in the inn's courtyard with the long-handled iron pump. In one of the top floor rooms lived a candied-fruit maker, in another, a shoe-polish blender. As soon as it was daylight, from Tanburaji Inn's vaulted gateway, every kind of huckster rushed to the streets. I enjoyed this animated, mobile life. And everybody there knew me. Everyone treated me with courtesy, as if I were older than I was, even as if older than themselves.

Bashchi Ibrahim

Bashchi Ibrahim was from Edirne. He was thin, middle height, a gentlemanly tough. Like everyone in Tahtakale, he carried a knife. But he wasn't one of those brawling bullies. He ran most of his affairs with his head, with shrewdness, and planned well. (Those who suspicioned that they might be attacked ar assaulted by their enemies didn't carry their knives in a sheath, because it takes time to pull the knife from its scabbard. A knife fight happens with the speed of lightning. Therefore, they put a bottle cork on the pointed tip of the blade and placed the knife in the left inside coat pocket so the handle stood up.)

When writing Turkish with Arabic letters (Old Turkish) it was easy to make mistakes. If a person could write old Turkish without mistakes, or even with few mistakes, it meant that he had a good education. Bashchi Ibrahim from Edirne used to write smooth, very readable Old Turkish, almost without mistake. So he'd had a rather good education.

He wore either a black or navy-blue suit, a white shirt, but never a tie. He was called "Bashchi" Ibrahim because he cooked and sold sheepheads.

There were four or five *bashchis* in Istanbul. Each one of them employed a number of peddlers. In the evenings, these hucksters went to sell at their special spots where Istanbul's night life went on. Theirs was night work. Istanbul's five or six *bashchis* had divided Istanbul among them into territories for the purpose of sales. Some of the territories were good for sales, some were worthless. Within the territories, sales spots were the same way. For good sales, the hucksters were as important as the sales spots. If one of the *bashchis* crossed over into the other's bailiwick, or muscled-in on a sales point, or tried to proselyte another's expert salesman, bloody knife fights resulted. I had witnessed these fights.

Bashchi Ibrahim had control of most of Istanbul's places where sheepheads and pilaf were sold. His best sales spots were Tahtakale, Galata, Arap Jamisi, and Karaköy. He assigned his most expert hucksters to these four places.

Every day, near noon, a porter would bring one or two baskets full of butchered, skinned sheepheads to the Tanburaji Inn. Bashchi Ibrahim's workman would light the big fireplace at the back of the inn courtyard. He placed the great copper pot on the fire, filled it with water, and threw in the heads. The boiling of the sheepheads finished near afternoon prayer time. Then he would take the pot off the fire and leave them to cool. Upon cooling, a layer of grease formed on the pot's surface, a finger or two thick. This grease was poured off into another pan. The collected tallow was sold separately.

In the broth in which the heads were cooked, chickpeas were boiled first. Later, pilaf was cooked in this same broth and mixed with the chickpeas.

The salesmen wipe the glass of their showcases with hot soapy water, then polish them. They properly cut up the steaming heads that they've taken from the boiling water. At the time they're cut up, worms—swollen in the boiling water— fall out from the inside of the sheepheads. Striking the top of the head and shaking it, they extract these worms and throw them away.

Bashchi Ibrahim said that these worm eggs are laid in the sheep's nose and enter its head; there they feed and grow.

I spent all that time with Bashchi Ibrahim at the Tanburaji Inn, but to this day I've never eaten sheephead meat.

They clean the heads, divide them into pieces, and arrange them around the outer sides of the glass case. The middle of the case is filled with mounds of chickpea pilaf. Before this, onions have been finely diced and mixed with parsley. Little white plates, forks, and spoons have been put in the drawer under the case.

The hucksters put a case-base (a round cushion made of cloth, which they call a *simit* [bread-ring]) on their heads, then raise the case on top of that. Grasping the tripod in one hand, they take off to their own sales spots.

Until midnight, Bashchi Ibrahim makes the rounds of the sales places and checks on his peddlers. Then he returns to the inn and goes to bed. The hucksters make sales until four or five in the morning. When morning comes, they return to the inn and settle accounts.

All-Night Coffeehouse

The *sakatchi* (seller of the butchered animal's head, legs, and entrails, which are called *sakatat*) who sold sheepheads to all the Istanbul *bashchi*s, was an Albanian by the name of Haji. Among the *bashchi*s, Haji favored Ibrahim the most. Ibrahim was always in debt to Haji. Haji would get angry at him over this, yet would again give him credit. The accounting between them was never quiet. Haji used to holler and yell. Ibrahim, who always conducted his business shrewdly, would feign humility to soften Haji up. Grinning, Haji would make a note of Ibrahim's debt, which grew a little every day, in his account book.

Above and adjacent to Tanburaji Inn, was the shop of a Turkoman prayer-bead maker; next, a grocery; and above the grocery, a teahouse. Across from this teahouse was another inn. Lined up on both sides of the inn were the shops of woodworkers. Further up, the street was full of sellers of second-hand clothes and shoes. In that inn opposite was located another *bashchi*. This *bashchi*, by the name of Shükrü, worked for Ibrahim some time back, as a huckster. He left and started working for another *bashchi*. Then later, he went into the *bashchi* business himself in that inn across the way. He became Bashchi Ibrahim's major competitor and archenemy.

I used to see Shükrü around there. In the whole sense of the word, he was a despicable fellow. He would drink and drink, then come in front of the Tanburaji Inn, staggering from side to side, yell, and make provocative remarks about Bashchi

Ibrahim, and taunt him. When trying to start a quarrel however, due to Shükrü's shrewd reckoning, Bashchi Ibrahim wasn't to be found; but even if he were around, he acted as if he didn't hear a thing.

Ibrahim employed a young salesman named Ali. And it was Ali who couldn't stand Shükrü's impertinence, who, every now and then, jumped up and wanted to go after the man, but Ibrahim restrained him.

Ali was from Ünye. He hadn't yet done his military service. He was no more than eighteen or nineteen. His moustache had just recently sprouted. He was a big, handsome youth.

Bashchi Ibrahim and Ali shared the same bed. In the mornings, Bashchi Ibrahim would get out of bed, and Ali, who returned from work at this hour, would leave his case in the courtyard, climb into the empty bed, and sleep until afternoon.

The nights I stayed in that room my bed was the wooden bench by the door.

They tried to keep me from noticing, but I knew that both Bashchi Ibrahim and Ünyeli Ali smoked hashish. Due to the great respect they felt for my father, whom they courteously referred to as "Efendi Father," they didn't want me to know about their habit. Few living in those circles didn't use it. Hashish usage was very widespread, but heroin was used much less in those times. Ali and Ibrahim smoked hashish, but weren't excessively addicted to where they couldn't endure being without it.

Ünyeli Ali was a very good salesman. His sales spot was on the Karaköy end of the Galata Bridge, the corner right in front of the Agriculture Bank. Ibrahim, who visited his other hucksters during the night, would drop in on Ünyeli Ali last, and return to the inn from there. Ünyeli Ali would finish selling the meat and pilaf in his case by three or four o'clock in the morning, then would sit in an all-night coffeehouse, not going back to the inn until later in the morning.

On nights I stayed in that inn room, what could I do there all by myself? A dirty, half-dark room... There was no place to study my lessons. So I used to go with Ünyeli Ali to his sales spot in Karaköy. A few nights, I stayed with him there till morning.

One night—it must have been four in the morning or so—Ali had sold off all the goods in his case. The Galata Bridge had been opened so the ships could pass into the Golden Horn. There was no crossing the bridge after that. It was necessary for us to wait for the bridge to be closed and the road opened in order to go across. We entered an all-night coffeehouse on the street behind the Agriculture Bank. This was the first one I had seen. In those coffeeshops, after midnight, they used to charge the customers a little extra in addition to the cost of what they'd consumed.

Inside the coffeehouse, thick smoke, dirty smells... Full of old men and young boys. Long-haired, bearded vagabonds hunched over, with their heads on the tables, because it was forbidden to lie down and stretch out... To one side, those who smoked doped cigarettes. The tea man was bringing the dope smokers tea, steeped prison style, in little thin-waisted glasses so the opium wouldn't knock them out.

I was scrutinizing my surroundings with great interest in what I saw.

Of all those people filling the teahouse to the brim, very few spoke, due to their being tired, exhausted, and sleepless. The eyes of those not asleep were squinting from the opium, and the heads of some rose and fell on their chests.

Five heads had been leaned together on the filthy marble of the table beside me. They'd nodded off. The police must have forbidden sleeping in the all-night coffeeshop, because the waiters were endeavoring to prevent it by yelling, making a racket, and nudging the customers.

One of those at the table beside me raised his head from the marble. His face was hidden by a beard. He squinted from the opium and sleeplessness, but you could tell by his eyes that he wasn't old. He focused his eyes and stared at me. I was wearing the Orphan School jacket. His gaze was on my jacket collar, which had the school insignia.

"You're from the Orphan School?" he asked.

"Yes," I said.

"It's a good school." he said. "I went there too, as far as the ninth grade. Then I was led astray and ran away from school. So I fell into this road, where I'll stay to the end. Just you never run away from school... Study! You can't find such a school. It's like a mother's embrace. I couldn't know..."

The last of his words came from his mouth as if he were talking in his sleep. Then he leaned his head against the marble again and slept.

Soon the door opened. A man entered. With the opening of the door, the wind—clean and cold as ice—made the dead, thick, smoke-laden, breath-fouled, dirty air, that filled the coffeehouse, undulate.

The man who came in was yelling, complaining; but what he was saying couldn't be understood. In those days, they collected toll money for both going and coming across the Galata Bridge. Men known as bridge agents stood at both entrances to the bridge and collected tolls from those who passed through. The bridge agents wore an apron of gray cloth, like a smock, which was put on over the head and buttoned in the back. The man who came into the coffeeshop, yelling and complaining, was wearing such an apron. Obviously, he was one of the agents who did his last duty tour at the Galata Bridge just before it opened for ships to enter the Golden Horn. He was drunk. He appeared between forty and fifty years of age, a fat guy with plump cheeks and a long mixed-gray beard. After some time, one could understand what he was trying to say. A *babajimji* boy had stolen his pocket watch. And the agent was making the rounds of the all-night coffeeshops in order to find the boy thief.

I was hearing the slang expression *"babajimji"* for the first time. Very young deviate boys, who sat on warped old men's laps, exclaiming, "Daddy, my daddy!" [*Babajim*]—loving, caressing, deceiving, and bringing pleasure to the old guys— were called *babajimjis*. The *babajimji* deviate boys "lifted" what was in the pockets of the warped old fellows on whose laps they sat, and also stole other odds and ends.

The bridge agent, without any embarrassment, was visiting the all-night coffeeshops, looking for the *babajimji* thief who'd stolen his pocket watch.

The sun rose; it was daylight. The sea sparkled. Ünyeli Ali and I went out into the fresh, clean cold. Ali set his showcase on his head and picked up his tripod. The Bridge

123

was open to pedestrians. We crossed the Bridge and came to Tanburaji Inn in Tahtakale.

Emine did the laundry for the bachelors in the Tanburaji Inn. She was a large, vigorous woman, over forty, whose wild beauty had aged in the hands of coarse men. While Ibrahim was receiving his clean laundry and giving her the soiled, he made very loose jokes with Emine. I listened like those who don't hear, and saw like those who don't watch.

One day, Ünyeli Ali and I had gone to Galata. At that time, there were brothels in one section of Galata. We went into one of the coffeehouses in the brothel district. Those in the coffeeshop knew Ali. They greeted each other and exchanged jokes. A tiny, dainty young woman, wearing an apron of shiny black material, with a white lace collar, like a student from a girls school, came in. She talked and joked with the customers. She came over to Ali and joked with him too. Of what they kidded about, only this remains in my mind: Ali (patting the girl a few times below the belly) asked, "Girl, is your machine out of order?"

And the woman replied that she'd just come from an examination; her machine had been repaired at the hospital and was now in fine condition. The woman's comparing herself to a machine by saying "I just came from repairs... brand new..." amazed me.

All of these sexual subjects were things I sensed, as if I knew all about them, when actually I knew very little.

Banana Thieves

Cold, a very cold night... Ünyeli Ali, at his place on the Agriculture Bank corner in Karaköy, was selling his customers plate after plate of pilaf and head-meat. The glass in the showcase was sweating with the steam from the hot pilaf; the pilaf served on the plates was steaming. Ali was cutting the head-meat with his sharp knife on a board at the front of the showcase, putting it on the plates and adding a little chopped onions and parsley on the side.

I had no overcoat, only my jacket on my back. I was walking back and forth with my hands in my pockets. A boy, younger than I, ran past and took shelter at the corner or the bank wall. He whistled. Both the boy's furtive behavior and clothes caught my eye. He was barefoot. In that cold, he was stepping in the mud and water with bare feet. His pants were so ragged they couldn't be called pants. The tattered shirt on his back couldn't cover his nakedness.

Another whistle answered the whistle of this boy hiding at the corner.

I pulled back a little in an effort to find out what went on, or what was going to happen. On the corner of the opposite side street, another boy lurked. He too was smaller than I. They were communicating with each other by whistling. Whatever the boy near me signaled with whistles, the boy on the opposite corner carried out. There was a fruit store on the street. One boy started walking toward the fruit store, which was well-lighted—probably with carbide lamps—and had the best of every kind of fruit. He went right up to the fruit man and told him something. At this point, the boy nearby, agile as a cat, moved toward the fruit store. The boy who was talking with the fruit man must have said something very bad to him, because he began chasing him, cursing and swearing. While the one boy, swift as a rabbit being chased by a greyhound, was escaping from the fruitman, the nearby boy, with that catlike agility, snatched two large bunches of bananas, which hung from two long springs, jiggling up and down, and made away with both.

The fruit man, who lost hope of catching the boy he chased, returned panting to the store. He wasn't even aware that his bananas had been stolen. Who knows when he would find out?

Underbridge Boys

In those times, the pontoons for the Galata Bridge at Karaköy had their covers open. There were two places in Istanbul where homeless, orphaned waifs could find shelter for the night: the Kilichali bathhouse in Tophane and these bridge pontoons with their covers off. One paid to enter the Kilichali baths and sleep, whereas getting into these pontoons was free; so many boys filled them that there wasn't even sitting room left. Then the gangs of boys already occupying the pontoons prevented any others from getting in. Only by force could anyone muscle his way in. Even big strong men couldn't do it, let alone a child.

One time, on a cold winter night, I went into one of these pontoons. In my life I've seen many places, many incidents, which I could describe as loathsome, evil, ugly, fearful, but never before nor since have I seen anything like I saw that night.

One entered the pontoon by hanging from a round hole, so narrow that a fat man couldn't pass through, and descended to the bottom by grasping iron handholds on the pontoon's inside wall. The pontoon's bottom was probably a few meters below the surface of the water. Immediately upon entering, the most overwhelming of foul smells hit a person in the face—the nauseating odor of iron rust and the vomit-inducing smell of poisonous paint. Piled here and there on the iron floor of the pontoon were things like dried grass, straw, and kapok. On every pile, five to ten kids sprawled, as if stuck together. The children in every group were so tangled, so wrapped up, so clamped together, that they resembled a creature—not human—with eight or ten arms, eight or ten legs, and four or five heads—a giant reptile. Among them were even six- or seven-year-old kids. The pontoon had the dimensions of a very large salon. In one corner a few boys were lighting wood by burning dry grass and straw to warm both themselves and the pontoon. One boy was shouting advice on how to blow to make the wood flame, warning them they would suffocate from the smoke. They were trying to warm the pontoon under the sea with smoke and flame.

These children, who really did live under the bridge inside these pontoons below the sea, were called the "Underbridge Children." A tragic, tear-provoking novel, *The Underbridge Children*, was written about them. The book had wide sales. The author and publisher made a lot of money. Then an equally tragic, tear-provoking film was made, also entitled *The*

Underbridge Children. The film-maker made a lot of money too.

No one in power could prevent these homeless, orphaned waifs from frequenting this place nor their falling into these circumstances. But one very important move was made. The entrance holes of the pontoons, which those poor children entered in the winter cold and found some degree of shelter, were closed up. There are still children like that today, and their numbers are even greater. But they can't find a pontoon to go into like the underbridge children of forty years ago.

Thievery

Apparently, I wore rubber *mests* [light boots] in those days. I recall this through an incident. It was afternoon. In just what connection, I don't know, but Bashchi Ibrahim said that he could hide my boots in the room in such a place that I wouldn't be able to find them. In this tiny room, where could the boots be hidden so they couldn't be found? We made the bet.

I went out of the room. Shortly, Bashchi Ibrahim called me. I entered the room. It contained only two or three pieces of furniture. I searched all over the place but couldn't find my boots. I'd lost the wager. Bashchi Ibrahim took my boots from their hiding place. He'd folded and folded my boots, which were very light, and stuffed them into the teapot! Never had it entered my mind that he could stuff a pair of boots, big enough to wear on my feet, into a small teapot, so I hadn't looked there.

I used to go to school two or three days a week. One day at school I hadn't eaten lunch. When I left in the late afternoon, I was very hungry. I was dizzy from hunger. I figured that when I went to Bashchi Ibrahim, he would give me something to eat, as usual. I walked from school to Tahtakale and entered the inn. The door to Bashchi Ibrahim's room was open. On the workbench beside the window, change was piled, a lot of yellowish twenty-five *kurush* pieces. I waited a while. No one came or went. I walked outside and looked around the courtyard; neither Ibrahim nor Ali was in sight. I went into the room again, took two of those brass twenty-five *kurush* pieces, and went out. Down the street a little was a bakery. I bought a quarter-loaf of bread. (In those times, a quarter- or half-loaf of bread was sold at the bakeries.) I bought a small amount of *kashar* cheese and two hundred fifty grams of *yapinjak* grapes. After all these purchases, a little money was left over. I ate the cheese and grapes with the fresh bread. Upon returning to the room, I put the change on the workbench beside the other money. There still was no one around. Some time later, Ibrahim arrived.

Was what I did thievery? Certainly, because I didn't tell Bashchi Ibrahim that I'd taken any money from there.

A Perverted Relationship

Ünyeli Ali disappeared. Bashchi Ibrahim looked everywhere for him. At first, he thought that the other bashchis—his competitors—had hired his most expert, trusted salesman away from him to work for them. He searched and combed, but couldn't find him. There simply was no Ali anywhere...

Why was Bashchi Ibrahim so greatly interested in Ünyeli Ali? He was saying, "Because..."

Because he wasn't going to be able to find another salesman as skilled as Ünyeli Ali. Generally, one couldn't tell for sure if a showcase full of pilaf would yield eighty or a hundred plates. There is a real trick to pilaf-dealing, a typical huckster trick. (Ünyeli Ali was a very trusted salesman; he never stole from his boss.) Ünyeli Ali had such a talent at putting pilaf on the plates, that from the pilaf another salesman could dish up, let's say ninety plates, he was able to make a hundred or hundred ten plates of pilaf.

Because he was a young man who trusted his fists. As long as Ali was around, the other *bashchis* couldn't move in on his territory.

That's all there was to it... Just like that... Because Bashchi Ibrahim loved him as a brother, a son, not as a salesman.

Anyway, that's what Bashchi Ibrahim said. He dreamed up a lot of other compliments about Ünyeli Ali too.

Was what Ibrahim said true? At that time, I thought it was.

From the day Ünyeli Ali disappeared, Bashchi Ibrahim had been miserable, had acted crazy. And in his searching and combing, Ibrahim had neglected his business. The other *bashchi*s even took over his sales spots. Only the Agriculture Bank sales corner in Karaköy remained his. Ibrahim took care of the sales there himself. But these things held no importance; it would be enough if Ali were found, if he would only come back. Then they would cooperate and make more money than they used to.

Finally, Bashchi Ibrahim learned that Ünyeli Ali had gone to his home town. Ibrahim wrote Ali letter after letter— long, long letters... In the end, Ali came back. Ibrahim was extremely pleased. He immediately had a navy blue suit tailored for him.

Later on, I thought about this event and the relationship between Ibrahim and Ali, which I hadn't dwelt on at all at that age. What was this close tie?

Well, you know our people: when making judgments concerning incidents they don't definitely know the details of, they preface their remarks about the person they accuse with, "It's on his head." And now I'm saying the same thing: It's on their heads, but I think that the relationship between them had a perverted aspect. Perhaps, however, this wasn't entirely a perverted relationship. In the old language, the older men called their love for young boys—which was a weak love— "*mahbub perestlik*," which means "worship of beauty." I think the love that Bashchi Ibrahim had for Ali was, in all probability, such an eccentric love.

A Crime In Tahtakale

In the evenings, Bashchi Shükrü, from the inn opposite, rolling and lurching as he passed the Tanburaji Inn, would yell and direct suggestive remarks at Ibrahim and Ali. Sometimes he would go even further; he'd enter the inn courtyard to shout and call from there. From his manner, it was becoming quite obvious that a knife fight was imminent... The old-clothes dealers in front of the inn gate, the regular customers of the coffeehouse on the opposite corner, the traveling peddlers, all were anxiously waiting for something to happen, for someone to get killed. In that tense atmosphere during those days, one could sense a silent discomposure in the people of the quarter, like that in animals before an earthquake.

When Shükrü shouted outside, it was evident from Ibrahim's twitching, taut face muscles that he clenched his teeth.

Every time Ali rose to go out and fight with Shükrü, Ibrahim held him back.

This tense atmosphere and Shükrü's annoying tactics continued for days.

In Tahtakale, no more than ten or fifteen days passed without knifing and shooting incidents. The inhabitants were accustomed to it, and expected more of the same.

After Ünyeli Ali returned, Bashchi Ibrahim's business started to improve; Ibrahim said so himself. Then he remarked (after all, he did everything he could for Ali), "I had a navy blue suit tailored for him. I also put a spanking new pistol in his pocket!"

Ünyeli Ali, in those days, always had a folk song on his lips, sung in his half Black Sea accent: "I'll decorate the handle of my pistol with roses; with roses I'll decorate it." Ali now walked with his left shoulder high, the right one low. He skipped rather than walked. Between his cap—which he tipped to the left—and his ear, a red carnation was tucked. He swaggered along, tapping out a dance rhythm on the paving stones with his egg-heeled shoes—a show-off! He threw his jacket over his shoulders; and when he placed his two hands on his dark red cummerbund, his elbows akimbo, with the navy blue coat stretched over his arms, he looked like an eagle ready for flight. He *was* just about to fly... Every day, he went to the barber and got a close shave, just as if he were a bridegroom. He knew that no matter how often he shaved, his beard would still grow out as fast. However, he didn't have his dark brown moustache cut, and it was slowly growing longer.

130

It was an afternoon. Bashchi Ibrahim, Ünyeli Ali and I were in the room. Drunken Shükrü was again yelling and cursing at the inn gate. Gradually, his yells were heard closer by. He'd entered the inn gate, obviously. His curses were most obscene. Ali, jaw muscles twitching, arose with painful effort and went to the door. This time, Bashchi Ibrahim didn't hold him, didn't stop him. Ali paused a moment at the door, then Bashchi Ibrahim stroked his back. Ali opened the door and dashed out. With one leap he landed in front of the opposite wall. Those in the passageway, leading from the inn gate to the courtyard, scrambled in every direction. Swaggering and yelling, Shükrü came at Ali. His right hand rose into the air with such speed that I saw the flash of the knife in his hand as an ascending steak of light.

All of this occurred in a few seconds.

Knife in hand, Shükrü closed with Ali.

One after another, three pistol shots were heard. I saw yellow flames spurt from the pistol's muzzle. Ali flew along the passageway like an arrow, then disappeared through the gate...

This was Tahtakale; there was no cry of "Hold, arrest him!" The killer killed; the one who was hit got hit...

Shükrü, screaming, "My God! I'm hit; the guy got me..." collapsed. Blood flowed onto the ground from his wound.

There's no trace in my memory about how I got out of there, how I came home.

Upon my arrival home, I told my father nothing of what had happened.

Haji Became A Murderer

Haji, the *sakatchi* who sold sheepheads to Bashchi Ibrahim and all the other *bashchi*s in Istanbul, made good money from this business; he was rich. He had a young, beautiful wife. Haji wasn't old either; I think he wasn't yet forty. Haji's wife was playing around. She was having an affair with a deputy from the Grand National Assembly. Haji became suspicious of his wife and started following and watching her, neglecting his business to do so. Finally one day, he accosted this deputy—his wife's lover—as he was getting out of an automobile on Bank Street, and pulled his knife...

After hearing of this crime, I always envisioned Haji in a bloody-red setting, cutting off and skinning the heads of cattle and sheep with the knife in his hand.

Haji knifed his wife's lover in fifteen or twenty places, filled him full of holes and killed him on the spot. Screaming and shrieking, his wife escaped. He'd intended to slay her too, but found her gone when he turned around...

Haji ran up one of the side hills on Bank Street and got away. They couldn't find him anywhere...

Although the incident was written up in the papers of that time, it probably was not publicized that the man who was killed was a deputy.

Where would Haji go? With whom could he hide out? He took refuge in the bravery and help of Bashchi Ibrahim, with whom he'd fought almost daily over his debt. Bashchi Ibrahim truly was a person who could be trusted, a loyal friend, one who would throw himself into the fire for the sake of a pal without hope of profit, without expecting anything in return. Bashchi Ibrahim planned to smuggle Haji out of the country. He was going to get him aboard a foreign freighter in the Istanbul harbor.

After organizing his escape plan, Ibrahim found a go-between to carry it out. He gave that go-between the necessary money, which he'd gotten from Haji.

The go-between said that on such-and-such a date, a foreign freighter was arriving; and on such-and-such a date, it would leave the harbor. And the freighter actually was anchored in the harbor on that date. The agreement was made with the freighter's captain. A boatman to row them from the dock to the ship was also found.

Ibrahim and Haji came to the Tophane dock at the early morning hour agreed upon. The go-between was there. They climbed into the boat waiting for them. Everything was working out... There was the freighter, thirty or forty meters ahead... Even in the thick morning fog, it could be seen that the foreign freighter's ladder had been lowered. They intended to come alongside the freighter with the rowboat, and Haji was going to climb the ladder to the ship. Ibrahim could then return easily to the dock. A little later, the ship would pull anchor and sail.

The man who was acting as go-between for the escape was sitting in the back of the boat. The boatman pulling the oars was in front, and Ibrahim and Haji sat in the middle. But what was this? The boat, after leaving the Tophane dock, instead of proceeding to the freighter, turned its prow toward Sirkeji, away from the ship. Before Ibrahim, revolver in hand, could demand, "What's this? Where are you going?" the rower dropped the oars and pointed his pistol at Ibrahim.

"Don't try to move! You've been surrounded on all sides by police boats!"

One of the launches concealed in the dense fog approached the boat. Resistance by neither Haji nor Ibrahim was of any use... They took Haji and Ibrahim from the boat into the police launch and handcuffed them.

The man Bashchi Ibrahim had engaged to be the go-between for Haji's escape attempt, and whose word he trusted, apparently was a police informer.

Bashchi Ibrahim was under arrest in the Sultanahmet Prison.

To me, at that age, weeks seemed as long as months, and months as long as years. It was as if a year had passed since Bashchi Ibrahim went to prison. I had to go and visit him. But with whom?

The Visit To Prison

One day, I went with someone to visit Bashchi Ibrahim. I can't recall with whom. There was a rather big package in my hand. It was a present of five or ten packs of cigarettes and a little fruit.

We went to Sultanahmet Prison on visiting day and entered the gate easily.

If I hadn't written about this event forty-five years after living it, I wouldn't have felt the necessity of saying "easily," because I used to think that I would always be able to enter the gate easily.

133

We easily entered the gate, and easily went into the prison yard. We climbed the marble stairs on the left and came to the second floor. All of these things were accomplished with ease. But I didn't realize they were easy until forty-five years later, after I experienced with what difficulty these same things were done while living as a prisoner in that same jail.

We sat on a wooden bench on the staircase landing. There were other visitors too. Also, prisoners who had visitors were there. The place was very crowded.

Ibrahim came. He'd always been sickly and thin. Frequently, he had stomach aches; the pains used to last for hours. In prison he'd become terribly skinny; his cheeks were sunken, his face even more pallid. Haji was in another section of the prison, because he was under a heavy sentence.

Ibrahim ordered us tea from the prison galley. While sitting there chatting with Ibrahim, from where?—how?— could I have known that years later I would stay in this jail as a prisoner and spend youthful years there, years which should have been life's most beautiful.

I can't remember what Ibrahim said that day. Only one of his remarks left an impression on my memory: he said, "I won't get out of here alive!"

According to my judgment at that age, the guilty one was Haji. Ibrahim had no guilt. What had Ibrahim done? He'd helped a friend even though that friend was a murderer. That is, he had done what any human should do. His being a prisoner seemed an injustice to me.

The day I visited Ibrahim in the Sultanahmet Prison, I had seen a man. That man, in his entirety, lives in my mind. He was very tall—perhaps 6 feet 2, or even 6 feet 6 inches... Big, very handsome, also very charming. But he kept such a frown on his face that, doubtless, he was trying to conceal that charm. And his color? He was jet black... He wore navy blue clothes and a white shirt. Despite his charm, his size and gaze—with the whites of his eyes rolling—frightened a person. Who was this handsome negro? A notorious bully, whose name is in the history of bullies and who holds a place in the history of prisons... He was the prison "con-boss" at that time.

Years later, when I was in prison, among the tragic tales about many famous brawlers that I heard from the seasoned old cons were tales of Marmara Hasan. That handsome black bully's end came about in an evil fashion. In prison he started on heroin. As soon as a ruffian began using heroin, it meant he was through, that he'd become a clown...

That day, Ibrahim said several times, "I won't get out of here alive."

He didn't leave jail alive. Where were his father and mother? Didn't Ibrahim have anyone at all? No, there wasn't a soul to give the deceased's personal effects—a tiny bundle—to.

Börekchi Mehmet Efendi

A two-story building on one of those narrow mixed-up streets in Tahtakale... Börekchi Mehmet Efendi works on the top floor. He's either from Daghistan or Turkmenistan. His eyes are slanty, his cheekbones prominent. His tongue is flavored with the accent of his native land. From his speech it's evident he isn't a Turk from Turkey.

Mehmet Efendi, an acquaintance of father, did me a lot of favors. On my every visit, he gave me money.

In making *böreks* [pastry turnover with cheese or other filling], Mehmet Efendi's expertise at rolling the *yufka* [thin sheets of dough] was something to behold. This was such a remarkable talent, it seemed to me that if Mehmet Efendi were to set up his table at a circus and roll the *yufka* in front of spectators, they would—as if witnessing an unbelievable magician's trick—watch with fascination and enthusiastically applaud him.

A large table with zinc-covered top... His sleeves rolled up, Mehmet Efendi wore a work apron which passed over his head and hung from his neck. He would take a handful of flour from the pan at his right and put it on the table. Adding oil, he would press, knead the dough, and spread it out. As the dough spread, it became thinner and broader. Mehmet Efendi would take the *yufka*, broadened now and thin, by the sides with his two hands and, twirling it above his head from one side to the other, slap it down on the table's zinc top. Every time it struck

135

the table, it grew wider and thinner. In Mehmet Efendi's expert hands the *yufka*, as it took off into the air, would undulate and fly about like silk crepe, like a veil. The *yufka* became paper-thin and was finally ready to be made into böreks or *baklava* [diamond-shaped pastry with many layers of *yufka*, honey, nuts, and so on]. Mehmet Efendi dipped his hands into a pan of olive oil, then took another handful of flour. His hand was so accustomed, that the dough was always of the same weight.

Mehmet Efendi would prepare ground lamb, plain, or cheese-type *böreks*. The *böreks* were placed in great black baking pans and sent to the ovens.

Eight or ten people worked with him. Of these, three were his assistants, the rest were peddlers. One of the peddlers was a Moslem Indian, with a long curly black beard and a great turban on his head. Since he'd recently come to Turkey, his speech was still broken. He had a portable glass showcase, whose handles he carried with his arms, from which he sold *böreks*. The other peddlers had showcases, mounted on rubber-tired carts, which were pushed by hand.

After Bashchi Ibrahim was imprisoned, I stayed at Börekchi Mehmet Efendi's house. Mehmet Efendi lived on top of the steep hill between Tahtakale and Süleymaniye in one section of a big old mansion. That house, with its high ceilings and walls, was decorated in various colors and as clean as a flower. He had a very ladylike, meticulous wife. This lady used to prepare excellent meals.

In contrast to all her good aspects, she had an unendurable, intolerable habit: it was a "talking sickness." I would become stupified from listening to her. Though she constantly complained about her husband, he never used to say anything bad to her. So what was she complaining about? I couldn't really understand. But, according to what I could infer, Mehmet Efendi wished to be a father. His wife, older than he, was not bearing children. Because of this Mehmet Efendi wanted to separate from her, but being a kind-hearted man, he just couldn't do it... The woman was deeply troubled, her nerves shattered. Among the things that she related in great detail, and which she repeated again and again, was something I approved of very much. Together with Mehmet Efendi, the woman had shouldered life's burden; they'd worked as a team, had persevered through bad times, and survived difficult circumstances. Thus Mehmet Efendi had arrived at his present-day situation. He was making good money. But now, after finally reaching the shores of salvation, he wanted to divorce his wife.

So it was within this limited area that the woman's remarks wandered around repetitively, as she talked on for hours, for days. And I had to acknowledge that she was right. When, one day, I got married, I figured on having a wife who would share with me all the burdens and difficulties of life. Whatever success we won would be neither mine nor hers, it would be ours. Even at that age I was planning to have such a wife.

I felt that the woman was right, yet I couldn't find Mehmet Efendi in the wrong either. What should the poor fellow do? His wife wasn't bearing children.

My First New Suit

Until I was in my thirteenth year and a student in the first class of middle school, like children of my age, I'd worn neither a ready-made or a custom-made suit of new clothes.

I believe it was the eve of a holiday. Börekchi Mehmet Efendi was going to buy me new clothes. Together, we left Tahtakale and passed through Chakmakchi and Bakirji. We came to the Bayazit entrance of the Covered Bazaar but didn't enter the big gate, going instead into the adjacent Flea Market. Inside, there were rows of new and used clothing shops. We entered a store that sold new clothes. It was chockfull of clothes on hangers. The clerk laid out a number of suits before me which would fit. Mehmet Efendi said, "Nusret, pick a suit you like."

This wasn't possible, it was unbelievable, I was as if in a dream!

Though Mehmet Efendi said to pick whichever one I wanted, I hesitated to pick the best, the most expensive, thinking it would be unmannerly. I would be ashamed to abuse the man's desire to do good. So under this pressure, I chose the one I liked the least, rather than the best. But the one I liked the least looked mighty nice on me. It was light in color, a creamy brown suit of linen cloth. A suit with long pants, what a handsome thing!...

Mehmet Efendi's goodheartedness didn't stop with that. He bought me shoes too. There were other suits in the store that were nicer, that I liked better than the one I selected; but, in the big shoe store we next entered, there were no shoes that I liked better than the ones I got. I had chosen the nicest ones. They were neither yellow nor brown. My shoes were of a beautiful color that hadn't a name, a blend of yellow, red, and brown.

Oh, dear Lord, were these really mine!

And in return for this good deed of Mehmet Efendi's, what did I do for him?

He had me write a letter to a close relative in his native country. He dictated, I wrote. I was just about to write the address on the envelope. Mehmet was dictating the address (I've forgotten his relative's occupation), but when he said "at his *karhane*," I couldn't bring myself to write the *karhane* phrase on the envelope. When he saw me hesitate, he explained smilingly, "Where I'm from *karhane* means factory, business place, workshop..." [*Karhane* or *kerhane* means brothel in Turkey.]

So I wrote the address. He put in the letter and handed me the envelope. He also gave me the money.

"Mail it," he said.

But I didn't mail the letter for Mehmet Efendi, who'd done all those nice things for me. I spent his postage money. My intention wasn't bad. Until I had money to post it another time, I put the letter in a book for safekeeping. Either today or tomorrow... A lot of time passed by. And finally? One day, while going to the Island, I tore the letter into bits and threw it from the steamer into the sea.

What's the punishment for this sin? Whatever it is, grant me the heaviest there is! Now whatever heavy punishment you've decided on, I've continually suffered for years, in my conscience, one which is much heavier.

The punishment I've suffered—and will suffer the rest of my life—is a lack of faith in others when it comes to the type of offense I committed. Regardless of whom I give a letter to mail, I worry that they won't post it. This means that if a person accuses someone else of a misdeed, without having any evidence, then that person has either committed the same offense, or is capable of it. Lack of trust is like that; when a person lacks confidence in another, without sufficient reason, it reveals that he himself isn't trustworthy in a like situation.

Mehmet Efendi's business gradually improved. He opened another shop in Bakirjilar and, later on, in other locations. He always treated me well, did me favors. His last store was on Taksim Square—below the Eftalipos Coffeehouse (which burned)—facing the statue. I think he opened this shop with a partner.

...I had become an army officer. I hadn't been able to call on Mehmet Efendi. Then I was separated from the service. I wanted to visit his store one day and kiss his hand. But I kept on saying, "Let's wait until my situation improves a little, then I'll go. Let my situation improve a little, then I go. My situation a little... My situation...

Mehmet Efendi died.

I couldn't kiss his hand.

That *börekchi* shop still stands on Taksim Square.

At times, even those closest to me are puzzled at some of my behavior and think that my actions are stupid. Due to my inability to tell them in a few sentences, I can't explain the good things Mehmet Efendi did for me. If I become very depressed, with a lump in my throat, I yell at those who think my behavior stupid, "A lot of good things were done for me!"

Of course they don't understand what I really want to say.

At no time, in no way, no matter what we do, can we repay those who do us a good turn, for the good things done us. But in doing good to others, we can try to pay for the good done us.

I can't forget the creamy-brown linen suit, the light brown shoes... (And later, the letter which I didn't mail but tore up and threw into the sea)... nor Mehmet Efendi who bought them. Not even once did I enter the Börekchi shop and kiss his hand. For shame, shame on me!

What Was It That Saved Me?

I lived under very harsh living conditions in places that could be called sewers. Why wasn't I carried away by the current? Why didn't I become a bum? What was it that saved me? Was it only Chance working on my side that saved me? I accept that Chance did save me from a number of evils, but there must be other reasons outside of that too. While writing these memoirs, at the age of sixty, I want to mull over these reasons and understand myself.

For a person to analyze and, without bias, interpret himself, is so difficult as to be nearly impossible. We're all biased about ourselves. But, still, I'm trying to understand my salvation from the morass, both at that age and later on too. I wasn't carried away by the current, and felt no inclination toward becoming a vagabond. There are, I think, three important reasons in my life for this.

First, from time to time, my father behaved roughly toward my mother, but he loved her very much. And Mother knew that she was loved. My mother and father, who loved each other, treated me with great affection. One thing that saved me from many evils was the affection I experienced in childhood from my parents.

Second were my mother's last words as she lay dying. I'll never forget that she said she'd not die disappointed, because I was in a boarding school. Whatever happened, whatever filthy pit I fell into, I would hear my mother's last words in my heart and try to save myself from that pit. I would realize that I was not keeping faith with myself and my mother, and struggle to be saved from that disgrace.

Third was my father's endless trust in me, his pretending not to understand my guilt, and his forgiveness. In the face of such endless trust, no matter where he is, one will be ashamed of himself, and try to be a person to be trusted absolutely.

And today, I feel that whenever I was able to save myself from fearful, evil conditions, certainly Chance worked on my behalf, but I must say too, that my mother and father's behavior was even more effective.

...I was running away from school; I couldn't study my lessons. It was like this and that... No matter how I wanted to, I couldn't save myself from being left idle. I couldn't get organized. Still, I hoped to be promoted to the next grade. I was always going to pass... I was going to pass but... The requisite *sülüsan müddeti* not being filled, they wouldn't even let me take the examinations. Without entering the exams, I was being retained in the grade. The Arabic word *sülüsan* meant "two-thirds" in Turkish. It was necessary to go to school more than two-thirds of the school year. Those who went to school less than two-thirds of the time lost their rights to take the exam. Thus, I was retained in grade. One-third of the school year was more or less three months. So, at that time, they were more reasonable with the students than they are today. Today, students who don't attend school twenty-one days are retained in grade.

As a matter of fact, when I started the Vefa Middle School, I was so determined to study hard, to pass my class, so definitely determined to cover my previous lack of success...

Without support, by yourself, of what use is determined decision? What use is desire only?

A Few Recollections of Vefa

A few recollections from the Vefa Middle School made an impression on me... We were reading Süleyman Shevket's book entitled *Beautiful Writings*, a book with a red cover. Our Turkish teacher was Enver Kemal Bey. Our geography teacher dressed in a fashionable manner, but he never smiled. His name, Ruknettin Nasuhioghlu. Later, he became a deputy in the Democratic Party's administration, then after that, Minister of Interior. Our director was Selahattin Bey, who was a big man with heavy eyebrows. The director's assistant was the physical eduction teacher, Badi Ekrem. A teacher called Tatar [Tartar] Arif came to the zoology class.

In a class ahead of us (later on, he was retained with us) was Muhteshem, who—at that age—played on the Vefa soccer team. Subsequently, he became a player on the national team. Due to an accident in a match, he lost a leg in an operation.

At that time there was a famous ruffian called "Chamur" [Mud] Shevket, and it became popular to call every other person named Shevket "Chamur" also. From among my classmates at the Vefa Middle School, "Chamur" Shevket, "Gambot" [Gunboat] Muzaffer, and Kemal were with me later in the military school.

I was retained in grade. My father knew about it too. He didn't get angry at all.

What was I going to be? What would I do?

We Are Moving to Istanbul

Winter had passed. We were just going into summer. A few people were moving to their summer places on the Island. While everyone else was moving there, we were going to move away from the Island.

Though it was never discussed among us, we knew my father had long been looking for work. Again, one evening, he came home, carrying as usual his kerchief and basket full of vegetables, fruit, and bread. He was a person who didn't show his feelings much. Yet we sensed that he was pleased. As we sat on the floor for the evening meal, he told us he'd found work. He was going to be caretaker of a garden at Chapa in Istanbul. He described the garden to us: it was fairly large; in it, there was every kind of fruit tree. There was a vineyard. My father was to cultivate this garden, and we could use the crops. In return for this, what were we going to give the owner? Nothing, that is, practically nothing... Just look after the section of the garden planted with flowers; he wanted that section kept up, that's all.

Father began working in that garden. His going in the morning and returning in the evening was difficult.

One day, he took me there. It was surrounded by high walls, at a place called Uzun Yusuf, between Chapa and Shehremini. Just in front, there was a little cemetery with cypruses. At one side, a public bath... On the other sides, lots in a burned-out area, occasional tiny houses...

One, two, three—yes, the garden had four gates. Three of them had two wings, very large. Inside were two mansion-like houses. The garden was divided in two, called the bottom garden and the top garden. Stone stairs, with five or six steps, descended from the top to the bottom garden. The owner's house was in the bottom garden. A little beyond the two-story house in the top garden was a single-room house. To even call it a house wouldn't be accurate. The place, in its entirety, used to be a *tekke* [Dervish lodge]. The one-room house, once the lodge's kitchen, held a great stove, and on a raised area, a room. Evidently we would move into this old lodge kitchen. Compared with our house on the Island, it was a very poor place.

But the garden truly was beautiful. It contained every species of fruit tree: French grapes, Japanese plums, varieties of figs, quince, pears, and even pinion pines; many trees I was acquainted with, and some not... A pond in which fancy goldfish swam, stairways, arbors, water tanks, trellises, flowers, vineyard and many other things... Like a fairytale garden. But there was another aspect to this fairytale garden.

To tend the flower section of the garden, maintain it, would necessitate the constant care of an expert gardener and a gardener's apprentice. Therefore, Naji Bey, the owner, would have to pay a rather good wage to a gardener and his apprentice to do all that work. Father had agreed to perform the work of both a gardener and apprentice free; and in return for his labor, he could keep the produce he raised in the garden. Obviously, Naji Bey was going to profit more from this arrangement than Father would. After he started to work, he'd learn that much more clearly. But Father was so desperate that he considered this work proposal of Naji Bey's—a tight-fisted man—a great favor.

Naji Bey, the last sheik of this lodge—which was closed after the Republic, like all the lodges—was the branch director of the Istanbul Office of Finance. Not bearded, very well-dressed, a dapper man, he appeared to have no connection with a lodge or being a sheik. Due to his being almost beardless, his age (perhaps forty-five or fifty) was hard to determine, and he looked younger than his years. I wondered how many clothes he had because, to my surprise, he changed them every two or three days. He always smelled of lemon cologne. A bachelor, he had an adopted girl.

Probably I didn't interest myself in our move to Istanbul because I didn't like the old lodge kitchen we were moving into. Little by little, perhaps every two or three days, a piece to be taken to our house was moved. At the end, the goods left over were moved to Istanbul in a motor launch. Thus we were moving for practically a month. Still, a number of our things and a bed were left in the house on the Island. We didn't completely move our household possessions.

Naji Bey and my father quickly came to a better understanding of each other. In a short time, Naji Bey learned that my father wasn't just any old gardener looking after his garden. As a result of this closeness between them, Naji Bey, of his own volition, gave permission for us to live on the bottom floor of the vacant two-story house.

Hayret Abla

Every boy of my age has memories of a "Hayret Abla," which fill the years from twelve to fifteen—a warm recollection that flows gently in his heart. The names of these "Hayret Ablas" change with every boy.

The name of Naji Bey's adopted child was Hayret. Her real name was something else. Naji Bey had taken her in when she was very young. She had no parents, no one. So fast was she with her hands and feet, she did her work so quickly, that those who saw her speed, industry, and skillfulness cried in amazement, "Hayret! Hayret!" [amazing]. And when Naji Bey also began calling her "Hayret! Hayret!" the name stuck.

When I became acquainted with Hayret Abla, she was twenty years old, but even at that age she was considered to be late in getting married. It was being said: "Naji Bey doesn't let the girl out of the house so the poor thing can meet someone, so how can she find a husband?" Naji Bey had forbidden her going outside the home, even to the grocery. In every meaning of the term, the girl was imprisoned in that house and garden.

144

The gossips didn't stay idle: "Naji Bey... That fellow wouldn't even let a female fly escape. He didn't raise that girl all these years for nothing... It's surely for his own pleasure..." His not letting the girl out isn't for nothing; it's so she won't see someone and get acquainted... Look now, he neither gets married himself nor marries off the girl."

These gossips thus revealed their own secret desires, what they dreamed of doing were they in Naji Bey's place.

Hayret Abla really was an amazing girl. All by herself, she managed the big house where Naji Bey lived. No servant, laundress, nor cook entered that house. Hayret Abla did all of the work. Naji Bey was a very clean, meticulous man. In all my life, he was the first man I'd seen who changed his underwear every day. His shirts would be starched, his suit pressed, his handkerchief like new, and his shoes polished. Inside, his house was kept brand-new clean. On the weekly holiday—Friday at that time—guests used to fill the house. Food was eaten; coffee, tea, fruit juice, and sherbets consumed. All of these, every job, Hayret Abla accomplished by herself.

With all this, her work still didn't end; after Naji Bey went to work every morning early, she had to milk the sheep and goats. Naji Bey owned seven or eight sheep of the Sakiz breed, and seven or eight Malteze goats, which give a lot of milk. After milking the sheep and goats, Hayret Abla turned them over to the shepherd, who came to the gate. Then she looked after the chickens.

Hayret Abla, who did by herself the work that four or five industrious persons could do, definitely was a girl who amazed people. What's more, she always laughed; she invented things to laugh about. Her laughter echoed in that big house, resounded in the large garden. What a beautiful, tinkling laugh, as if a large precious crystal vase had fallen from the top of high marble stairs and, rolling from step to step, tinkled as it shattered a little more on each one, spreading, breaking up, until its sound muted and died out at the bottom of the stairs... Her trills of laughter fluttered in the garden like butterflies of sound.

Hayret Abla was as pretty as she could be. However, hers was not the type of beauty that would take first place in a beauty contest—a different kind of loveliness, a charm that radiated warmth, pleasure, and liveliness around her. With the light sparkling in her eyes, she set fire to the blood of those around her. Somehow, I fancied she was an Albanian girl, and perhaps that was so. I may have thought this because of her blondeness, the pink glow in her cheeks, her freckles, her plump build.

The outside walls of Naji Bey's house were covered with ivy. The leaves of ivy, lively green in summer, upon turning bright red in autumn took on a reddish tinge especially at sunset, making the whole house look as if trimmed in flames. Near winter, the red leaves turned yellow, and the flames died out.

In everyone's recollections there are scenes, events—like colored decals they paste on children's wooden school desks, book bags, book covers—stuck to the mind or the subconscious. These are the things that intrude into our dreams. That ivy-covered house of Naji Bey's, like a colored decal, impinges upon mine; that house, in changing forms, I see still in my dreams.

One enters the house by way of a staircase with a number of marble steps. A wide entrance enclosed in colored glass, then an outside door of heavy wood. A big salon filled with valuable antiques. On one wall of the salon hung a huge mirror with a carved frame gilded in gold; in front of the mirror was a table with carved legs and a top of veined, colored marble. In the middle of the salon, a large table with fringed cover of purplish-brown velvet... On this table, a big spiral vase... The first room on the left was Hayret Abla's. The furnishings in her room were nice too; her clothing, her attire, were also beautiful, and the clothes closet full. She had many shoes. In every respect, Naji Bey treated her as if she were his own daughter, not like an adopted child. And guests too, whether they liked it or not, had to treat Hayret Abla as if she were a true daughter of the house. From other later events, I learned that Naji Bey covertly profited by treating Hayret Abla as his own daughter. To behave that way was to his advantage. Were she considered a servant—a servant who did the duties of several people—rather than the daughter of the house, she would have had a salary for this service, and thus been more expensive for Naji Bey. Although she performed the duties of a maid, cook, laundress, and manservant, through being treated

146

as the daughter of the house, she came a lot cheaper—just like my father's coming to Naji Bey was a lot cheaper than a gardener.

Hayret Abla loved me a lot. Perhaps her love for me sprang from her lonesomeness at always being locked up in this big house. Naji Bey had forbidden her venturing out into the street, talking with the neighbors, or even going to the grocery. She could only meet and talk with his acquaintances who came to visit. It may be for this reason that she liked me very much. I went in and out of her room. She called me "Chakiji" [knife maker or seller]; "Chakiji," with the meaning of village dandy, swashbuckler...

As a matter of fact, by no stretch of the imagination could I have been described as a dandy or swashbuckler. Her calling me Chakiji was not because I possessed those characteristics, but must have come from her wish to picture me that way.

Hayret Abla was the girl for whom I felt my first male desire, a secret feeling that I tried to hide even from myself, at every appearance of which my face burned in flames of shame. Every time my eye slipped to what was forbidden, at my every furtive glance, I felt an indescribable shame, which took spark from the collision of feelings of sin and desire, and blazed up. Obviously, Hayret Abla knew, or sensed, this feeling I nurtured for her. She had a brazen side to her too. Otherwise, what reason could she have had for being particularly immodest in front of me, as if she thought me unimportant? Whenever I evasively looked at her full breasts—even more visible as she leaned over, necessary or not—what other reason was there for her smile when she perversely caught me in the act? She sensed the feeling she awakened in me and secretly enjoyed it; also, she was testing her trust in herself. Anyway, that danger she looked for, expected, and longed for, was not going to come from me.

When Hayret Abla was milking the sheep and goats in the stable, I used to be there too. It was my job to be there. I held the heads of some sheep and the legs of some ill-tempered goats so they wouldn't upset the milk pan. When milking, what was the reason, as she squatted right in front of me, for Hayret Abla's holding her calves open all the way up? When I sneaked a peek, she was going to catch me in the act and enjoy it... "I won't look; honest, I won't look..." I didn't look.

Like a naughty boy, she climbed the fruit trees clear to the top. A few times, from the top of the trees (with a patent wish to say, "Please take a good look!") she yelled, "Don't look at my legs, Chakiji!" and broke up in laughter. Then the earth swallowed me in my embarrassment.

Naji Bey

In Naji Bey's house, I had duties too. After all, my father was going to use his garden, so both my sister and I would also have work to do for Naji Bey.

Hayret Abla put the milk she'd milked from the sheep and goats into a copper jug, which had first been washed with lye water, then with hot soapy water and soda. Every morning, I used to carry this milk in the jug to an ice cream man in Beyazit. Ice cream made with sheep milk was extra good. Therefore, the ice cream men would pay a high price for the sheep milk. Every morning, I walked from the house to Chapa, rode the streetcar to Beyazit, measured the little jug of milk with my liter measure, sold it to the ice cream man, and returned home with the empty jug.

Naji Bey liked to work with the garden, flowers, trees, and animals a great deal; so much so, that on the morning of his day off, he entered the stable and milked the sheep and goats, while I helped him. One morning, while milking the sheep, he remarked: "You know, this sheep smell, the smell of this stable, I'm very fond of it."

I couldn't tell Naji Bey, "I do too..." The thing we both had in common was our love for animals, plants, and nature. Though Naji Bey, who always smelled of lemon cologne, was a man as meticulous as any could be, still he liked to visit the stable and milk the sheep, and work in the coop with the chickens. He enjoyed those smells.

In the top garden was a small vineyard of well-tended grapevines. This vineyard was like a grape collection, with almost every variety represented, two vines of one type and four or five of others: Chavush, Yapinjak, Kara Üzüm, Bardak Üzümü, Misket, Razzaki, and other different flavored grapes I was unfamiliar with. When the clusters ripened, the wasps hung around, stuck their needles into a grape, sucked the juice, thus shrivelling and drying up the cluster. In order to protect the grape clusters, Naji Bey had bags of muslin sewed, like those tied to the udders of sheep and goats to keep their young from suckling. A bag was put on nearly every cluster to protect it from the wasps. Some varieties of grapes matured late. And there were clusters without bags on too. Naji Bey gave me another assignment: it was to kill the wasps which perched on those grapes. He demonstrated, himself, just how to do it. With a small pair of scissors in hand, you look for the wasp. When the wasp alights on a grape, he loses touch with this world. Well then, you know, the wasp's waist is narrow; that's where you cut him in half with the scissors. The two halves of the wasp fall to the ground... they move and squirm for awhile.

Naji Bey promised to give me a *kurush* a piece for each wasp I killed. Hunting wasps was an enjoyable job. Furthermore, I didn't feel sorry for the wasps I killed, because they were good for nothing. There were days when I killed up to a hundred, in between my other chores. At first, I was filling an empty cigarette box with the heads of those I'd cut in half. But I never did take them to Naji Bey to show how many I killed. Perhaps I may have been embarrassed at asking for money, or maybe I sensed that Naji Bey's offer of pay was just talk to make me try harder, or because I somehow knew, that on some pretext, he wouldn't pay me anyway. So, for whatever reason, I never told him how many wasps I murdered.

From time to time, I ran Naji Bey's private errands. He used to send me to people or places on business, or to obtain something he wanted delivered to the place he worked. His office in the Istanbul Finance Building seemed very luxurious—magnificent—to me.

There were visitors who came often to Naji Bey's house: a retired general, he called "Pasha"; a retired civil servant, who ran a grocery store in the Air Force Association Apartment in Laleli; fancy but elderly, ladies... From time to time, the remark came out: "This Friday, the lady whom Naji Bey is

149

going to marry will come..." They came, these ladies, but Naji Bey didn't get married. My father, angry because Naji Bey never married and had children, called him "a fruitless tree."

In summer, the guests used to sit in the flower garden, in the center of which was an enormous flowerbed. All of the pansies around its border reminded me of people's faces, to my amazement. On one side, broad shady camellias. Iron chairs with soft cushions. A great iron table, marble on top... Here, the guests drank the cold juice Hayret Abla made from the fruit of the garden. Naji Bey enjoyed introducing me to his guests. He wanted to show them that I was an intelligent boy. At this time, my school work was discussed. What school was I going to go to? Could I be taught at a free boarding school, or a trade school?

While I should have liked these conversations, they troubled me a lot. At that time, I certainly couldn't properly evaluate Naji Bey's conduct (which today I understand much better), but with my child's mind, at least I sensed that his aim was not simply to do me a favor.

As with Hayret Abla and my father, he wished to get his work done cheaply. He wanted, through his own intervention, to have me enrolled in school, so I could still do his leg work—run here and there for him at the same time. Even though I didn't understand it would be that way, I sensed it.

Hayret Abla Marries

The word went around that Hayret Abla was going to get married, and to a captain too. I'd seen the captain she was to marry, one time. He was a swarthy, handsome young officer. Since word of her marriage started going about, Hayret Abla hadn't been seen; she had stayed cloistered in the house.

Hayret Abla's departure from the house is before my eyes. She wore a lovely bridal gown and looked absolutely gorgeous. Her slippers were white, and she had long white gloves and a white hat. That day, the house was very crowded. Many pictures were being taken—on the steps, at the flowerbed in the garden, at the camellias, by the pine tree, in front of the house, beside the pool... While the pictures were being taken, she called me a few times, and we had our pictures taken together.

They got into the cars at the gate, and all left together. Her husband was stationed at Izmir and they'd gone there. I was so happy that she'd married a handsome captain, that perhaps next to her, the most pleased at this marriage was I.

After her marriage and departure, I saw Hayret Abla twice.

Only two or three months had passed since her wedding. She had come from Izmir with her husband to visit Naji Bey. In this two or three months, an unbelievable change had taken place in Hayret Abla. Before me sat a beautiful but flippant, fickle, extravagant woman. She was telling about going to parties and balls with her husband in Izmir; how the men there showed interest in her and announced they loved her; and while telling this, she seemed to fly with pleasure. She was delighted at all the men's liking her. The dentist in Istanbul who treated her teeth had given her an appointment that day and was expecting her. And more remarks of this kind... I could see that Hayret Abla's marriage was not going to last very long, and felt sad. Upon being rescued from her loneliness and depression, stuck for years in this house and garden, she was enjoying her freedom as much as she could.

Poor Hayret Abla... She was uneducated too... I don't know if she could read a book, but she didn't know how to write. She couldn't cope with a happy marriage. What happened, when faced with kind treatment? She lost her head!

Afterwards, six years passed. Hayret Abla had long since separated from her husband and come to Istanbul, but Naji Bey wouldn't take her in. She was ill. I learned her address and went to see her. At that time, I was a student at the Kuleli Military High School.

It was a winter day. In bed in her single-windowed, low-ceilinged room in a house, half-house half-shack, on the muddy side street, heated by a charcoal brazier, a woman with her head bandaged... Something unbelievable!... Was this Hayret Abla, that beautiful woman of one time? It was as if she had aged thirty years in seven.

I thought of the Hayret Abla in the top of the trees; the Hayret Abla who laughed with tinkling laughter; the Hayret

Abla who caught me in the act of looking at intimate places while she was milking; the Hayret Abla in bridal costume, snow-white from her hat to her slippers, and the Hayret Abla, who, even though a married woman, rushed as if flying to her date with a womanizing dentist.

Okka Roses

I mentioned this recollection of mine on Heybeli Island in the first volume of my book: there was a lame white Arab who looked after the twins, Ferit and Feride. Perhaps Ferit and Feride's father, as governor in an Arab country, had brought home this young Arab when he was a child.

One day I saw that Arab servant shining shoes in Aksaray. While I was having him shine my shoes (my brown shoes that Börekchi Mehmet Efendi bought), I talked with him. They'd fired him from his job in that house where he worked. Why? He didn't know why; they hadn't said. Perhaps because the children had grown and it was thought they needed a tutor; or, perhaps, due to a lame servant's being useless. Perhaps the economic depression, which shook society, had reached as far as that house, and they'd fired the young Arab from his job.

I asked him how business was. He complained that it was bad. He had a very poor shoeshine box.

I told him there was room for him at our house; he could stay there if he wanted.

I took the lame Arab youth home and explained the situation to Father. My father didn't say no. We settled the lame boy in that old, one-room lodge kitchen. We gave him a bed. He set his old shoeshine kit by the door. Daytimes, he picked up his box and went to work; at night, he returned and slept there.

Naji Bey's garden was, altogether, only three or four *dönüms* [a dönüm is a quarter-acre]. One section held a flower garden, one a vineyard, and another an orchard. Very little space was left for Father to plant and harvest. There was no possibility of our getting along on the crops we planted and sold from that tiny space.

The summer was hot. In the garden were roses of the Okka variety, highly perfumed and pink, the petals of which are used to make rose jam. They were plentiful. Five or six kilos of rose petals on the bushes were being lost every day. Father asserted that these sold for a good price; therefore, we must get the value out of them. With the help of the lame young man, we could sell petals for rose jam. First, I purchased a long, broad basket with handles. Early one morning, I got up and picked Okka rose petals, pulling them off and filling the basket. Father had a scales, which I took. I hooked the basket onto the lame boy's arm.

Father said, "There's no one on the outskirts of Istanbul who will buy Okka roses; you must take them to Beyoghlu. The Greeks and Armenians, who live in the apartments of Beyoghlu and Shishli, will buy lots of them."

The lame one and I set off... Limping along, he hastened to keep up with me. We were on foot. We went to Beyoghlu and cut off at Kuledibi. We covered everywhere, including the back streets, the side streets of Tarlabashi, Taksim, Harbiye, Osmanbey, Shishli...

Truthfully, perhaps in the conceit of my childhood, or with feelings of inferiority born of our living among the rich on the Island, I was ashamed of peddling in the streets. I was ashamed, but I knew I had to do this job.

I told the Arab, "Yell!"

"What should I yell?"

"Yell, 'Okka roses!'"

I was ashamed to shout myself.

The lame boy yelled loud and often. Our first buyer was a Greek woman who came out of an apartment on the street back of the Beyoghlu fishmarket. She probably bought two hundred fifty grams. Actually, they bought these Okka roses in small amounts. No one showed up who purchased a half-kilo—they all were buying a hundred grams, two hundred grams. As the rose petals were fluffy, two hundred grams made a big pile and took up a lot of room. I believe we were selling a kilo for two or three *lira*. We were giving a different price to every customer and trying to get the best price we could. I think, in those days, when bread was ten *kurush* a kilo, two or three *lira* wasn't a small amount of money. After our first sale, we both put out more effort. After the second or third sale, I forgot my embarrassment and shyness and started yelling away with the lame Arab: "Good roses, perfumed roses... Okka roses... Roses for jam!..."

Near evening, the basket was empty and we'd made considerable money. We'd walked so far that I had water blisters on my feet. The lame boy was limping badly.

The next day, again we filled the basket with just as many rose petals. Now we had learned the business. We were earning good money. The Okka roses in the garden yielded a bountiful supply of petals. The big difficulty in selling roses was our being forced to do a lot of walking and a lot of yelling; there was no one who bought a large quantity. Selling them little by little, we were getting extremely tired.

The rose production slowly started to decrease. One morning I got up and saw that the lame Arab had picked up his shoeshine box and left. The poor cripple couldn't take it. He was right, it wasn't to be endured. I had imposed upon the poor lame lad so I could make some money.

I still see that lame Arab here and there in Istanbul. At present, he's working at a publishing house on Istanbul's Ankara Street, running errands. What a surprising thing! We don't show that we're acquainted with each other. He passes me by as if he doesn't see me, and I turn my head the other way.

The Second Running Away From Home

What should I do? What should I do? What should I do?

I was thinking about it day and night, and couldn't find an answer to this question.

What was I going to do? Nothing. How was I going to study?

From time to time, I was seized with the fear that I'd lost everything; I was whipped. For no reason, I was ashamed of my father and the endless trust he maintained in me.

In general, children between eleven and fifteen years of age, especially boys, for various reasons (or, if not, for excuses they invent), live through a period of running away from home, and go through depressions.

I ran away from home twice. And both times there had been no quarrel, no clash with my father or home. My reason for running away was not that anyone scolded or lectured me or disliked what I did... Both of my flights were to find a way out, a road to success. I wanted to reach the road to success and get rid of the shame of my old failures. Had there been someone to show me the way, to get me settled in a school, I would never have left home. Because all I wanted to do, my one desire, was to go to school and study. Frankly, I thoroughly believed that if I could study, I would become an important person. But I had to surmount obstacles beyond my control, and study.

When I decided to run away, I had no plans beyond that. All I knew was, as the first important step, I was going to my Uncle Galip's. Uncle Galip had become a teacher in a village in the Akyazi district. In the letter he sent my father, which began with "Brother," he wrote that he'd finally brought his mother to live with him before she died. I had Uncle Galip's address with me. I was going to go there. That would be my first stop. After that, I didn't know where I'd go. But no matter what happened, I didn't intend to return without entering school or getting a job.

Again, on the sly, I took a little money from my father's pocket. I think it was two-and-a-half—perhaps even five—*lira*, but no more than that. I left home in the morning, wearing the suit and shoes that Börekchi Mehmet Efendi had bought me. I had a straw hat on my head too. Where this straw hat came from or why I wore it, I don't know now. It must have been a rather funny costume, with that straw hat on my head.

After leaving home, I remembered two things. First, there were six postcard photos I'd had taken a week before at a photo shop, which had to be picked up that day; and second, my father's old felt hat that had been left with the hatter to be blocked. In view of my not knowing when I would be in Istanbul again, I had to pick up the photos from the photographer, and Father's hat from the hatter.

At that time, there were a number of shops adjacent to the Beyazit Mosque gate that opens onto the Book Market. One of these was the photographer's. I picked up my pictures at his shop. I came to Karaköy. From the hatter, at the lower end of Yüksekkaldirim, I got my father's hat. The hatter wrapped and pinned the hat in tissue paper. Carrying that felt hat, all wrapped in tissue, I crossed over to Haydarpasha. After paying the photographer and hatter, my money was almost gone. Also, I didn't know how to get to Akyazi. I figured that when I got to Adapazari, I could walk half an hour—at the most, one hour—and arrive at Akyazi. I bought a ticket to Adapazari, and when the time came, boarded the train.

One Who Doesn't Know The Region's Geography Makes Such Mistakes

A year would pass after making my journey on the train as a traveler into the unknown. A year after this train trip, I was an eighth grade student in the military school. At school, after supper, we withdrew to the classrooms for study hours, which we called *"müzakere"* [Arabic: conference] or *"mütalea"* [Arabic: study] those days. At these *mütaleas*, some of our comrades studied and some didn't... Generally, those who didn't study were in the majority. Sometimes, not even one student studied his lessons. At those times, the noise and ruckus from the classroom would reach all the way to the class officer's room. And the class officer would come. The class monitor was held responsible for the noise in the classroom.

One night, we were in the *mütalea* and I was the monitor. Many of the students were pushing, shoving, and creating a lot of noise. If the class officer heard the noise and came, he'd be angry with me. In this situation, I had to either go to the class officer and complain against those who were making the noise, or be satisfied with the punishment the class officer would give me. One of the laudable traditions of the military schools was that to complain about a comrade to a superior, whether right or wrong, for whatever reason, was considered the greatest cowardice, the dirtiest trick. Such students lost all standing with their comrades.

I couldn't quiet my friends, yet I'd rather die than go to our class officer and report them. One or two boys wanted to study, but those who didn't want to—being in the majority— prevented it.

I went to the lectern, like a teacher and pounded my fist, "Boys," I said, "I will tell you how I ran away from home."

Suddenly they were quiet. I started to talk. While listening to me, they didn't make a peep. In our classroom, no teacher had been heard with such attention, such silence. They were listening so attentively that although the recess bell rang, they didn't go out; they wanted me to continue the tale.

After this experiment of mine, other monitors, if they couldn't put down the noise in the classroom at study hour, asked me to tell of how I ran away from home. While in the eighth grade, I related this adventure of mine a number of times to my comrades. They knew what I was going to say, but still they listened. And later on, if there was something I forgot or skipped, in view of my having told it before, some of my friends would correct me, saying, "You forgot this"— "You skipped that!"

The part of my adventure they found most interesting was this section: in order to better see the places the train passed and keep them in my memory, I stretched my head out of the open window to watch outside. I'd bought a third-class train ticket so it would be cheaper. Not only was it cheaper, but I was used to it. I couldn't even think that a train ticket other than third-class could be bought, so didn't consider it. On the steamer, second-class sections are in front. On the trains, the third-class places are in front. Why? If the train has a collision, becomes derailed, or meets with some other accident, the lives of the first-class passengers in the rear are saved—let whatever happen to the second- and third-class passengers in front; after all, they don't have money in their pockets to buy first-class tickets, so they will come face-to-face with danger first.

The compartment was on the left. While looking outside the open corridor window on the right, smoke coming from the locomotive's stack, right in front, was hitting me in the face. In order to see the seashore the train passed by, to glimpse those beautiful views, I didn't pull my head inside; squinting my eyes to escape the soot was enough for me. There, opposite, were the islands... There's Heybeli Island... Our house would be some place around there. Who knows when I'll be able to see my home again?

I got a cinder in my eye from the locomotive's smoke. It was indescribably painful. Tears streamed from my eyes. No matter what I did I couldn't get that cinder out. The only way to stop the pain was to close my eyes and not move my eyelids. Even when a person closes his eyelids, how hard it is for him not to move or roll his eyes... I sat down on the wooden bench in the compartment and closed my eyes. The train stopped at the station. It departed from the stations. I didn't open my eyes. After what seemed a long time, I opened them. The cinder had either dissolved or come out. My eye hurt less. Upon looking out the compartment window, on the left in relation to the direction the train was going, I met with a surprising view. There was the sea before us! How could that be? Before I got a cinder in my eye, the sea was on the right. How could the sea on the right cross over to the left? Or had the train turned around? And I couldn't ask anybody anything.

I wouldn't learn that the sea visible on the left of the train's direction was not the sea but, rather, Sapanja Lake, until my return to Istanbul, again on the train.

So while telling this travel adventure to my friends, the place they were interested and laughed the most, was this mistake.

"The sea was on the right. And when I opened my eyes and looked, the sea had crossed over to the left... Aaah, how could the sea cross over from the right to the left?

Every time I told this, my comrades laughed.

Zeybekzade Mehmet Efendi

I had received the address of that kind-hearted man who did me a favor. I'd always wanted to write a thank-you letter to him. For years I had felt this wish, but I really hadn't been able to fulfill it. While saying "soon," years passed, and I lost his address. He was, at the most, fifteen years older than I.

158

He must be seventy-two or seventy-five now. He had sons; perhaps they will read this writing of mine and realize that I've not forgotten his big favor. What a man! Zeybekzade Mehmet Efendi, without thought of gain, showed hospitality to a strange boy.

I got off the train at Adapazari. It was near evening and I was hungry. *Simits* were being sold at the station. They weren't like those in Istanbul; though round, they were flat and wide. After buying two simits, I didn't have any money left. How far it was from Adapazari to Akyazi, I didn't know. I thought that if I walked—at the most, for an hour—I would arrive at Akyazi and go to the village where Uncle Galip lived before nightfall.

I asked this person and that where one went to Akyazi. "That way," they said. I walked. In my hand was the large hat package. The tissue paper wrapping on my father's felt hat was torn here and there, and the pins had fallen out. It was hard to walk with such a package in my hand. Best I wear this hat on my head. I'll fold the old straw hat I'm wearing and wrap it in the paper... And that's what I did.

His age thirteen, height one forty [one meter forty centimeters] at most, one forty-five, a boy with a great felt hat on his head... What a ridiculous costume—I must have resembled a circus midget.

I walked and walked and came to the picnic place called Chark. It was the weekly holiday, or something, for a big crowd was there. Since it was evening, they were returning home, some walking, some in phaetons... I kept asking the way: "Is this the road to Akyazi?"

"Yes."

"How far?"

"Eh, it takes six hours; but the way you're going, it'll be eight or ten."

I neared the Sakarya River. A young man who caught up with me gave a greeting: "Peace be upon you."

"And upon you, peace."

"Good luck."

"Thank you. Same to you."

"Where's the journey? What direction?"

"To Akyazi."

"What? To Akyazi? On foot, right? And after this hour?"

"Yes"

"Why didn't you take the bus from Adapazari?"

I couldn't say because I didn't have the money, so I had to make up a lie: "I didn't know there was a bus to Akyazi."

"Impossible... Where'd you come from now?"

"From Istanbul. I just got off the train."

"Say, that's too bad. If you'd only stayed in Adapazari in a hotel! Shortly, very soon, it will be night... If you walk until morning, you can't make it to Akyazi. Come spend the night at our village. Be a guest in our house. Look, that's our village over there; you can see it."

Automobiles and buses didn't go buzzing down the roads as they do now. Every half hour, or hour, an oxcart or horse wagon perhaps would pass, or someone on a donkey. It was an old road—if you could call it a road—in bad shape.

We crossed the Sakarya Bridge. To the right, a village with trees which appeared emerald green after sunset. I forgot the name of the village, but not the name of the good-hearted man who showed that hospitality: Zeybekzade Mehmet Efendi.

He was asking, I replying. I was going to my teacher/uncle in Akyazi's such-and-such a village—I can't recall the name of that village now either.

He asked, "What work did you do?"

"I'm a student."

"In what grade?"

I told such a lie to Zeybekzade Mehmet Efendi!... "I'm in the ninth grade."

Why had I told this lie? Was this lie necessary? I think I invented such a story to appear big and gain respect in the eyes of this man who treated me like a grown-up and invited me to spend the night in his home.

Zeybekzade Mehmet Efendi was amazed at my being in the ninth grade. Allah Allah, at this age too! Praise God...

We were going to his home. A beautiful village house. It was clear that Zeybekzade's situation was good. We entered a room on the second floor. Children of my age and older came into the room, either Zeybekzade Mehmet Efendi's sons or his brothers.

160

"Look," he said, "he's in the ninth grade..."

Upon entering the room, I took off the felt hat and set it aside. Tears were still coming from my eye which had gotten the cinder in it on the train, and I was quite troubled over this.

In Zeybekzade Mehmet Efendi's house they were treating me with respect, as if I were a big man. Mehmet Efendi said: "Tonight, you'll stay here. You'll get a good sleep and rest up. In the morning, early, the bus that goes to Akyazi goes through our village. (Maybe, he'd said, the next morning a truck was going to Akyazi.) We'll have breakfast together, put you on the bus, and see you off."

As soon as he said, "We'll put you on the bus," my heart thumped. I hadn't the money, so how was I going to ride the bus or a truck? And I couldn't tell them I didn't have the money. We talked at length, but my thoughts, my mind, were on the bus that was going through there early the next morning.

A meal was set up in the center of the floor. Very nice food was arranged in bowls on a tinned copper tray. We filled our stomachs well. We talked for some time more. They spread out my bed on the floor. A clean, soft bed.

You know, a person has an internal clock that works like an alarm clock set for a certain time. Any hour you want to get up, it will awaken you. In the fear that the bus would come early in the morning, and I would be a scandal to the driver because I had no money, my internal clock worked in such a way that it awakened me before daylight. I quickly arose, dressed, and rushed outside. In villages, everyone wakes up early. I must have gotten up so early that there was no one awake. The cool blue-black of morning glowed everywhere. What if a dog barked or someone should awaken... Heavens! if someone saw me and asked, "Where are you going so early? At least, stop and let's have breakfast," or "Wait until the bus comes..." I'd be scared to death; after all, I was running away...

When I got some distance from the village and came to the place where the village road joined the highway, I was soaked in sweat, but I was saved.

Upon Zeybekzade Mehmet Efendi's awakening early and not seeing me there, who knows how surprised he was, and what the people in the house thought... How could they know that I ran away from the house because I had no money?

Perhaps they've forgotten me after so many years, but I can't forget their hospitality.

Forty-eight or forty-nine years have passed, and I still have the desire in my heart to go and see Zeybekzade Mehmet Efendi. I keep on thinking about talking things over with him. Is he alive? How is he? Where are his children? Years ago, when I was an officer, I passed through that area. It had changed so that I couldn't even recognize their home.

I hit the road. Gradually the heat grew oppressive. The road was awful. Along the roadway, the ground was soft, flour-like dust. At every step, *lap lap*, on the dust, from under my feet a sound would come, *fosh fosh*. I was benumbed by the rising dust. Though it was seldom, when a vehicle, a truck, or even an oxcart passed, the rising cloud of dust—due to the weather's not being windy—remained awhile, as if it were hung in the air. I looked at those in the vehicles that passed me; their eyebrows and eyelashes were painted dust-gray color, as if they'd put on masks. In the afternoon, the sun poured its roasting heat on the dusty road. Going outside the borders of the road, where the ground was weedy and hard, was easier walking than on the road. I had some money in my pocket, even if only a little. If I raised my hand to halt the passing trucks, maybe one would stop and pick me up. But I hesitated to stop the buses or trucks, because they might want more money than I had. We hadn't yet heard the term "*otostop*" [hitchhike] then. In my childhood I didn't have the self-confidence and courage of my son who hitchhikes around Europe. Plug along... On the left of the road a grove... Among the willows a stream flowed, leaping and jumping over the boulders and stones, foaming and hesitating. It would be one of the small branch streams which emptied into the Sakarya. The stream spread and widened in places. In the shadows of the willows, I undressed and threw myself into the water.

I recall the way I traveled and how I arrived at Akyazi. I can't forget that after arriving, in order to take a shortcut I was told about, from Akyazi to the village where Uncle Galip lived, I went into a big cornfield and fell down in the recently well-watered, soft swampy soil; got confused as to my directions because the corn was so tall; had to struggle a great

162

deal to get out of the muddy field; and got my clothes all muddy.

I've forgotten the name of that village where my Uncle Galip was the *imam*. It was one of two neighboring villages which carried the same name, but were distinguished from each other by descriptions such as "up," "down," "big," "small." The village houses had been built on high poles. Yes, you climbed up on a wooden ladder.

Uncle Galip, who suffered the torment of separation for years, had brought his mother to his side. They were living together. She was a village woman, with years of sorrow sedimented in her looks and a thin face whose lines and wrinkles told the story of her tribulations.

Even though she had forgotten how to laugh, it was apparent that she was happy to be joined with her son. However, my Uncle Galip, despite the reunion with his mother, which he'd longed for for years, didn't appear happy. The reason for his unhappiness was his inability to provide a life for his mother on the level he wished. Their getting along on the village *imam* salary was difficult. This wasn't the life he wanted. He seemed to have aged a lot in a short time; he was broken down. There was a great difference between the teacher, Uncle Galip, whom I saw at the teachers' course in Izmit, and the village *imam*, Uncle Galip. My uncle, who shaved every morning when he was a teacher, as village *imam*, had let his beard grow.

The houses in the village were far apart. It was vacation time for school. I didn't know anyone in the village, and didn't become friends with any of the children. But I was happy by myself. I'd become so absorbed in sauntering about, enjoying myself, that many times I forgot my hopelessness, even that I had come here to find hope.

Return Defeated

Uncle Galip had given me my travel money for the return to Istanbul. Upon my arrival at Istanbul, at night, I had no money left. I was hungry too. If I went home, what was I going to say to my father? Until late hours, I wandered around town. After midnight I came home, walking. It was a very dark, starless night. I jumped over the wall into the garden. Feeling with my hands, I found the big apricot tree behind the house. Its branches were hanging down. I ate the apricots I picked. Then I entered the one-room house that was formerly used as the lodge kitchen, and in which we'd lived for a while. I struck the match I found at the stove. I didn't light the oil lamp so there wouldn't be any light. I found a pan full of apricot jam. Since the pan had not been emptied, the jam must have been boiled that day. Spooning up the jam, I ate until I was full. I climbed the four or five wooden steps from where they began in the kitchen and led to the raised area that was used as a room. There were sheepskins, pillows, and cushions there. I was so tired that I immediately lay down. I planned on leaving home early in the morning, before my father awakened. I was going to look for a job for myself, no matter where or what kind of work... Until I found a job and had a place to live, I was going to secretly come and stay here at night. I fell asleep.

"My little son!"

It was my father's voice. I awakened. Father was looking at me with all his affection. There was no possibility of getting up earlier than Father! He'd long since been up, and while the morning prayer was being called, performed his prayers.

With the pleasant manner he always displayed only to me, my father asked why I'd slept here, why I hadn't come in the house. I followed his lead, adopted his natural manner of speaking, and talked easily, as if I hadn't run away from home, as if I had no guilt at all. I explained that I'd returned late and didn't want to awaken and disturb anyone at that hour.

"You got chilled here, my boy..."

"No, I wasn't cold."

"You're hungry, my son..."

"No, I'm full."

We were having breakfast. After a while, Father asked me, as he would an acquaintance who had recently come back from a trip, what I'd been doing all this time. I told another lie, just like before; without thinking, a lie suddenly slipped out of my mouth: I had gone to Izmir and won the entrance examination to enter a boarding trade school. When school opened, I was going to that trade school.

Gradually, I developed that lie further. In a few days I was almost believing my own lie. From where did Izmir—which I'd never been to nor seen—suddenly pop into my mind? Lies, lies, lies... I was very troubled and depressed because I told a lie. I wanted to tell everything straight. But a person, especially a child, in order to tell the truth, has to be in a position where he can tell the truth. Well, I was searching for that place. There was but one thing I wanted to do with all these lies of mine: to come to a healthy place where I would no longer lie, where I wouldn't feel the necessity to lie.

Now, while writing this section of my memoirs, in my sixtieth year, I want to get personal, as a father, and tell of the deficiencies in my fatherhood. I couldn't be as good a father to my children as my father was to me. While both my physical and mental possibilities were much superior to my father's, still I was unable to show my children the understanding and affection he showed me. That father of mine couldn't be affectionate to anyone other than me. It wasn't because of any characteristics, such as my being intelligent or industrious or good; no matter what I was, without any question, he loved me simply because I was his son. It was an unadulterated father love, just that...

Apart from the above lie—my going to Izmir, winning the competitive examination, and entering the boarding school—I had to reckon with a real fact: Naji Bey was cajoling me and putting me off, saying he intended to enroll me in school. Time was going by, and I was forced to choose my own way.

The Davutpasha Middle School

The schools were about to open. Those who had finished elementary school were being enrolled in middle schools. Was my winning the exams for the boarding school in Izmir forgotten, or had this lie never been believed? Or hadn't I gone because the place was far away? Anyway, I was enrolled in the Davutpasha Middle School, which was the nearest one to our house. I was eager to succeed. My school number was 317.

Well do I remember how we were separated for the foreign languages we were going to study. The students of the middle school first class had been assembled in the school's bottom floor salon. The director's assistant, who was standing on the stairway landing, wished to separate those who wanted to learn French from those who wanted to learn English.

Practically none wanted English. The great majority of the students chose French. With considerable difficulty, he collected enough students to fill a classroom for the English section. I had separated myself into the English division because I'd studied English in the previous year's class.

Only a few years had passed since English classes had been started in the schools. The most-taught foreign language was French; German was next. They were providing the English teachers from retired naval officers, for it was difficult to find English teachers. For example, our English teacher at the Davutpasha Middle School was the *imam* at a small mosque in the Fatih quarter. He was a bearded man with a smiling face. He wore a low-collared shirt without a tie. During one of his classes, he'd told us: in World War I, which he joined as a reserve officer, the English, into whose hands he fell as a prisoner, took him to India. While there two years as a prisoner, he'd learned English.

Our house was rather far from school. While going back and forth, I had to pass through wide areas that had been burned. Because these old Istanbul fires, which raged for days, had burned and reduced many of Istanbul's wooden residential neighborhoods to ashes, the burned areas between Beyazit and Topkapi were larger than those which had houses. Things like brick walls of mansions which had burned, bath domes, and kitchens survived in the burned areas. Vagabonds, dope peddlers, gamblers, and destitute prostitutes took shelter in these ruins, in cavities, and among the walls. Because of this, those burned places were rather scary for children. We used to hear from our schoolmates who'd seen it that an old woman—who lived in a shelter in the ruins of a brick wall, which had a dome remaining on its top, in one of the big burned-out tracts on the right when going from Aksaray to Chapa—would for a *kurush* from the students spread her legs and show them her sexual organ. We also heard that there were students who had sexual relations with her for five *kurush*. Mocking and laughing, his friends, who witnessed the incident, used to tell of how a student in the class above ours had gone to her for sexual relations and stuck stinging nettle in the old woman's crotch, and of how she yelled in pain. They used to say that this ancient crone's skin was all wrinkled up. She was living inside a ruin fifteen or twenty paces from the road. When we passed that ruin on the way, we climbed a mound and spied on it from a distance. An old sack covered the hole which served as a door to that cavity in the brick wall.

It was rumored that dope was sold and taken, in the row coffeehouses a little beyond the Hekimoghlu Ali Pasha Mosque, which I also passed on the way back and forth from school, and one sensed that it was so... The whole area was a vagabond neighborhood.

Our schoolyard was adjacent to a cemetery.

I retained no knowledge from my lessons in the previous year's class. It was as if I'd never attended the sixth grade. However, I started school with great determination. I listened to the teachers with rapt attention, studied my lessons under conditions which were not very good at home, did my school assignments with care. My first serious study started there.

My Teachers

In that grade, the teacher I loved most was our Turkish teacher, Sami Bey. His hair was gray. One of his legs was short, or perhaps bent, for he walked with a slight limp. He was one of those Turkish teachers who wanted to be a man of letters, but couldn't make it. Perhaps I liked him so much because he liked my composition assignments. I couldn't forget an anecdote of his, which he told in class; I used that story in one of my writings.

167

A pardon had not yet been granted the One-Fifties.[*] Riza
Tevfik of the One-Fifties had not yet returned to Turkey from
exile. In one of his classes, while Sami Bey was speaking of
Riza Tevfik, he related this incident: "Above the street in
Shehzadebashi, there is a shop that sells wood and charcoal.
This woodman used to arrange the wood that he'd neatly cut, in
an orderly pile, one piece on another. One day, when Riza
Tevfik was passing by, he stared and stared at the neatly
arranged wood in front of the shop, then said in a loud voice to
the friend beside him, 'Look, imagine such a country!... In this
country, a place is given even to wood...' In a roundabout way,
he was complaining that no room was given him." Our teacher,
a student at that time, chanced to pass by and heard these
words of Riza Tevfik's. He told us of this incident to illustrate
Riza Tevfik's pride and conceit. But I hadn't interpreted it
that way at all.

A holiday, and I had gone to Sami Bey's house with two or
three friends. He was living in one of the small brick houses
which had just started to be constructed, here and there, in the
burned-out area in Findikzade. The brick walls of the house
weren't plastered on the outside. It was a pleasant, neat house.

Our art teacher was one who made you hate art. Couldn't
he, at least, have made art, which was the most easily loved
course, liked? That subject of conversation wasn't for me
though, because I liked to draw pictures and was being
successful enough to please the teacher. He used to take the
earlobe of mischievous students between his thumb and index
fingernails and squeeze hard. The kids said this hurt like a bee
sting. I think that during my era as a student, art and music
courses were considered unnecessary, and their teachers were
made fun of and belittled by the students, so our art teacher was
forced to act very strict in order to make us consider his subject
important. He tried hard to teach us perspective. I learned
perspective first from him.

Our physical education teacher was Kemal Bey. I think
this was his first teaching assignment. In the winter, even in
snowy weather, he wore no overcoat. To avoid getting chilled

---

[*] tr. The "One-Fifties" are the one hundred fifty intellectuals
permanently exiled from Turkey in the Twenties.

in the cold, he advised us to put newspaper on our backs and chests, underneath our underwear. He opened his shirt and showed us. He didn't get cold because he had newspaper on his chest and back. In those days, I too tried putting newspaper on my back and chest to protect myself from the cold. Kemal Bey was well-built, wore a navy-blue suit, had a deep voice, and was the teacher who supervised us in sports in addition to physical education classes. He had all of us get white gym shoes, shorts, and athletic shirts for sports. I played volleyball then for the first time. I think it was in the year 1960, when I was invited as a judge in a girls high-school debate, that once again I saw Kemal Bey, as assistant director of that high school. I tried in vain to make him remember me. I told him of his advising us to put newspaper on our backs and chests, which had left an impression on my mind. Either he'd forgotten, or seemed to have. I was amazed, just as those in the generation after us are amazed at many things about us...

I can't remember the name of our mathematics teacher. His name wasn't mentioned; somehow he was called by the nickname of "The Coalman"... He was old, or of an age that appeared old to us. Like a ponderously working machine set up in front of the blackboard, he gave the lesson. Between him and the students, there was no bond, warmth, nor rapport; he had no other contact than giving his lesson. I fancied that at home he would speak to his wife, children, and visitors, with the impersonality of a machine, just as he did with us, and would unceasingly teach them mathematics and geometry.

In one respect, the man who directed me—in an indirect way—toward writing plays, was our music teacher, Hulusi Bey.

Our history teacher, who also taught at the Maltepe Military High School, was Memduh Bey.

Zat-i Devletleri İbish Hazretleri
[Prosperity Ibish, His Excellency]

In Shehzadebashi there were the Ferah and Millet theaters, facing each other. During that school year, I went to these theaters two or three times. I was particularly fond of Nashit. In the theater opposite where Nashit played, Ismail Dumbullu's troupe used to perform.

One day, while passing through Shehzadebashi, I read an announcement, written on muslin and hanging above the entrance to the Ferah Theater. The theater had organized a play-writing contest, open to everyone. The play which won the contest would be performed at the Ferah Theater. Either the theater was genuinely searching for a good play with this contest, or they'd opened a competition to attract the interest of their audience. As soon as I saw that advertisement, I became enthusiastic. I immediately took it into my head to write a play. But how could I write a play? I had seen only two or three *tuluat* plays [popular theater, where actors improvise] and one theater-in-the-round show. With the inspiration of whatever remained in my memory of a *tuluat* play I'd seen when eight years of age, I started writing a play. Of course I couldn't do it. I was only able to scribble one or two pages. So, this unfinished play was my first attempt at writing, at the age of thirteen.

In 1957, when my play entitled *Biraz Gelir Misiniz* [Will You Come Here, Please] was published as a book, my friend Kemal Tahir,[*] after reading it, told people that I wrote this type of play in order to belittle humor. And Tahir Alangu dared to take advantage of his remarks by using them to criticize me in his critique of a book of stories. This judgment, so mistaken, still continues. In one of our arguments, Kemal Tahir yelled, "You want the first play you wrote to be a masterpiece!" In order to appear to be in the right, he asserted, boastingly, that writing novels was enough for him; that he'd never written anything but novels. I didn't argue this subject with him because, as a matter of fact, I knew that, long ago, Kemal Tahir had unsuccessfully tried to write plays. In the book *Nazim'dan Kemal Tahir'e Mektuplar* [Nazim's Letters to Kemal Tahir] there are things Nazim[*] said to Kemal Tahir concerning the plays he wrote. Yes, I didn't argue with Kemal

---

[*] Kemal Tahir (1910–) Novelist, journalist and literary critic.
[*] tr. Nazim Kurshunlu, a contemporary playwright.

Tahir on this subject. I hadn't felt the necessity to tell him
that I hadn't just begun writing plays, that before *Biraz Gelir
Misiniz*, I had at least fifteen plays, which were written but
not performed nor published, and that I started my writing
career with a play.

But this rumor which he started, that I wrote this kind of
play in order to belittle humor, went on, and goes on. I wasn't
able to write the play for the contest at age thirteen, but many
years later, in 1971, still inspired by that *tuluat* play I saw at
age eight, I wrote the Play called *Zat-i Devletleri Ibish
Hazretleri*. Herewith, I quote a portion from the introduction
to this play:

> On Monday, 24 May 1971, I was confined by myself
> in an empty Quonset hut as a prisoner at Maltepe
> Barracks. Being denied books, paper and pencil was my
> greatest hardship. In such situations, in an effort to
> remain optimistic, I either think of the past or plan for
> the future. Pacing back and forth in this long barrack,
> given as American aid, I was living my memories... I
> am forty-eight years in the past. I am eight years old.
> The first summer after the liberation of Istanbul... We
> are renters in a room of an old two-story frame house on
> a side street in Jerrahpasha. An Aunt Fatma'nim, one
> of our acquaintances, lived there. She was the wife of a
> *hallach* [a cotton or wool fluffer]. She cooked in homes
> of the wealthy. One night, when she came home with
> time off from the place she worked, she took me to a
> *tuluat* play being staged in a garden. This was the first
> theatrical play I saw. Those in the audience were
> splitting their sides with laughter, but I was the one
> who laughed the most. A little scene from that
> theater-in-the-round is still very much alive before my
> eyes. In the play, when an old man put on a fur coat, it
> was as if he turned into a monster. And in their fear,
> the others, trembling, carried out every nonsensical
> command of this dictator and worshipped him in the
> manner of primitive tribespeople. If that callous man
> took off the fur, he became a good-for-nothing. When
> the manservant of the house found a chance to put on

the fur coat, he started to take over; he even mounted the back of his master, whom he forced to go on all fours, then became master himself.

As I am pacing back and forth in the Quonset hut, the rounded, sheetmetal roof conducts increasing heat. I am coming further this side in my memories. I am thirteen years old. Though I'm now a patron of the theaters in Shehzadebashi, I've not yet gone to the City Theater, but will go there the first time, in five or six months. The year would be 1929-30. I am a student in the sixth grade in the Davutpasha Middle School. One day, above the door of the Millet Theater, I saw the announcement that a play contest had been opened, which prompted me to write my first play. Thus, my writing career had first begun with writing plays. Its subject was that humorous scene which remained in my memory from the *tuluat* play I saw when I was eight: the ruthless oppression of the others by anyone who got hold of the magic fur coat and wore it. But I couldn't write and complete the play.

I am thinking now, that play I saw in my childhood, whose effect still stays with me, was possibly adapted from the play-in-the-round, *Büyüjü Hoja* [The Teacher/Sorcerer], or, perhaps, the *tuluat* version of the play, *Tahir ile Zuhre* [Tahir and Venus].

The Istanbul City Theater

Although I gave a great deal of importance to my lessons and worked hard on all of them, I just couldn't see the importance of the music course. I didn't believe in the usefulness nor the necessity for music. Not only mine, but the opinion of all of us in the class lay in this direction. Therefore, my generation, like the generation before us, doesn't know how to sing songs and marches together. As a matter of fact, an incident is told which touches on this. Whether true or not, this incident reveals a fact. Before the Turkish National

Anthem was composed, at an international sports meet in which we participated, the athletes of every country sang their own national anthems. Our athletes didn't know how to sing a march or suitable song together, yet they'd be disgraced if they didn't, so, when their turn came—knowing that the audience wouldn't understand Turkish anyway—they sang as their anthem the folk song, *"Hamsi de koydum ta ta tavaya— Uchtu da gitti ha ha havaya..."* [So I put the smelts in the fry fry frying pan—They flew and went into the air air air...]. Supposedly, it was well-received.

In music class, I went along with my friends and made a lot of noise.

Every school year examinations were given three times, and a report card was issued each time. We were in the days of the first examinations. Our music teacher was Hulusi Bey. He was a well-dressed, serious person. He was determined to teach us music at all costs. Before then, we'd figured that when you said "music class," it meant the teacher would teach us to sing a march or two. Those who had a good ear and nice voice and sang the march they'd memorized well, got top grades; and those, like me (who wouldn't be failed anyway in a mere music class), used to get a middle grade. My voice was as bad as it could be, and having no "ear" for music, I could never sing the folk songs, melodies, and marches. Thus, I'd never be able to learn music and, for me, it was a subject taught in vain.

Generally, ridicule is a cover to protect the unsuccessful person's ego, to hide his lack of success. The reason for children's being excessively mocking and disapproving— especially in the years preceding adolescence—is their struggle to protect their personalities by hiding failures. This is the reason for lazy students being more mocking and mischievous. If I'd had some small hope of being successful in music class, I would have been just as attentive and industrious as I was in other classes.

The first report cards of the school year had been distributed. I got "fives," which was the top grade, in all subjects except music, where I received only a "two." I was very unhappy. In all my school life, that was the only bad grade I'd gotten. After that, once again, I drew top marks in all the grades and every subject.

How could I have known that this "two" I got in music was going to direct me toward the theater?

Hulusi Bey didn't stop with teaching us songs and marches; he also taught us the notes, their position on the staff, and how to read them. These things I could learn.

In music class, my eyes were on Hulusi Bey's lips. I listened intently to him. And he noticed my attentiveness. At one class, he'd written notes on a staff drawn on the blackboard with chalk. He had the students stand up, asked them the notes, then had them sing a scale. He called on me to recite. I read all the notes with ease. When it came to singing the scale, I started making noises like a crow, like a hawk. My friends laughed out loud. Maybe they thought that I was making those ugly noises on purpose, to mock the teacher. Especially on high notes, like "la" and "ti," my voice grew ragged, hoarse, completely hideous. Hulusi Bey sounded "do" and wanted me to repeat. I repeated; rather, I thought I was repeating. Who knows what kind of noise I was making? Hulusi Bey ignored the kids, who were choking with laughter. He struggled mightily to get a true "do" note out of me. Finally, he had me take my seat. I was very angry with myself because I couldn't make it. And I was unhappy to have tired Hulusi Bey that much. However, as a result of this failure of mine, Hulusi Bey took notice of how very hard I worked in his music class.

On my report card for the second and third quarters, I received a "five" in music. At the end of the school year Hulusi Bey gave me a big envelope as reward for my hard work in his class. On the envelope was written both my given and surnames. Upon leaving Hulusi Bey's classroom, I excitedly opened that thick, beautiful, paper envelope. I drew out an invitation printed in gold. He was inviting me to a concert to be given at the *Darülbedayi* in Tepebashi (the City Theater, which later burned). How pleased, how happy I was; the world was mine!

I didn't even know where the City Theater was. On the day of the concert, I put on my best clothes. I put on a tie. I went to the City Theater. This was my first entrance into such a theater building. I really enjoyed showing the invitation in my hand and going in. Upon entering, I was enchanted by the splendid appearance of the hall. It seemed to me as if there couldn't be a place more beautiful than this. The floors were spread with soft carpets. The rounded folds of the huge, dark-purple curtain caressed the eye of the beholder. Carved, gilded decorations framing the stage and loges dazzled the eye. Above the stage frame, in the center, was a relief symbolizing the five arts. A warm atmosphere. Such a large crowd, but they walked in and took their seats silently. Respect was in the air itself. In the audience was no one of my age, all were adults.

The concert began. This was the first concert I'd heard. When I saw that the leader of the musicians was our music teacher, Hulusi Bey, I was very surprised. He was wearing a tuxedo too. For the first time outside the movies, I was seeing a man in a tuxedo. Suddenly, in my eyes, Hulusi Bey became the greatest man in the world. To me it seemed, with that baton in his hand, he was directing the whole world, rather than ten or fifteen musicians. How did it happen that such a man came to give lessons in music to such miserable wretches as us students, and we dared to ridicule him!... I last saw Hulusi Bey from a distance at that concert, but never again. At that time he hadn't taken his surname, Öktem, because the surname law hadn't yet been promulgated. Only much later did I learn that my teacher was Hulusi Öktem, who he was, and of his great personality. A large space is devoted to Hulusi Öktem in the encyclopedias of music: the founder of the first chorus in Turkey, founder of the Istanbul City Band, founder of the forty-member National Ottoman Band by 1914, director of the boarding school division of the Municipal Conservatory... And Hulusi Öktem knew five foreign languages fluently. He wrote books on the subject of music. I think about him more now than I did in the old days: why was a man of this caliber trying to teach music, in vain, to lazy sixth-grade boys at the Davutpasha Middle School? In this section of my memoirs, in telling of my teachers I pay homage to them. If old age consists of not liking the present and longing for the past, I can comfortably accept the fact that I am old on the subject of teachers. Yes, the teachers of my student era, in general, were truly idealists. Compared with today, idealistic teachers were in the great majority during that period. The reason for this, first of all, was their having idealistic feelings about the newly founded Republic and enthusiasm for the recently won War of Deliverance. Thus, in 1928, the 36-year-old Hulusi Öktem was not trying to teach music to these twelve- or thirteen-year-old bums—who dared to make fun of him—but struggling desperately to have them taste and like it. His music classes were of no use to me at all. But with Hulusi Bey's invitation to the concert, I first learned about the City Theater and then became a continuing patron of the plays there. This interest slowly directed me toward writing plays. From this aspect, I remember Hulusi Öktem with great respect.

I Am Writing A Novel

My seat mate was a boy named Reshat. He was slim, tall, dark, and handsome. Every day, he wore a navy-blue suit, a white shirt with a starched collar and a tie. According to the style of the time, the knot on his tie was small. He was from Izmir. He used to tell me, all the time, about Izmir and his life there. I had learned from him that there was a park in Izmir, called Bahribaba. Bahribaba was the place he praised the most. Although his family lived in Izmir, somehow he stayed, as a renter, in a room of a house in Aksaray. Perhaps it was the house of a relative. Both Reshat's food and care were provided for at that house. Money was sent him from Izmir, month by month. In Izmir, his father was either an advocate or a lawyer. Reshat secretly whispered to me that he was having sexual relations with a widow woman in the house where he stayed as a renter. Sexual relations? For me, and those like me, this was as fantastic as gathering stars from the sky and playing marbles with them.

Inspired by what my seat mate, Reshat, told me, I had begun writing a novel. Its name was a laughable thing, such as "A Pair Of Wells" to describe a beautiful woman with deep black eyes. The incidents in my novel took place in Izmir, which I didn't know at all, hadn't even been to. I wrote one notebook full and had started on the second. I wanted my novel to be very tragic. As I wrote, I read it part by part, to my father. In a few places, touched by my novel, Father's eyes filled with tears. That meant my novel was as tragic as I wanted it to be. I had succeeded. I even wrote letters to the big publishing houses of the day on Sublime Porte Street [the publishers' row of Istanbul] and asked them whether or not they wanted to print my novel. Three of the publishers I wrote to come to mind: Hilmi Kitaphanesi, Ikbal Kitabevi, Kanaat Kitabevi... In my letters, I described the theme of my novel, in summary. I tried to give the impression in those letters that I was a grown man. An answer even came from the Ikbal and Kanaat Kitabevis. The replies, written on printed letterheads, started with *"Muhterem Beyefendi"* [Esteemed Sir]. They had considered me a writer whom it was necessary to answer with *"Muhterem Beyefendi."* Principally, this was the thing that made me happy. I saved one of those letters until recently. In one of the replies was written a rejection, something like: "Due to our year's schedule being full, unfortunately we won't be able to publish the novel." Though my novel wasn't being published, I was still happy, because a big publishing house, thinking I was an honest-to-goodness, adult writer, had answered my letter. I had also informed them in my letter that, "If desired, I will send my novel." Actually, there was no novel as yet. I'd only been able to write a one-notebook section.

I can't recall the subject of that notebookful that I wrote on my novel. But my classmate, Mehmet Karahasanoghlu, remembers it because, at that time, both of us had decided to write a novel, and both of us had bought thick notebooks for novel writing. He didn't write a thing. In the novel I wrote, I was evidently telling about the life of a girl who was unattached, footloose, and fancy free.

In every school there are students known as good writers. In the Davutpasha Middle School there were two students in the class above us who were known as men of letters. One's name was Tahir, the other's Hüsamettin. I became good friends with Tahir. His house was on one of the hills that goes down to Samatya. Sometimes we went there together. Tahir was a boy with the dress and air of a teacher. Tahir, who read the sections of my novel that I wrote, made me acquainted with Hüsamettin. Hüsamettin's father had a pickle store in Kojamustafapasha. Hüsamettin was a very serious-minded boy who was a perfect gentleman. My novel had been left with him for a few days so he could read it. I was writing the novel in Old Turkish. Only one thing stayed in my mind from Hüsamettin's criticism when he returned the novel: "You wrote *alev* with an *ayin*, it has to be written with an *elif*."

I was quite upset at this criticism because I was of the opinion that I wrote Old Turkish without error. How had it happened that I wrote a letter wrong? In truth, wasn't *alev* written with an *ayin*? How was it possible? Alev was Arabic, wasn't it?

Forty-seven years have passed since that day, and I'm going to look it up in the dictionary with Arabic letters, right now, to learn whether *alev* is always written with an *ayin* or an *elif*... I just looked it up in the dictionary now, while writing my memoirs. *Alev* is written with an *elif* because it is a Turkish word. If it's written with an *ayin*, it's a corruption. The dictionary explains it like that.

Yes, that Hüsamettin is now a well-known writer friend of mine, called Hüsamettin Bozok. I told Hüsamettin Bozok that he read my first novel, and mentioned this *ayin* and *elif* incident. But he didn't remember anything, and didn't even think he knew me at school. It's always like that: we live the same event, but it enters the biography of one of us, not the other.

We Move To Uzun Yusuf

There were three buildings in Naji Bey's big yard. He lived in the one in the front garden, and we were living in a room on the ground floor of the two-story house in the back garden. The third building was the old lodge kitchen. As a kitchen, it was very large; but as a house, very small. Naji Bey rented the two-story house in the back garden, in which we were living. The renter, called Molla Bey, according to what I learned later, was rather famous. We were forced to move elsewhere when the house was rented. We moved to a house, near the old one, in a place called Uzun Yusuf [Tall Joseph]. My father was still going to work in Naji Bey's garden. He was taking care of Naji Bey's garden and flowers and getting no pay for this, but he sold the vegetables he raised in the garden on his own. So our money situation had rather improved over what it had been. Also, my sister was milking Naji Bey's sheep and goats. Since I'd started school, I no longer took the milk to the confectioner in Beyazit.

In Uzun Yusuf, we had again moved to a house adjacent to a lodge. There was a cemetery beside the lodge, and beside the cemetery was our house.

In Istanbul at that period, we were living with cemeteries, one upon the other. There were so many cemeteries among the neighborhoods that the windows of many houses looked out on them. The living were familiar with the dead. There were many lodges and many small mosques, and every lodge and mosque had a cemetery. In addition, there were tombs. The deepest impression remaining in my memory from that era in Istanbul is of the lodges, the graveyards. Even if I were to say that the number of gravestones from Eminönü to Topkapi (called Old Istanbul) was greater than the number of people in those places, I wouldn't be exaggerating very much. There were many black women too, who were important in our life. And each neighborhood had its special lunatic. Hardly any quarter was without a "crazy." These lunatics possessed various eccentricities; each neighborhood nut was individual and, as a lunatic, resembled no other. They were harmless. The neighborhood looked after them. Those lodges either burned, or were torn down, and disappeared. Those graveyards were done away with and became apartment house sites. But what became of those black women? Were they mixed and crossbred until they melted away? Very well, how about the lunatics, so special to each neighborhood? Aren't any left now, so they're no longer seen?

Like all the other lodges after the Republic, the lodge beside our place had been closed too. The sheik of the lodge wasn't a man with enough dignity to be called a sheik. When "sheik" is mentioned, a respectable person comes to mind, one who is dignified, whose remarks are listened to, who makes himself heard, who knows much but says little, is generous and frank. Naji Bey was among the last of such sheiks. However, the sheik of this lodge was shabby, untidy, broke, tight-fisted, knot-headed, and sort of crazy. The elderly woman who owned

179

the house to which we moved, was a lady and was sister to this sheik. Her daughter's name was N. Hanim. N. Hanim, who was separated from her husband, had a son and a daughter. N. Hanim dressed and adorned herself at a much higher level than those circles in which we lived. Not only in outward appearance, but in knowledge and experience, education and learning, the young lady was above her circle. She was lovely. She had a beautiful face. She was of the type called "a woman like cream cheese" in those days. Her husband, from whom she'd separated for non-support, ran a private school. I was angry at her husband because I admired N. Hanim. I used to think, "How could anyone ever divorce such a woman?" My feelings for N. Hanim were a different kind from those I had for Hayret Abla. This was more of a feeling like Ahmet Muhip Diranas[*] describes in his poem *Fahriye Abla*. N. Hanim was a woman I respected and exalted.

This place we moved to was a two-story, old, frame house. In the one fairly large room, to the right of the street door as a person entered up two stone steps, we lived for a very small monthly rent. They were living in the three rooms on the top floor, that is, N. Hanim, her mother, son and daughter. N. Hanim's daughter had beautiful curly hair. She was only four or five. Since I was in my thirteenth year, she was eight or nine years younger. But, like all boys of that age who feel as if they're grown, it seemed to me as if she were thirty or forty years younger than I. I liked this little girl a great deal. When I didn't have lessons to study, I enjoyed amusing her.

The room we moved to was suitable for me to study in. When I was alone there, I studied my lessons out loud, even shouting. N. Hanim liked me, cared for me a lot. She pointed me out to everyone as a model. Although I didn't like being pointed out as this kind of example, her praise didn't bother me.

From rumors, I knew that N. Hanim had a boy friend who was a student at the *Mühendis Mektebi* (Technical University). One evening, while I was playing in the hall with N. Hanim's

---

[*] tr. Ahmet Muhip Dranas (1909–) one of the best known poets in new Turkish literature. His poem "Fahriye Abla" is well known in Turkey.

daughter, she came in with that young man. N. Hanim
introduced me with great praise to him. He was a
distinguished, refined, fashionable youth. But I felt I mustn't
like nor care for him; I even felt compelled to be angry with
him.

That pretty little girl got sick. It was meningitis. Two or
three times during her illness, I stayed beside her. Her head
ached. In a very short time she died. N. Hanim was
overwhelmed with grief. One day shortly after her daughter's
death, weeping, she told me she'd planned on marrying her
daughter to me when I grew up. How was that possible? After
all, in my eyes, there was a vast age difference between me and
that beautiful, angelic child. I was a big young man, whereas
she was still a tiny girl.

I maintained friendly relations with that family for a long
time. Even when we lived far apart, when I was in high
school, at the Military Academy, and when I was an officer, I
went to visit them. N. Hanim remained with me as a sad
memory. I always thought of her as a person who couldn't find
a suitable husband, who was unhappy, but richly deserved to
be happy. Later on, I came to know of many women who, due to
their wrong choice of mates, or because they couldn't find a
husband, didn't attain the happiness they deserved, whose
lives were wasted, and whose value was not sufficiently
appreciated. Of course, there are such men too. But I've always
felt a lot sorrier for that kind of women.

In the French Section of the sixth grade, we had a
classmate who was either older, or appeared older, than us.
Tall and well-developed, he dressed nicely and wore a bow-tie
every day. He resembled a teacher more than a student because
he wore broad-rimmed spectacles. They told us about a joke he
pulled by taking advantage of his appearance—if it could be
called a joke.

In those days, when the memories of the War of
Deliverance were fresher, in Istanbul there was a dislike for
the Greeks, and, likewise, a reserve was felt among the Greeks
toward us.

Fifteen or twenty students from French sluffed school
together. That one who wore the glasses took the lead.
"Follow me!" he said. He carried a walking-stick in his hand,

as if he were grown-up... Between Davutpasha and Kojamustafapasha, at a place between the burned-out areas, was a church. The group went to that church. The one who had glasses summoned the church's priest. Talking big, he told the priest, that as a practical class, he was going to tour the church and show it to his students. The priest respectfully opened the door to the church. They went inside and wandered about. The student with cane and glasses, in the role of the teacher, scolding students who made a noise from time to time, really convinced the priest that he was the teacher. At this point, some students stole ikons and candle sticks when the priest wasn't watching. The so-called teacher shook hands with the priest and thanked him when they left.

They told this incident with lots of laughs. I think that student's name was Zeki. After middle school, he went to survey school and worked at that occupation.

Private French Lessons

Among my classmates was a boy who said his "r"s with a sound like a "gh" [as they pronounce them at Harvard]. It seems to me now that his name was something like Halit. He wasn't a successful student, but was fond of friends, very kind-hearted—a good, generous boy. From his clothes, it was plain that he was poor. His poverty was particularly evident from his heavily patched shoes, which had been resoled, one on top of the other. The clothes he wore were too big for him. It was apparent that they were clothes once worn by an adult. Either they were "hand-me-downs" from some rich person, or he'd bought second-hand clothes, cheap, at the flea market. Despite this, he had no feelings of inferiority. He accepted his situation as natural, and neither tried to hide his poverty nor advertise it. He was a quiet boy, always pleasant. When he laughed, his pearly white teeth appeared. My intimacy with him began with my desire to get my shoes soled, and if we bought the shoe leather from the tanner and soled them ourselves, it would be cheaper. According to what he said, he soled the shoes of those in his family by himself.

So this is why I went to my lisping friend's house. They were living in a house in a biggish yard, with walls half-fallen down, between Aksaray and Jerrahpasha. It resembled a squatter's shack, but was large. This place seemed more like a garage, with its cluttered interior—like a hangar, a materiel storage depot. Broken-down, cast-off furniture and old tattered goods filled the house. Inside were children, both boys and girls, of all sizes and ages. My lisping friend was the biggest of his brothers and sisters. As I remember, they were from Erzinjan. His father, who did any kind of work that came along, was a jack-of-all-trades. My friend soled my shoes. I wasn't surprised at there being a hammer and last in their house, because—in that houseful of carpenter tools, blacksmith tools—even a doctor's operating instruments might be found. From the smallest to the largest, the whole family were genial, generous people. Whenever I went to their house, they never let me go without food and drink, or, in any case, without giving me tea. Amid this confusion of tattered, broken, and cast-off things, they were living with optimism, noisy good humor, and warm affection. The love overflowing from all of them beautified the shabby, old, broken cast-offs in that hangar-like home.

Later on, from time to time, I happened to run into that lisping friend of mine. The last time we met, I was a student in the military high school, and he was an N.C.O. in the artillery. He'd grown tall, filled out, and become a large young man. He wore spurred boots of thick, raw leather. Yet he still spoke with that small boy's lisp, scattering rays of affection. After our meeting in front of the Aksaray police station (long since torn down, a place where the winds blow now), I never saw him again, but I never forgot him either... Him and their crowded home, which overflowed with love and affection.

Upon getting "five's" in all my subjects, including music, on my report card after the second exams, with the greed which success gives and a hunger for learning, I had become dissatisfied with what I learned at school. I was seized with a passion to learn more. English, we were studying in school. However, I must learn French too. But to take private French lessons, one had to be rich.

My lisping friend's mother knew our mathematics teacher, Kömürjü. I think this acquaintance came about through her going to our mathematics teacher's home to do housework. My friend said that someone who lived in the same house as Kömürjü gave private French lessons, and gave them very cheaply too. The price of the lessons was so small that I would be able to save from my scant pocket money and pay for them. If not, I could ask my father for a little more.

On a winter evening, when darkness fell early, upon leaving the last class, I went with my lisping friend to the house of the man who gave private French lessons. It was a four-story house with a narrow front on Tramvay Street, where one turns from Aksaray toward Samatya. Our mathematics teacher lived on the top floor, and on the floor below him, the man from whom I would take French lessons. He had a wife, a daughter, two sons—three children. On the first night that we went, there was no lesson; the time was spent in general conversation. I learned that the French teacher was a painter. Soon after us, our mathematic teacher's daughter arrived. Two girls were present that evening. Either both were Kömürjü's daughters, or one of them was the daughter's friend. The name of one of the girls was Piraye. (The choosing of names by an author for the heroes in his stories and plays is rather an interesting psychological affair. A relationship exists between these names and the author's life. These names aren't put in our writings haphazardly. We find these names after an intellectual procedure. Generally, we extract the names from our recollections. I've used this name, Piraye, many times in my stories and novels. I gave that name only to definite types.) Since Kömürjü, our mathematics teacher, had no contacts nor relations with us outside of teaching the class, I was very surprised at his having such a daughter. He seemed like a living robot to me.

Piraye was an American College student. In that era, to be an American College student was a distinction in itself. She was studying the History of Art, or some branch of that field. What don't they study and learn in some schools! What wonderful schools there are... The teacher gave Piraye an assignment in art history. As a part of this assignment, she had to draw a picture of an old Greek statue. Probably Piraye had drawn a picture of Apollo's statue. In order to have the drawing critiqued, she'd brought it to the artist who also gave private French lessons. The artist explained to Piraye how the picture must be drawn, and corrected what the girl had done.

At nightfall, I went home.

I planned to take a one-hour French lesson, three days a week. On those evenings, after the last class at school, I would go to the French teacher. I was very happy. I thought I was going to be able to learn English at school, and French from the private teacher.

I had forgotten his name. Now, while writing my biography, I suddenly remembered. The name of the man who gave French lessons at his home was Hüseyin Hüsnü. He's one of the very special people I've known in my life. After I'd gone to his house where we met, one or two times, they moved from there. The house they moved to was in Yenikapi at Etyemez. There, he lived in a house in the vicinity of a dirt field one encounters after passing under the railroad bridge. The brick house had three stories. They were renters of the middle and top floors of that narrow house.

At home, Hüseyin Hüsnü wore brief trousers, called "shorts." At that time, the English "shorts" hadn't even entered our language. No custom of men wearing short trousers existed; such a thing hadn't been accepted. His short pants were of colored material. Obviously, his wife had sewn them. Therefore, I thought he was wandering about, and meeting us in his underwear and found it strange. Afterward, I grew accustomed to it. He treated me as one of his own family, like one of his grown-up children. Maybe that's why he met me in short pants. (Since age thirty, I've been wearing short pants at home—from the beginning of summer, on—because I am very oppressed by the heat and can't stand it at all. I'm aware that some of my guests are uncomfortable with me in this garb. I don't mind, because clothes are simply clothes to me, just a necessity. One cleaning woman actually didn't want to work in our house, because I wandered about in shorts. Also, a writer I liked—as if he didn't have anything else to write about—to make fun, wrote in a newspaper article that I went about at home in my underwear.)

Hüseyin Hüsnü Bey participated in the War of Deliverance. In some connection, he was in France and had learned French very well there. He'd left the army when he was a captain of cavalry. His wife was a general's daughter. The general didn't want his daughter to marry this captain. In spite of this, they got married, because they loved each other deeply. I had the impression that their marriage had some effect on his separation from the army. Both he and his wife were angry with the father-in-law. His wife was a beautiful, young, blonde lady. She was mature and dignified enough to be called a general's daughter. Hüseyin Hüsnü Bey was lightly swarthy, chubby, a man with sparse body hair. They had three very handsome children. The youngest was a four-year-old girl. One of the boys was ten, one eight. Hüseyin Hüsnü Bey was not sending his children to school, because he didn't like the education methods of the schools, nor the textbooks.

He was going to educate and teach his children himself. He believed he could give better education than the schools. He'd even taught his older son considerable French.

Hüseyin Hüsnü Bey had a general discontent, the reason for which I couldn't understand. In later times, I observed a similar discontent in other teachers of mine; and much later, I seemed to sense the reason for it—to be more exact, I analyzed it myself. Among the comrades of these disgruntled teachers were some who had extracted a high price for their national service. There were those who, exploiting the national service they'd rendered (or appeared to have rendered), whenever possible went into politics, then peddled their political influence for personal profit. The idealists were defeated by these profiteers. They became withdrawn and sullen. Even though they were offended, some of these idealists continued pressing their idealistic efforts without rebelling.

Hüseyin Hüsnü Bey invariably treated his wife with love and respect. In their house, life flowed on with affection and love. But they were angry with the father-in-law general. The pasha had not forgiven his daughter after her marriage to Hüseyin Hüsnü.

They were rather poor. Their house was practically without furnishings. But they lived in harmony. Hüseyin Hüsnü was supporting his household by painting pictures. He

186

would buy rectangular pieces of velvet of every color, thumbtack them on his easel, and with oils, paint on them. Painting a picture on each velvet required one, or at the most, two hours. He produced three or four a day. He could do even more, but the demand wasn't large. The landscapes he drew and painted on the velvet were from memory. They were romantic pictures, with moonlight, silvery brooks, emerald meadows, mountains with clouds or snow at their crests, bubbling waterfalls, and beautiful village houses fit to spend a honeymoon in. I was amazed at how he could paint from memory all of these different scenes. I especially liked his portrayals—painted on black or navy blue velvet—of the full moon, and those of the full moon reflected on the quiet water.

Once a week, he sold these velvets he'd painted, wholesale, to merchants at the Covered Bazaar. For most of them, he couldn't get his money in advance. At times, he received special commissions. If I remember right, the pictures were one *lira* per velvet. Occasionally, he rendered large pictures on cardboard and plywood. He sold one of these to a fish merchant in Aksaray. He couldn't get all of his money, and the fish merchant paid off his debt in fish. The fish-man became a watermelon-man in the summer. Whenever I passed the melon shop, I used to stop to gaze at that picture for a while.

The French teacher grew bored with his students and dropped them, except for me. He liked me. He claimed he had a French teaching method that was his alone. He gave a lot of weight to grammar. By putting them in tables, he taught the conjugations of the verbs easily.

One evening, when I went for the lesson, Hüseyin Hüsnü hadn't yet returned home. His wife told me to wait. A little later he came. He was dressed up. He was wearing either a bow-tie or a plastron. He returned home full of joy. He'd been invited to discuss the prospects of a job with a French company or association. He'd just come from there. The Frenchmen were pleased with his French. That's why he was so happy. But somehow he didn't start the job, or they didn't take him.

Their way of life was opposite to the way we lived at our house. When they had little or no money (and many times it was like this), everyone ate bread and *katik* [anything eaten

with bread, such as olives, cheese or *helva* (a cereal sweet)],
and no one complained or fretted. However, as soon as they got
some money from a job, they would eat *baklava* and *börek*. The
money on hand was spent without ever thinking about
tomorrow.

In those days, eating *baklava* and *börek* at home was
considered a sign of wealth. I didn't approve of their
impulsiveness. I used to think to myself, "Instead of your eating
bread and *katik* for three or four days, then *baklava* and *börek*
for one, why can't you find the middle road and eat beans and
rice everyday?"

Between my classes in school, on one hand, and my hour-
long French lessons, three times a week, on the other, I was
getting exhausted. While giving the lesson one day, Hüseyin
Hüsnü Bey read my fatigue in my eyes. Perhaps my eyes were
burning and watering from lack of sleep too. He advised me on
how to rest: "Lie on your back in the grass or on the ground,
driving all thoughts from your mind; look into the endless blue
depths of the sky." I took his advice. I used to lie on the sand
and pebbles at the seashore, and aimlessly gaze at the blue of
the sky without seeing it. This is a marvelous way to relax; at
times, I still rest with this method.

I was still walking to and from my lesson. Darkness would
fall as I was on the way home. The road passed through
burned-out areas and gardens. One night, while coming back, I
was going by a garden wall, and as I turned the corner of the
wall in the dark, suddenly a man loomed in front of me. You
know, there's a saying, "Boiling water poured down from my
head"; well, that night, I really felt as if boiling water poured
down from my head. As a matter of fact, the man I suddenly
faced at the corner of the wall was merely another pedestrian;
he just continued on. But I couldn't walk, and leaned for a spell
against the wall. I'd been terribly frightened.

During the long summer vacation I also took private French
lessons. However, upon entering the boarding school, I never
went to Hüseyin Hüsnü Bey again.

Istimna Bil-Yed

Currently, it's expressed in French: masturbation. In those times, it was said in Arabic: *istimna bil-yed.*

Masturbation, *istimna*, or onanism, means to obtain sexual pleasure by hand or with some other means. *Istimna* is a word derived from the root *meni*, it means to bring semen. And *bil-yed* means "with the hand." *Istimna bil-yed* thus means "to bring semen by hand."

During my school days, among Istanbul's colorful characters, there was Doctor Lokman Hekim. He was an elderly doctor. He wrote health information in the newspapers and published health brochures that were easy for the people to understand. In that era, when owners of private cars were pointed at in Istanbul, he had a private automobile. This car was so old that we used to see it often broken down on the Istanbul streets. To illustrate how old that automobile was: the factory that made the car, in an effort to get this model back—of which there were no others left in the world—offered to give Lokman Hekim a brand new car in addition to a lot of money, but it was said that Lokman Hekim wouldn't accept. Well, one of the health brochures that this Dr. Lokman Hekim often wrote for the people in the newspapers, especially in Jumhuriyet, announced "The harm from pulling thirty-one." Just as there are those today who feel that saying "pulling thirty-one" or *"abaza"* in Turkish is vulgar, and say "masturbation" in order to be more refined, there were people in those days who preferred the term *"istimna bil-yed."*

I didn't know what this was or how it was done, but I heard it often. It was secretively whispered around, all the time, that one shouldn't do it and it was very bad for the health. A year later, and during my entire life as a student, some of our teachers, instructors, and officers would inform us about—and wildly exaggerate—the harm from "pulling thirty-one," so much so, that every boy who did this as a natural thing developed a psychosis, as if he'd committed a terrible sin, and feared he would die or become stupid.

In our class in the Davutpasha Middle School, we had a classmate who came to school once a week or every ten days. He was exceedingly skinny; his skin looked as if it had been

189

clumsily rumpled and pasted on his skeleton. His eyes were sunken in their sockets, and the circles around them had turned purple. Since his cheeks were sunken, his cheekbones protruded. His skin was of a tobacco-yellow tinge. While, at first, he used to come to school every week or ten days, later on, he attended even less frequently. Every time he came to school, he brought a sickness report. He coughed all the time. Because of his skinniness he appeared tall. One day, at the noon recess in the schoolyard, this classmate of ours related, at length, to his comrades gathered around him, how he had the habit of "pulling thirty-one" and was sick because of it. In their curiosity, the boys clustered around him let loose a torrent of questions. The sick boy asserted that he really couldn't break the habit. He had tuberculosis. The doctors said that if he didn't quit this habit, he was going to die. And he knew that he was going to die because of it. But even knowing this, he still didn't quit. What's more, his habit was getting worse... That whole noon period, I listened with sadness to what that boy said, and saw his inability to quit the habit as being stupid.

He began coming to school even more infrequently. Finally, he didn't come at all. Later on, we heard from someone: he died!

My Classmates

There were two Reshats in our class. One was Reshat from Izmir, whose tale became the subject of that novel I tried to write, and the other was Külhanbey [vagabond] Reshat. Külhanbey Reshat was an overly high-strung, aggressive boy. He was tall, with a tiny face. He had blond hair, blue eyes, and freckles. He spoke with a wry face. He was, perhaps, two or three years older than us. He walked with a swagger and carried a knife too. But he was kindhearted, a good boy. His big brother, who supported the household, was a slipper-maker. Reshat was very unsuccessful in class. I don't remember for what reason, but he pulled a knife on the assistant director, Sait Bey, and stabbed Mehmet Karahasanoghlu, who stepped

190

between them, in the leg. In the eyes of our age-group, he was a
mature boy. He used his fists well in a fight and also employed
a blackjack. I tried to help him with his lessons. Forty-two
years after those days, I saw Külhanbey Reshat in Eminönü
Square. I recognized him immediately, and he knew me too.
He'd become a shy, timid, nervous man. I asked him what job
he did. He said he worked at the museum. He was something
like a janitor or servant. He acted so embarrassed and
uncomfortable while talking with me, that I soon left him in
order not to trouble him further. But I couldn't walk away from
Reshat's life, which I fantasized... The burdens of life had
climbed on his back. Maybe he had three or four children.
Perhaps his wife... Who knows? I always think of Reshat.
Reshat in whom no one else is interested. But I see him as the
hero of some unknown drama. When he was talking with me,
he was so troubled, that it was obvious he wanted to get away
as soon as possible. The thing that touched my heart was that
not a trace remained of his old bravado.

There was an unlikable, spoiled classmate, whose name
I've forgotten. He was the son of a major. All of his showing-
off was done because of his being a major's son—his sole
enjoyment came from that. He considered himself highly
superior. Does it happen to you too? I definitely recall a letter
found in some names that I've forgotten. I can't remember this
boy's name, yet I know full well that there's the letter "H" in
it; he had a name like Hadi, or something similar. He'd
gotten a volleyball because he had money. He felt that having
a ball proved his superiority, and got on the volleyball team
because he had the ball. He was as awkward in class as he was
in sports. To downplay his clumsiness in sports, he wore better
shorts, more expensive gymshoes than ours. One day, secure in
his egotism over his ownership of the ball, he threw one of our
classmates, who played good ball, out of the game. When this
occurred, I quit the volleyball court on my own. The other
players followed behind me. The major's son, left alone,
grinned and called other kids to play. He thought that
everyone he called would come running. Not one boy went. The
major's son threw the ball and caught it a few times, then went
inside. I can't forget this rebellion which abruptly and
spontaneously happened.

Many of those boys of our age had the warped tendency to invent stories to the effect that some of the teachers were sexual deviates. Perhaps this is a symptom of immaturity. Such lies were invented especially about teachers who were mild-mannered, and who established close relations with students. They used to say this about our zoology teacher. They interpreted our classmate Z's going to this teacher's house in that light.

Another boy I can't forget was an introvert with an honest face, who seldom spoke, never played, never fought, and never smiled, yet was likeable. His name was Ihsan. He lived as if he were enclosed by a hard, invisible shell. Once, he did open up to me. He had a stepmother. His father, a municipal policeman, had recently married. Ihsan was very afraid of his stepmother. He was cowed because of her. I felt sorry for him. So many years have passed, yet if I read in the paper that someone by the name of Ihsan has a good position, a good job, I pray that it is my childhood friend, Ihsan. I want Ihsan to be in good circumstances.

Then, also, among my friends was Mustafa. He was industrious, a Tartar. His family lived in a tiny one-story house, that resembled our present-day squatter shacks, in the open space where the Shehremini Bazaar was established. I went to their house once. From her features, it was evident that his mother was a Tartar. And how clean that tiny house was... Snow-white cambric curtains, white spreads... For all these years, it seems as if I've never seen a cleaner place than that. While I was a student at the Military Academy in Ankara, someone came up to me in Ulus Square and shook my hand. I didn't recognize him. He told me his name was Mustafa, that we'd been in the same class at the Davutpasha Middle School, and that now he was a student in the Agricultural College. I still hadn't recognized him and told him so. Perhaps he thought I intentionally, as a slight, said I didn't know him. Suddenly, he got angry, turned around, and left. As soon as he left, I remembered. How could it happen that I couldn't recognize that Tartar face, that industrious Mustafa, this boy from the cleanest house in the world! I looked after him. I wanted to run and catch him, to call him, but I couldn't. This incident embarrassed me greatly. Even now, at the most inopportune times, I remember Tartar Mustafa, his angrily leaving me, and I am embarrassed.

It is theorized that during the early adolescence of our children the male and female hormones are in balance, that the male hormones are not in a dominant situation; however, in some children this balance becomes disturbed. I believe this view is correct. For the first time in the class in that school, even though it was subsurface and secretive, I observed symptoms in some of my classmates of deviate tendencies for one another. Previous to that, outside of talk, I was innocent about such things. And no preventative had been thought of that would protect us from this. This deviate tendency, which was in very few of us, was obscure and existed only on the emotional level.

My benchmate's name was Müfit, a dark-skinned boy. We used to take the same way home with another classmate, whose name I've forgotten. This friend, who was quiet at school, for some reason kept annoying me on the way home. I paid no attention to his impudence because I've never liked to get into a fight. But he finally pushed me so far that I was forced to shut him up. Every time he got hit in a fight he would angrily cry and curse. Yet the next day, he'd do the same thing, and take a beating again. It seemed as if he were deliberately trying to make me beat him. I was very unhappy. If I ignored his annoying tactics, then he cursed horribly, obscenely. One day, I was again trying to shut him up. He slipped out of my grasp. He escaped and, weeping, started throwing rocks at me. I was terribly afraid of rocks. I think it stems from when I was quite young and saw someone with blood flowing from his head after being hit by a rock. Once, too, when I was four or five years of age, the corner of a garden hoe punctured my forehead, and blood squirted out. Perhaps my fear of rock-throwing came from these incidents. I really was afraid of those rocks my friend was throwing. By going another route, I avoided the rocks. And never again did I go home the same way with that boy.

In my relations with others I didn't show it, but when I was that age, and by myself, I was a very romantic child. Sometimes, for no reason at all, I was seized with such deep emotional feelings that it must have been what they call "meditation." At those times, I used to think, "I never want to forget this moment!" As a matter of fact, that moment, quite likely, was not a never-to-be-forgotten one, but rather a commonplace, ordinary moment. The setting of one such place, when I said, "I never want to forget this moment," in a time of extreme sensitivity, is before my eyes now. I was going home from school, was on the way. To my left rear stood a two-story frame house with three steps leading up to the street door; and in front of it was a small single-story house, its exterior painted white. A wagon wheel leaned against the wall of the little house. The place was a rather wide dirt road and the ground was muddy. The setting of that place where I said, "I never want to forget this moment," remains in my memory in all its detail. Yet it was neither a memorable nor an unforgettable place. I don't know why I was that way; perhaps it was the sensitivity of that age, the unnecessary emotionalism. In years following, I was never seized by such feelings.

My best and closest friends were Mehmet and Sh. Mehmet and I were in the same classroom. Sh. was in the French section.

Mehmet was from Divrik. Because his father had died, he was staying at the house of his uncle, a leather merchant in the Covered Bazaar. His uncle, Hüsnü Bey, was wealthy. Mehmet and I could reveal all our secret personal problems to each other. He was an organized, industrious, honest student. He was taller than I and strong. My friendship with Mehmet, with quarrels interrupting occasionally, has continued until this day. Mehmet is now a retired colonel.

Sh. is a friend who has influenced me from a number of viewpoints. He was a friend who had what the Americans call "a sense of humor" and a feeling for jest, which they consider a virtue. He would find and extract a joke from everything he saw, every incident he heard about. (In my whole student life, I knew only two friends who had a sense of humor.) He had very white teeth and a long nose.

By always laughing, he not only made himself pleasant as he could be, but even handsome. In the years before we were together, due to these qualities I've just mentioned, his friends had tacked the nickname of "Sharlo" [Charlie Chaplin] on him. Their house was on a short dead-end street, right across from our school. The frame house was old but roomy. They owned it. Sh.'s mother was a notable woman. His father was a porter. He did his work with a back-basket. But a porter such as he had never been seen in the whole world. Every morning at the same hour, just like a serious civil servant, he left the house. He went on duty at Aksaray. His portering was done in the vicinity of the Valde Mosque. He didn't take his basket home, but left it some place near there. Upon his return home in the evening—again, at a regular hour—he took off his work clothes and donned pajamas. When he wasn't portering, his clothes were different. He was rather elderly. He didn't look like a porter, but had more the appearance of a civil servant. He was a silent man. I think that this couple felt apprehensive about creating a feeling of inferiority in their only child because of the portering, which is considered an inferior job and might downgrade him in the eyes of his friends. If I'm not mistaken, Sh.'s mother and father were from Erzinjan. Sh. was one of the best and cleanest-dressed of our comrades. He always wore a suit and went around with a tie on.

In my view, satire and humor are a means of self-defense one uses to conceal his deficiencies and not reveal them to others. Although it isn't correct to tie it to a single reason, I think the basic reason for Sh.'s being a joker and critic was his father's job. He was defending his ego by laughing, making fun of, and also making others laugh. Perhaps his making fun was, indirectly, to compensate for his not being handsome.

Two of our classmates became generals. And each of them remained in a class behind ours, since they were held back a year: Class of '38, Lt. Gen. Mahmut Ülker, who is the General Director of Maps; also Class of '38 Military Academy graduate Maj. Gen. of Intelligence Faruk.

The Karabash Quarter

Living in the house in Uzun Yusuf, my father found his working in Naji Bey's garden both difficult and not sufficiently profitable. He started looking for another job to increase his income. In the Karabash quarter of Mevlanakapi, he rented a four-*dönem* [1 *dönem*=1/4 acre] garden plot rather cheaply. We intended to plant this garden and make a living selling the crops we raised. The garden contained various fruit trees. Formerly, there'd been a large mansion here. The only remaining traces of that burned mansion were the ruins of the bath. This ruin must also have included the cistern for the mansion bath. The remains comprised a four-brick-thick-wall, about two spans high from the ground. These walls had been only a meter high. Although the top bricks had fallen down, the remaining ones were solid. This place was an area of 2 x 3 meters, more or less. Its floor was of broken-up concrete. I'll tell you later why I dwelled this long on the ruined cistern of the burned mansion's bath.

Around the garden was a wall laid with mortarless rocks, which was called dry wall. As it had formerly been the mansion garden, the fruit trees were grafted with excellent varieties, and the fruit was of a quality rarely found. There were ten or fifteen pear trees. The income from these alone would be considered good. To one variety of pear—three of which would weigh a kilo—we gave the name of "Eggplant" pear. Since that day I've never seen this pear anywhere. The Mustabey pear was the best variety in our garden. Because its top was blunt, we dubbed it "Noseless" pear. There were pears of different aromas, different flavors; there were speckled ones, extra juicy ones, and some that melted in your mouth like butter. In addition, there were two big trees of mulberries, three walnut, five pomegranate, five or six fig trees, about ten quince, large grape trellises, and other fruit trees too. This garden was truly marvelous. On the hottest summer days a nice breeze blew in the shadows under their broad branches. And, as it was very breezy, there were no flies under them. It was a most suitable place for an afternoon nap on hot summer days. The garden had a well too. Father constructed a windlass for it. This garden's only imperfection lay in its not having a roof in it to shelter our heads. My father built a house in the garden, by himself—if it could be called a house... I say he built it by himself because the man he hired as a stonemason was no more skilled than Father in laying a wall. My sister also worked on the construction of the house. It could be said that no foundation was dug. The walls were laid on a foundation one or two spans deep. But for mortar, neither lime nor cement was used. And the stones, other than a few in the garden, procured from here and there, were of odd shapes and most were small. While the wall was being laid, mud mixed with straw and grass was chinked between the rocks. (Later on, grass sprouted from the walls.) Father had bought the cheapest old door and window sashes from the junkman. The roof was covered with old style tiles, called *a la Turk* tiles, also purchased from the junkman. A lot of tin and sheet iron was used on the roof and some places in the walls. The tin and sheet iron weren't new either. Well, that's how the house we were going to live in was built. One entered the room directly from the street door, through which a fairly tall person could enter only by ducking his head. But no one in our family had to duck his head while entering that low door. This room, right by the door, was floored with used lumber, again obtained from the junkman. One went from this room to an adjacent one. The floor of the second room was of earth, packed hard by continuous use. Adjacent to these two rooms, but with its door on the outside, my father built a stable. In front of the stable, he erected an outhouse, into which the wind, cold, rain, and snow came in. This toilet was the most ramshackle part of a ramshackle house.

Going to this outhouse was torment for me, especially on rainy winter mornings. I disliked its crudeness more than the difficulty and discomfort it caused. We used the stable as a chicken coop and had quite a few chickens. In the room first entered from the street, there was a wooden bedstead. Later on, a wide iron bedstead, which had yellow knobs at the foot, was put in its place. This room had a single small window. In front of the window a platform was built of wood and was used as the sofa. The sheet iron stove, which was a problem to light on winter mornings and smoked when it first burned, was behind the door. This room was my father's. And I slept together with him in the same bed. As a matter of fact, until we moved to this house, I'd slept in my own bed. But here, there was no room for a separate bed for me. The adjacent room was my sister's. All of our belongings had been crammed into her room. It resembled both a bedroom and a storage depot. I can't remember whether or not this second room had a window. I think it was windowless, because it was always dark in there.

Well, this was our house. I was very ashamed of my family's living in such a house. Even the squatters' shacks built nowadays are better and more sturdily built than our house was. By convincing myself that there was nothing to be ashamed of, I conquered my embarrassment and was saved from the feeling of inferiority born of living in such a place, and comfortably invited my friends to our house—more correctly, not to our house, but to our garden—and there were times that I entertained them. But wasn't the thinking of this shame nonsense, and trying to conquer it a problem in itself? Having to defeat an erroneous thought means that it has already lodged in one's mind.

The garden wall would often fall down, and Father used to repair it. And during storms, rainwater leaked into our house. Father continually tried to repair the roof and shuffled the tiles from one spot to another.

In that period, the Karabash quarter was one of the places where those living outside the law, fugitives from the law, and toughs took shelter. Dope and heroin used to be sold. A little beyond us, in holes in the old city walls, horses and donkeys were butchered illicitly.

My father was working in the garden, wrestling with the soil. From time to time, he hired a day laborer to spade the ground. He planted every variety of vegetable: spinach, cabbage, leeks, tomatoes, cucumbers, lettuce, onions, and so forth. The first year, he planted more than half the garden space in romaine lettuce. The soil was very fertile. And it was abundantly productive because it hadn't been planted in a long time. Even during a light rain, a small stream at the foot of our garden flowed and brought lots of sediment, as good as manure, to the garden. That year, our lettuce garden was very productive and profitable. The lettuce was fat and the inside leaves were rich.

As soon as the fruit in the garden started to ripen, Father would sell it in bulk while it was still on the trees. Our money situation had improved a great deal over what it used to be.

Characters From Our Neighborhood

Very interesting people lived in the Karabash quarter. I've used many of them as characters in my stories. One of the most interesting types was a woman called Sheker Abla. It would have seemed more fitting if she'd been called Sheker Aga rather than Sheker Abla. I can't describe her by merely saying she was a mannish woman. Sheker Abla was a woman who was more masculine than a man. Everyone knew she was a lesbian. And it was impossible not to know this. She had the appearance of a tall man who was wearing a cape, or *charshaf*, as a change of costume.

She had a hoarse, heavy bass voice. Though slender, she was hard-muscled and vigorous. They used to say that she carried a knife. Even the toughs shied away from Sheker Abla. Her coat looked like a man's coat. She wore men's shoes. The way she smoked cigarettes, her movements, her cough, her swaggering talk, her walk, everything about her was masculine. Like many of our neighbors, she called Father either Hoja'fendi or Efendi Baba. It could never be considered that Sheker Abla had any relation to femininity. She lived in a one-story little house with a young woman. It was said that she took excellent care of the woman she lived with. The talk about her wasn't secret, words weren't spared; it was just frankly known.

Another interesting one in Karabash was a bearded character they considered miserly, whose name has slipped my mind. He had a rather large two-story house. They used to tell unbelievable stories about this skinflint's stinginess. I do know that this bearded miser left his house at dawn and until evening darkness, poking around in the streets, alleys, burned-out places, and vacant lots, picked up everything he found and filled his house with it. It was as if he thought there was nothing in the streets not to be picked up: paper, cardboard, pieces of wood, rusty nails, discarded screws, bolts, old odd shoes, rags, cigarette butts, food cans, empty bottles, and all kinds of things you wouldn't dream of... He piled what he collected in the house and later sorted it according to category. Those rusty nails collected in the streets were separated according to size; those who saw it said he had a room full.

Being a very devout Moslem, he was respectful to my father. When Father offered him his tobacco pouch, he would roll two cigarettes, put one in his pocket, and smoke the other. My father enjoyed making fun of his stinginess. As if he was going to take all the old junk he accumulated to the next world! The time came and went... In 1939, when the Second World War exploded, throughout the five war years Turkey suffered an unprecedented shortage of things. At the top of items not to be found came nails. Even used nails, rusty nails, crooked and bent nails were worth money. That bearded miser sold the houseful of junk and rusty nails, and at black market prices too.

Reliance On Animals

My father could make more money if he didn't sell the fruit and vegetables he raised in job lots, and peddled them himself. But for this he needed to buy a cart or an animal to carry the produce to be sold. Father bought a donkey. I loved the donkey in our yard at first sight. It was an easy-going lovable animal. I gave this well-bred donkey, even though she was female, the name of "Chelebi" [gentleman].

I liked to groom Chelebi. But I only groomed her a couple of times. In the end, this job fell to my father.

Every morning, he filled the baskets tied on each side of the donkey's pack saddle with fruit and vegetables from our garden and went off peddling. Sometimes he would take two baskets full of fruit to the covered fruit and vegetable market and sell them wholesale, as was. But he took the rare, choice varieties of fruit to the produce shops in rich neighborhoods to sell. After awhile, Father became accustomed to peddling. He even sold two baskets filled with honeydews and watermelons at the market. Father had many acquaintances, and he usually visited them and sold his products.

To protect the fruit and vegetables in our garden from the thieves of the Karabash quarter, we acquired a dog. My sister named the dog "Fanor." The pup Fanor became friends with the kitten of the house. The two of them played rough-and-tumble. Although Fanor didn't lose his playfulness as he grew older, the cat started to become dignified and lazy. She didn't want to play with Fanor like she used to. When Fanor, who just couldn't comprehend this, wanted to play, the cat would scratch and run him off. However, if Fanor wasn't naughty, the cat continued her friendship with him again. Usually, they slept beside each other, wrapped in one another's arms.

Fanor also became friends with Chelebi. From time to time, he would jump on Chelebi's back and nap there. If he wanted to play with Chelebi, he would pretend that he was going to jump on his back, and bark at his nose. Chelebi simply feigned indifference. Fanor was a good-natured, unusually long dog of medium build, with black, slightly curly hair, and chin whiskers like those of a sparsely bearded man. He knew from Father's preparations when he was going out, and went with him. He would follow Father to Shehremini, and when he boarded the streetcar there, Fanor would run along the street behind the car. Father said that Fanor ran all the way to Aksaray behind the streetcar.

We tried locking Fanor in the stable so he wouldn't follow Father when he went out. We managed this only two or three times. As soon as Fanor realized from his preparations that Father was leaving, he would rush out of the yard to avoid being locked in the stable, wait at a distance for my father, then follow him. What amazed us was that when Father was making preparations for something else, Fanor didn't act this way, only when Father was truly preparing to go out. So we used to lock Fanor in the stable before Father even came out of the house. If Father loaded the donkey and went out to peddle, and we hadn't locked Fanor in the stable, he would follow my father all day long behind Chelebi.

Our broody hens had hatched their chicks. They were wandering about the yard. The hawks continually circled about above our garden in order to snatch the chicks. If a hawk made a dive to grab one, the mother hen would give her warning call, which every one recognized, to protect themselves. When the chicks heard this warning, they tried to crouch some place and hide. At this warning call of the mother hen, the cat and Fanor, regardless of where in the house or yard they were, would quickly leap up and rush to the mother hen's aid. They not only refrained from snatching and

201

eating the chicks themselves, but, along with the mother hen, protected them from the hawk. While the mother hen ruffled her feathers, opened her wings and jumped at the hawk circling in the air, the cat by meowing and the dog by barking also tried to scare the attacker away. And the defense didn't stop at this. Chelebi, upon hearing the voices of the hen, cat, and dog, as though she too realized the danger, strove to free herself from the iron stake she was bound to by a chain around her foot, and, at the same time, braying, joined in the chorus of defense. We became aware from the combined chorus of the hen's clucking, the cat's meowing, Fanor's barking, and Chelebi's braying, that the hawks were attacking the chicks, and rushed out of the house.

One day, the mother hen, cat, Fanor, and Chelebi chorus began again. I dashed out of the house. I saw that Chelebi had freed herself from the stake she'd been tied to and was rushing to her friends, rattling the chain that was bound to her leg, dragging the iron stake at the end. She'd struggled so hard to go to the aid of her friends that she'd even pulled out the iron stake that had been hammered into the ground. Upon joining her friends, she pricked up her ears, and, like them, raised her head in the air, and started braying at the hawk. The hen, cat, dog, and donkey had organized a full defense chorus. Perhaps Chelebi's getting loose from the stake and going to the chicks was a coincidence. But I interpreted it to be the donkey's rushing to the aid of the other household animals.

One day when I wasn't there, Chelebi stepped on a rusty spike. Spreading iodine on, they tried to treat it. Chelebi collapsed to the ground and slowly stiffened until she was rigid. It was tetanus. The illicit donkey butchers asked to buy Chelebi, who had died from tetanus, from Father. Certainly my father didn't sell, but in the yard next morning he found Chelebi, whom he intended to bury some place that day, carved up with a knife. During the night, thieves had cut off and carried away the animal's hindquarters. Apparently, they hadn't been able to cut up more of Chelebi and carry it off because of Fanor.

A Room Full Of Books

Confucius implored God thus: "Oh, God! Give me a house full of books and a garden full of flowers."

At that age I didn't feel the necessity for a garden full of flowers. But I was burning with great passion for a house full of books; no, not a house, a room full of books, a little room. A tiny room full of books would do for me.

The dimensions of old Istanbul houses were large compared with today's. Rooms and halls were wide, stair steps rose gently, and ceiling were high. Later on, when the architecture of house dimensions diminished, old Istanbullus made fun of the new houses, saying, "Bean halls, chick pea rooms." Even the spacious toilets of the old Istanbul houses were as big as the bedrooms of today's houses; and the toilet ceilings were half a story higher. When I went into those large marble toilets, scrubbed white with hydrochloric acid, I used to think, "If only I had a room as big as this, it would be enough. I would fill it with books!" Unaware of the above quote from Confucius, I was imploring, "Oh, Lord! Give me a room, as big as a toilet, full of books!" I dreamed that it was a mansion, that I filled it to the ceiling with books. When I went into smaller toilets, I used to content myself by saying, "If it's only this big, still it will be enough!" I would even have been satisfied with a room as big as the toilet on the ferry, just so the roof didn't leak and the wind blow in... On Fridays, the weekend holiday (later it was changed to Sunday), I went to the public library in Beyazit and read books there. On the lunch hour the library was closed. I ate my lunch, brought from home, wrapped in a newspaper, in the university garden, then went back to the library and read books again in the afternoon.

In those days, a story I read in a library book influenced me greatly. It was either a Chekhov or a Gogol story. The summary of that story I read forty-seven years ago remains in my mind and goes like this: two rich young men of the Russian nobility make a wager. If one of them can remain locked up for twenty years, his friend who loses the bet will give him a large sum of money. If he can't endure twenty years by himself and comes out, he will pay his friend this large sum. The one who is locked up will be given everything he desires. A guard will be at his door.

One of the noble youths is locked up in a place that has one door and one window. There is a guard at the door. A few days later, the young man who is locked up requests a book. As the days pass, he increases his requests for books. He is given the books he asks for. Years pass. Meanwhile, the other youth loses his wealth through gambling and dissolute living. His entire hope rests on his locked-up friend's losing the wager as a result of not being able to endure living all by himself, coming out, and forfeiting that large sum of money. He does everything possible to induce his friend to escape, tells the guard to act as if he doesn't see, has him leave the door; but whatever he does is in vain...

On the last night of the twentieth year, he plans to kill his friend and make it look like suicide. Thus he will win the bet and get the money. With this intention, in the morning, before daybreak, he enters the room where his friend is confined. But his friend isn't there... And the window is open! So he escaped! In that case, he'll get the money... On the table, he finds a letter his friend has written to him:

> By leaving here one hour short of completing twenty years by myself, I save you from paying me the money. I do so because with the books that I have read over the past twenty years I've become so enriched that even the great sum of money you were going to give me now has no value in my eyes. For this unending wealth you've arranged for me, I thank you.

At that age, I was a glutton for books. Without choosing, not knowing how to choose, I was reading whatever I found. Thus, in those days that I longed for a little room the size of a toilet, full of books, it seemed as if I might have a chance to satisfy this longing of mine. The bath cistern in the yard of the old mansion, which had long been in ruins with only traces remaining... If a brick wall were to be laid on top of the ruined walls of the old mansion's six- or seven-square-meter bath cistern, and roofed over, it would make a charming library for me. Like a caterpillar, self-imprisoned in its cocoon, I intended to lock myself in this little library and ceaselessly read books. My library would have a small door. And for light, a tiny window would be enough. The ceiling would be built high, and I planned to fill it to the ceiling with books.

I told Father my plans. "All right," he said. After all, he never said "no" to any of my plans or requests... I meditated and formulated plans for years. I kept dreaming of the little library set up on the cistern's four ruined walls, and the big sheet iron roof it would have.

Small Incidents

I wasn't helping my father much on the garden work. Now and again, hauling water from the well with a bucket on the pulley, I did water the vegetables. It was tiring but pleasant work, this watering the sprouts. To see the sprouts growing taller every day, gave pleasure. In addition to the well we used, there was another, a garden well, on the lot. We were unable to cover the wide, wide mouth of this well. Occasionally, its walls would tumble and rocks would pour in.

In addition to pulling water from the well, once in awhile, though it was rare, I brought water for the vegetables from the fountain, still using those two copper jugs of ours. The fountain was nearby. Our irrigation water came from the well, and drinking water from the fountain. Kirkcheshme [Forty Fountains] water, Istanbul's oldest supply, was brought to the city by using dams, and flowed from the fountain in our neighborhood. Years later, Kirkcheshme was cut off by the city because bacillus was found in the water.

Some incidents can turn an ordinary day in our lives into an unforgettable one. Retired Colonel Mehmet Karahasanoghlu hasn't forgotten our going swimming in the sea on the 4th of April that year, nor have I.

On the last Sunday of October in 1975, I was in a night club in Yenikapi with fifteen retired colonel classmates of mine. There, Mehmet Karahasanoghlu said, "Do you remember our going swimming on the 4th of April?..."

A very unimportant event. But can I ever forget it? "Melon rinds hadn't fallen into the sea," that is, according to custom, one didn't go swimming yet in Istanbul. But it was such a beautiful sunny day... We three were of the same mind: Mehmet, Sh., and I. But, for some reason or other, Sh. didn't swim. We had gone to the seashore at Samatya. We couldn't withstand the temptation—Mehmet and I waded into the water, in our underwear, of course... We swam some too. Even though our hair stood on end in goose bumps, our skin was blotched, and our lips blue, in order to maintain our bravado, we tried not to reveal to each other that we were cold. Very well, why didn't we forget this unimportant incident? Because a week after we went swimming in the sea, on the 11th of April, snow fell in great flakes on Istanbul.

Shayin-i Takdir [Praiseworthy]

The result of my great effort was success, concrete enough to grasp. We had taken the final examinations for the school year and received our last report card. Other than the "2" I received on my first report card in music, I'd gotten the top grade, "5," on the three report cards for final exams in all my subjects. The school administration, not being content to note my success with the "5" grades, had also written along the border of the report, "Shayin-i takdir," that is , "Praiseworthy."

After this first success in my school life, during all my studies in high school I achieved the top grade every year in every subject. According to my present-day thinking, I don't consider it necessary for a student to get top grades in all his courses. But my situation was different. I'd entered a battle. I had one hope and that was to study... To study was my only weapon in this war of life. Otherwise, I well knew that this merciless life, whose back I'd succeeded in mounting only by the study and success I won—whom I galloped with spur and whip, whom I directed with the reins in my hand—at my first slip, my first failure, would shake and throw me off and I would be lost, ground, and trampled under the feet of the disorderly mob. So this is the reason I had to be first, always. And when they didn't make me first, I was still first. I wasn't first because I wanted to be, I *had* to be first. This passion to—without fail—get the top grade in every class came from my desire to take revenge, even though unconsciously, intuitively, on the opportunists and those who wouldn't grant me an equal opportunity. Every top grade was a seal that documented my revenge.

I think this anger exists in everyone who has been schooled and educated under the difficulties and restrictions of poverty. But this anger in most of them melts and is lost in the torpor of bourgeois happiness when they change levels and climb to a higher class. These are the ones who say, "Every sheep hangs by his own leg"; "The one who saves his ship is the captain." However, the anger of others continues lifelong. And this anger in some of them can change from individual emotion into social consciousness.

The Summer Vacation

We three friends were spending almost every day of our vacation together. I was apart from Mehmet and Sh. only on days I went to the public library. I read many of Hüseyin Rahmi's novels that summer. His first novel I read was *Shipsevdi* [Love At First Sight]. Old Turkish could lead a person into many laughable mistakes. Although I knew how to read and write Old Turkish very well, I had read it "Sheb-i Sudi" [The Profitable Night], because both were written exactly the same. It was many years later, upon its being printed in Turkish with Latin letters, that I learned this novel was *Shipsevdi*. (I was reading Hüseyin Rahmi's novels from the Old Turkish print.) I also made other mistakes similar to this in Old Turkish. The general heading for Abidin Daver's articles in the *Jumhuriyet* newspaper was "Hem Nalina Hem Mihina" [Hammer Both Horseshoe And Nail]. Until this heading was written in the new letters, I had been reading "Hem Nalina Hem Mihina," thinking it an Arabic expression, "Hem Na'lene Hem Mayhane" [Both Slipper And Tavern].

During the first days that I went to the sixth grade of the Davutpasha Middle School, I carried a small size dirk. Why? I don't know. I displayed the dirk to this boy and that, apparently showing off. To tote a dagger, was no doubt, a carry-over from my life in Tahtakale. I'd probably gotten the dirk from Bashchi Ibrahim's room in Tahtakale. This folly of carrying a dirk only lasted five or ten days. When I started to study my lessons, I developed a new personality.

During those summer vacation days, I had a beautiful little pocketknife. But I didn't carry this knife with the same aim as I did the dirk. I was only going to use it as a pocketknife.

The boys of that time were belligerent. If they were together in a gang, they'd mock boys passing through their neighborhood, grow belligerent without provocation, and attack. We met up with such an attack. Mehmet, Sh., and I were coming back from Samatya. Because we were dignified, we considered ourselves quite adult. While passing through a narrow street, about ten boys gathered there jumped us for no apparent reason. They started to beat up on us. Our strongest was Mehmet. But he couldn't cope with it either. A number of them piled on me. While I was down, I suddenly pulled out my pocketknife. Supposedly, I was going to open my knife and stick the guys on me. The pocketknife fell from my hand. Then I heard footsteps. The escapee was either Mehmet or Sh.. I started to get away too. If we didn't escape, we'd get a good beating. While we were running away, they booed us. Why had I taken that pocketknife out of my pocket?... I couldn't stab with it... And maybe the knife hadn't fallen—perhaps I had thrown it away.

We spent many days of the summer vacation at the Samatya shore and in the sea. I used to bring grapes, tomatoes, pears, and such from our garden, and would take bread, cheese, and boiled eggs from the house. Then I'd drop in at Mehmet's house. Together, we would go to the seashore at a place in Samatya, called Etyemez. It was always the same place, a little inlet surrounded by water. You went down a very steep hill, directly into the sea. We spent our entire day in the water and on the pebbles. Mehmet swam better than I. When swimming the crawl, he curved his hands and smacked the water so hard that he made the air between his cupped palms and the surface of the water explode. When the air and sea were calm, these incessant bangs from his overhand crawl were heard echoing in the distance. One day, cracking the air and swimming overhand, Mehmet had gone from the shore all the way to the fishing weirs, when suddenly the bangs from his swimming ceased, and his head started bobbing under and out of the sea. Then he called, "Help!" a few times. With his mouth full of seawater, he yelled, "I'm drowning..." Not far away in a boat were fishermen catching fish. And from the shore I yelled at the top of my lungs, "Come help! My friend is drowning..." and dived into the water. I couldn't see what happened then, because I was rushing out, with all my strength, to reach Mehmet, and the fisherman in the boat was standing on his feet, swearing like a trooper, and trying to hit Mehmet with his oar.

Mehmet had pretended he was drowning, as a joke. He'd fooled both me and the fisherman. And the fisherman, hearing my yelling from the shore, thought that I was in on the trick. Upon pulling the oars as hard as he could, reaching Mehmet and learning that it was a trick, he had got mad as a hornet. The fisherman chased Mehmet and me a long way in the water, and we had a hard time getting away from the man.

About fifty meters offshore there was a rock in the sea. Clams were fastened to its bottom. My friends used to tear off big clams from there, light a fire on the bank, and cook them in a can or on a rock. At that time, I didn't eat clams.

None of us boys who swam from that shore wore bathing suits. We all swam in our underpants.

From time to time, there would be a big explosion. We knew that dynamite had been thrown into the water. The fisherman used to throw dynamite into the sea from the city walls on the sea front. When the dynamite exploded in the water, all the fish in the vicinity would die, be knocked out, or stunned. They threw the dynamite into areas where there were schools of fish. Two or three fishing boats would be ready, waiting in the water, before the dynamite was thrown. After the explosive was thrown, the fishermen, ready in the boats, gathered in the unconscious fish with nets and scoops. They caught most of the unconscious fish floating on the surface. Gathering fish from the sea surface was easier than picking apples from low branches. The fishermen filled their boats as quickly as they could and hurried right out of there because it was against the law to fish with dynamite.

As soon as we heard the dynamite go off, we tied the pantlegs of our underdrawers tightly to our legs with twine we'd brought along, and went into the water. Five or ten of us boys who knew the place where the dynamite was thrown into the fish beds, would swim there together, overhand. By the time we arrived, the fishermen had filled their skiffs and gone. Otherwise, we couldn't have gotten near the place. The left-over fish were down on the bottom, because the fishermen had combed and collected those on the surface with their nets and scoops. Upon coming to the place where the dynamite exploded, we raised our heads out of the water, took a deep breath, and dived to the bottom. We caught the fish that were stunned by the pressure of the explosion, and filled our underdrawers, which were tied at the legs. It wasn't all that easy to catch those fish, because their grogginess had pretty well worn off while we were swimming there. We played tag with the fish at the bottom of the sea. Sometimes, just as we were going to catch one, the fish would slip from our grasp, or we would run out of breath and let the fish go. We would break the surface, fill our lungs with air again, and dive to the bottom. If we hadn't tied the legs of our underdrawers well, the half-live fish, flopping and struggling, would force open the tie and go off into the sea. The fish we stuffed into our pants wriggled and squirmed around. Sometimes we stuffed in so many that their weight made it hard to get back to shore. However, it was seldom we caught that many fish. And that was because three girls from three adjacent houses right on the sea, being closer to where the place the dynamite was thrown, got into the water before we did and collected the fish on the surface in sacks... These three girls were like mermaids, half-fish half-girl, and how pretty all three were!... Well, maybe they weren't pretty; possibly I was just at an age when I could see every girl as pretty.

There was a kids' gang that tyrannized the whole shore from Yenikapi to Yedikule—about ten to twelve kids. They were near our age, some younger than we. The leader of this tough group was a girl who dressed like a boy. She was hard on

those in her gang. Everyone feared them. Yet they were happy
kids; they laughed and played, smoked cigarettes, and enjoyed
themselves. Many times I saw them at the garbage dumps and
docks on the shore. I was scared they'd get me.

Jemal Nadir

The classmates of Sh., who was in the grade ahead, dubbed
him "Sharlo" [Charlie Chaplin] to tease him. Those who
compared the two of us in those days thought that he would be
the humorist, not I. Sh. was a boy who read. He was an
admirer of Jemal Nadir. He bought the *Aksham Gazetesi*
[Evening News] every day for Jemal Nadir's caricatures. And I
used to buy the *Milliyet Gazetesi* [Nation News]. But I think I
was buying a paper to keep up with Sh. Jemal Nadir was
publishing caricatures in *Aksham*, and Ratip Tahir in
Milliyet. Sh. and I were like partisans for soccer teams; one of
us was for Jemal Nadir, the other for Ratip Tahir. The
Milliyet paper was being published in a place at the lower end
of the Jaghaloghlu hill, where later the *Tan* newspaper
(whose owner was Halil Lütfi Dördünjü) came out. It's now a
tripe shop. The linotype was a very new typesetting device.
On the street floor of the *Milliyet* paper, set behind a big plate
glass, like a department store show window, were two
linotypes. A pair of operators worked at the linotypes, and
passersby used to watch in amazement at how these typesetting
machines, visible behind the glass, set type. And I used to be
among the spectators every time I passed there.
     Sh. learned where Jemal Nadir, whose admirer he was,
lived. Jemal Nadir was living on the second floor of one of the
narrow-faced apartment houses opposite the Laleli Mosque
when you go down to Aksaray from Koska. More than anything
else, Sh. wanted to go to Jemal Nadir's house and talk with
him. He wanted to drag us along with him because he didn't
have the guts to do it alone. Every time we three pals passed
by there, he mentioned this. One time, he really pressed us
hard. I told him to go with Mehmet; that I would wait across
the street on the sidewalk, and if they could get in, I would

come right along. Mehmet and Sh. went. From across the street
I saw them push the doorbell. They went in, and right out
again. The woman who opened the door—no doubt, it was
Jemal Nadir's wife—evidently gave them such a scolding that
they didn't know what they'd run into. Poor Sh. was utterly
humiliated.

Yarin

If I'm not mistaken, the *Yarin* [Tomorrow] newspaper was
being published in those days. Arif Oruch was publishing it.
At that time, the price of a paper was, I think, five *kurush*.
But Arif Oruch's Yarin was quickly grabbed up, ran out, and
sold for fifty *kurush* on the black market. I had seen *Yarin* sell
for fifty *kurush*. I don't know definitely whether it was that
year or the year before. But there is one thing I know for sure.
That scene is before my eyes now. One day, the walls along
Istanbul streets had been decorated with a poster like this: the
picture of a man with waving hair, wearing glasses. Above
this picture was written "Notorious National Traitor," and
underneath, "Arif Oruch." It was rumored that Ali Naji, who
was the owner of the *Milliyet* newspaper at that time, had
these posters printed and pasted on the walls. Ali Naji was a
partisan for Ismet Pasha's government. And Arif Oruch was in
opposition to the government. *Yarin*, in the beginning, was the
organ of the Independent Party. Either the day that these
posters were hung, or the day before, the papers reported that
Arif Oruch escaped to Bulgaria.
    Why did it sell so well, Arif Oruch's paper? In my
judgment, it was neither because of its being against the party
in power nor its being the organ of the Independent Party. The
Yarin paper, once every two or three days, wrote about
improprieties and theft in government offices. This was
something that had never been written, never been seen, before
that time. And this was the most concrete form of opposition.
This was why Arif Oruch's newspaper was being snatched up.
    Years later Arif Oruch returned from Bulgaria to Turkey.
After 1950, he again began to publish his *Yarin* newspaper. No

restraints at all were put on it. But the *Yarin* didn't sell well and went under from lack of sales. During this period, I became acquainted with Arif Oruch and wrote articles for his paper too. Why didn't *Yarin* sell when published the second time? In my opinion, the reason was this: when Arif Oruch reported news of improprieties in his paper, he ranged in the neighborhood of forty, fifty, or a hundred thousand *lira*, like he used to. As a matter of fact, during the years that had passed, a hundred-thousand-*lira* impropriety had become so common-place that it wasn't even considered an impropriety; a fifty-thousand theft wasn't considered theft—it was even considered modesty, being satisfied with so little (humility). As has been said, "What an honest man! He doesn't steal, more than 50,000 *lira*..." After 1955, there were even those among the public who said of some administrators, "Let him go ahead and steal, just so he does his job..."

When going up and down Jaghaloghlu hill, I used to stand long before the bookstore windows and gaze at the books. I read the names of the authors. I used to muse: "Some day, will I have a book among these too?"

Mama's Boy

Sh. and Mehmet decided to go to military school. And they definitely wanted me to go to military school too. We mustn't be separated from each other, being such close friends. Until that age, I'd thought of being many things, like an artist, a writer, a scientist. But being a soldier had never crossed my mind. I didn't like soldiering. I was going to finish middle school and high school, then study at the university. But I couldn't conceive of how I was going to be able to manage this. Under the restrictions we lived in—single room, sleeping with my father in one bed, studying in a little house with no table, under a kerosene lamp—how could I finish high school and study at college? It was impossible.

Sh. and Mehmet insisted repeatedly that we enroll together in the military school. One must take the necessary documents to the military school before the enrollment period ended. I made a stand against it. No, I wasn't going to be a soldier! As a result, my relations with Mehmet grew strained. We often argued this subject. But one day in our debates, Mehmet posed such an undeniable argument, that I couldn't say a word. Mehmet asked me: "Was the Gazi a soldier?" (The Ataturk surname hadn't yet been given.)

"He was a soldier."

"Marshal Chakmak?"

"A soldier."

In that period, almost all of those at the head of civil administration were soldiers. Mehmet was counting them off, one by one. Finally, he abruptly said, "Now, tell me a single great man in Turkish history who wasn't a soldier!"

I couldn't name any. In this argument, Mehmet had won. That meant, to be a great man in Turkey it was absolutely necessary to be a soldier. At that time, for us, to be a "great man" meant to be the President of the Republic—who at no time in history, and in no country, had any deficiencies—to be Prime Minister, Chief of the General Staff, President of the national Assembly, and so on. Well, all right, I wanted to be a great man. As the route to being a great man passed through soldiering, I was forced to be a soldier, like it or not. But it still didn't overcome my distaste for soldiering. Sh. and Mehmet really tried to talk me around to believing in being a soldier. Still, we couldn't agree. We were on that rather narrow road that runs from Davutpasha to Hekimoghlu Ali Pasha. They left me and turned back. And I took the road home. I was out-of-sorts...this was a disagreeable parting... I had gone five or ten steps, when I heard Mehmet's voice behind me: "Mama's boy!... He's afraid of being a soldier... It's too tough for him... Sissy!"

I turned around and stared at them. I was astonished at Mehmet's yelling at me like that, because he wasn't the kind of friend who would act so unmannerly.

One only ridiculed weak, frail, seedy kids with "mama's boy," "sissy," "milksop," "mommy's lamb," and "baby." And now they were making fun of me like that. A sissy, huh! Mama's boy! Who, me? I'll show 'em who's a mama's boy... So the reason I entered the military school was Mehmet's making fun of me, calling me "mama's boy," "sissy!" That was why I decided to go to military school. But it was a very good thing that I did! Otherwise, my going to school and getting educated would have been impossible. I always thank Mehmet from the bottom of my heart for this favor he did me—perhaps without his even knowing it.

Physical And Competitive Exams

The next day, I told Mehmet and Sh. that I'd decided to enter the military school. We were going together to take our documents for enrollment in the school. They had completed their papers. The required documents were a "request to enroll in school, six identity photos, a good-conduct certificate from the neighborhood notary, and a *tasdikname* [certificate] to be obtained from school." I got all the documents except the school certificate. The time had come for that. I went to our school. Only one duty teacher stayed at school and took care of the administration, as it was vacation. The day I went to school, our history teacher, Memduh Bey, was on duty. I entered his room. I told him I wanted a certificate so I could enroll in the military school. Memduh Bey liked me because I was one of his industrious students. He told me to give up going to the military school. And I said that I had definitely decided. Memduh Bey explained. He was a teacher at the Maltepe Military High School himself. He well knew the military school situation. If I entered the military school, I would be sorry. If I studied in civilian schools, in his view, I could develop into a true scholar...

Memduh Bey set forth a number of arguments to convince me not to attend military school. But there was one thing he didn't know: the circumstances of our home and the impossibility of my getting educated under those conditions.

Contrary to Memduh Bey's advice, I said that I still intended to enter the military school.

Memduh Bey yelled, "In that case, I won't give you your certificate!..."

I left his room sorrowfully. Two days later, the assistant director and Turkish teacher for the French division, Sait Bey, was on duty. I went to him and requested my certificate. He immediately put it in order and gave it to me.

Thirty-five, forty years after this incident, I was sitting in the pastry shop of the Park Hotel with friends one day. They introduced me to Memduh Bey there. He was now a retired teacher. I told about his not giving me my *tasdikname*. This incident, quite naturally an important point in my life, was of such insignificance to Memduh Bey that my remarks didn't even attract his interest. Probably he didn't even know my name as a writer either.

Our enrollment documents for the military school were ready. We three comrades went to the military high school at Halijioghlu and went through our enrollment procedures. They sent us to the Gümüshsuyu Military hospital for physical examinations, carrying the forms they gave us. The exams lasted a whole week because we had to have complete physicals. Eyes, ears, nose, throat, and so on... The boys gathered in front of the examining room door, were telling extraordinary tales. They claimed the specialist in external medicine tells the boy he's examining to pick up a coin he throws on the floor. When the boy leans over to pick up the money, the doctor can tell whether or not he's homosexual. How about the psychologist? He curses hard at the boy he's examining. If the boy shows a reaction to this swearing, he doesn't pass the psychological exam, because he's nervous. So even if the psychologist curses a person's mother, he mustn't say a word... One of the things that was mentioned was especially amazing and funny. The expression, "He leaves no ashes in the brazier," comes from this. The whole of the expression is: "Upon farting, he leaves no ashes in the brazier." They have the boy who comes in for examination make wind at a pan of ashes. To the extent the wind raises the ashes, he is considered that good, that brave. If the wind raises no ashes at all, very bad... Even though the expression, "He leaves no ashes in the brazier," was used later on as a mocking remark, it was said at that time to denote bravado and courage.

Hasan Amja, a generation before us, has written in his book, entitled *Nizaniye Kapisi* [The Barracks Gate], in which he collected his memoirs of the military school, that the same kind of conversation went on among the boys at the physical

examinations at that time too, just like ours. So these invented
rumors had been going the rounds for a number of generations.

All three of us had passed the physical tests. Now the turn
had come for the competitive examinations. On examination
day we went to the Halijioghlu Military high School. There
were more than a hundred students who had joined the
competition to enter the school. They seated us on benches in
two separate classrooms. The only thing that remains in my
mind of that written exam is that I didn't do as well as I hoped.
I made a mistake or two in my answers, even though I knew the
right answer and could do it.

According to what Mehmet Karahasanoghlu said only
recently, in addition to the written exam at the Halijioghlu
High School, we also took an oral one. There's not a trace of
this oral exam in my memory. I must not have done as well as
I'd hoped, for as often happens, this incident that I didn't want
to recall was scratched from my memory.

The results of the examinations were to be announced a
week or ten days later. We could hardly wait for the time to go
by. The three of us went together to Halijioghlu and looked at
the list, which was hung on the wall, of those who'd won the
competitive examinations. And I was among the winners. But I
had taken a place in the middle of the list. While I should
have been pleased at winning, I was trying to hide my
disappointment at getting average grades.

In coming and going to the same places for such procedures
as enrollment in school, the physical and competitive
examinations, some of us boys became friends. I think there
were twenty students who won on the exams. Among those who
became my friends and continued that friendship later on were:
Atif (Erchikan) who retired as a lieutenant general, and Enver,
who rose to the rank of general staff colonel. He was a teacher
at the Academy. On the "27th of May" they made him a
provincial governor. Enver, a friend who was overzealous of
his honor, killed himself because of an improper and unseemly
telephone conversation. Kemal became a flyer. He retired as a
colonel and died recently. Mehmet (Karahasanoghlu), who
was the reason for my entering military school, retired as a
colonel of engineers. We still see each other. Sh. retired as a
senior quartermaster colonel.

They handed us our school acceptance documents at the
Halijioghlu High School. Until that day, we didn't know at
which military school we were going to study. They told us to
go to the Chengelköy Military Middle School. We were to
report at school the next day.

The Contract

Sh., Mehmet and I set off on our way. We went to the
Chengelköy Military Middle School. We waited together
outside the big gate with iron bars. A captain came to the gate.
That great gate opened a little. If the procedures in the
documents were complete, the captain took the student whose
papers he scrutinized inside. The students were entering in turn.
Both Mehmet and Sh. entered. When my turn came, the
captain who looked at my papers said, "Well, where is it, your
contract? You have no contract!"
I thought the world had fallen in on me. What contract?
What sort of thing was that? No one had told me anything
about a contract. Upon my friends' going on the other side of
that great iron gate and just me staying on this side, I felt like I
would weep. The captain told me that it was necessary for me
to bring the contract from a notary, and that he would know
how to make one up. Someone whose property, money, and
economic considerations were trustworthy would give a contract
for me, certified by a notary. This man would contract to pay
double the money spent on me during the days I lived at school
if I were to leave or run away from the military school on my
own. The paragraphs of the contract didn't stop at this. Upon
finishing school and coming out as an officer, I agreed to
obligatory service of so many years, and would not resign before
that many years of service were up... A number of other
paragraphs. My father was going to be the guarantor of these
conditions and was going to sign the contract in my name as my
guarantor due to my age. It was also written in the contract
that, in case of failure, the boy who owed obligatory service
would be sent to a regiment and serve as a sergeant, and so on.

My friends entered the school and I stayed outside. They were going to sleep in the school that night, and I couldn't. I was thinking that if I didn't sleep at school that night I would die! Those who were sleeping there would snatch up all the great-men positions, the generalships, and nothing was going to be left for me. It's said, "I became a bird and flew." Well, I did just that, from Chengelköy to the ferry, boarded the streetcar from Sirkeji to Shehremini... Just how I came to the Karabash quarter I can't remember. It was afternoon. My poor daddy had lain down after lunch to take a nap. I woke him up in such excitement that he was confused. I must immediately find someone to be a guarantor for me, have the notary make up the contract, and take it to school that day! In vain, Father tried to tell me not to worry, that in view of my being accepted by the school, I could go the next day anyway. I realized that my father was anxious about my agitation and lack of understanding. But I was all worked up over my friends' staying at school that night and my not.

There were more than ten people who, by way of inheritance, owned that garden we rented. One of these was a man who had a locksmith shop on that narrow street beside the Rushtempasha Mosque in Tahtakale. His shop was filled with keys of all sizes and various locks. He was a squint-eyed, good-hearted person.

With my father, who dressed in a hurry, we went to that man. Father explained the situation. He agreed to give the contract. We went to the notary. Together with Father, he signed it.

The minutes seemed like hours to me. My biggest fear was that when I got to the school gate, they would say, "You're late. Come tomorrow!"

Holding the contract tightly in my hand so I wouldn't drop or lose it, I went to Chengelköy. Running, I climbed the long steep hill that leads to the school. It was evening, the shadows had fallen. I arrived at that enormous, fancy iron gate. A captain, who came to the gate, took the contract from my hand and pulled me inside.

And now, victory! I was the happiest boy in the world...

I am Mehmet Nusret Efendi, number 4162, a student in the seventh section, seventh grade, Chengelköy Military Middle School.

The End - Part III